PRIESTS, WITCHES AND POWER

In the aftermath of colonial mission, Christianity has come to have widespread acceptance in Southern Tanzania. In this book, Maia Green explores contemporary Catholic practice in a rural community of Southern Tanzania. Setting the adoption of Christianity and the suppression of witchcraft in an historical context, she suggests that power relations established during the colonial period continue to hold between both popular Christianity and orthodoxy, and local populations and indigenous clergy. Paradoxically, while local practices around the constitution of kinship and personhood remain defiantly free of Christian elements, they inform a popular Christianity experienced as a system of substances and practices. This book offers a challenge to idealist and interpretative accounts of African participation in twentieth-century religious forms, and argues for a politically grounded analysis of historical processes. It will appeal widely to scholars and students of anthropology, sociology and African Studies; particularly those interested in religion and kinship.

MAIA GREEN is a senior Lecturer in Social Anthropology at the University of Manchester.

Cambridge Studies in Social and Cultural Anthropology

110

PRIESTS, WITCHES AND POWER

The monograph series Cambridge Studies in Social and Cultural Anthropology publishes analytical ethnographies, comparative works and contributions to theory. All combine an expert and critical command of ethnography and a sophisticated engagement with current theoretical debates.

A list of books in the series will be found at the end of the volume.

Founding editors:
Meyer Fortes, Edmund Leach, Jack Goody, Stanley Tambiah

PRIESTS, WITCHES AND POWER

Popular Christianity after Mission in Southern Tanzania

MAIA GREEN

CAMBRIDGE
UNIVERSITY PRESS

PUBLISHED BY THE PRESS SYNDICATE OF THE UNIVERSITY OF CAMBRIDGE
The Pitt Building, Trumpington Street, Cambridge CB2 1RP, United Kingdom

CAMBRIDGE UNIVERSITY PRESS
The Edinburgh Building, Cambridge CB2 2RU, UK
40 West 20th Street, New York, NY 10011-4211, USA
477 Williamstown Road, Port Melbourne, VIC 3207, Australia
Ruiz de Alarcón 13, 28014 Madrid, Spain
Dock House, The Waterfront, Cape Town 8001, South Africa

http://www.cambridge.org

First published 2003

Printed in the United Kingdom at the University Press, Cambridge

Typeface Times 10/13 pt   *System* LATEX 2$_\varepsilon$ [TB]

A catalogue record for this book is available from the British Library

ISBN 0 521 62189 5 hardback

Contents

Maps

Preface

This book gives an anthropological account of popular religiosity in a largely Catholic community in Tanzania and of the shifting dynamics of its relationship with the Church as an institution enmeshed in the material world. The Roman Catholic Church is one of the largest Christian churches in Tanzania with some 9.3 million members out of a population recently estimated to be 63 million. According to the 1998 Catholic Directory of Tanzania it has a total of 9293520 members. Established in the country for over one hundred years and strongly associated with the provision of educational services in the colonial period, the Catholic Church is both widely respected and politically significant, counting among its public supporters leading statesmen and women, of whom the late president Julius Nyerere is the best-known example. Fully engaged in the post-adjustment political and economic transformations currently taking place in the country and still involved in the delivery of basic services, as well as education and training, the Catholic Church retains a position of some influence in post-colonial Tanzania. This influence is most pronounced in areas which have a long-established Catholic presence and infrastructure of mission. In such areas, often poor rural districts, even forty years after independence it is not unusual for populations to remain partially dependent on the Church for the delivery of some basic services and to seek, in their everyday relations with Church personnel and institutions, to perpetuate the kinds of relations of interdependency and obligation which were characteristic of colonial mission when the Church's need for Christians was reciprocated by popular desire for access to services and the public policies which channelled subsidy through Christian missions.

The context in which Christian churches now find themselves has changed since the missionary era. Churches must struggle to be self-financing and must seek local support to meet the rising costs of their expanded administration. Autonomy and localisation coexist with reliance on ex-missionary orders for funds and the persistence of what are essentially missionary structures and

power relations between the institutional churches and Christian congregations. This situation contributes to some interesting contradictions in the ways
in which Christianity is perceived and performed by its adherents, where those
who define themselves as Catholic continue to perform what the Church cate-
gorises as unchristian practice at the same time as Christianity is to some extent
now claimed as an authentically Tanzanian religion. As the Church attempts to
redefine itself as a civil society organisation for the twenty-first century capable
of mediating between state and family in a bid to maintain power in rural areas, it
must address the fundamental contradictions between hierarchy and legitimacy
and between institutional opulence and poverty if it is to achieve popular support. These contradictions may prove politically insurmountable, although they
can be and are recognised and addressed through the kinds of ritual practices
performed by Catholics and in their appropriations and interpretations of
Catholicism. An exploration of these in one part of the country, Ulanga, and
among a specific cultural group, Pogoro, is the focal point of this book.

Undertaking such an endeavour is not without its own problems and contradictions, especially in the politicised context of Tanzania where post-missionary
churches and their personnel are significant actors in a translocal political arena.
While the Diocese where this study was conducted was initially supportive of
the research on which this book is based, my analysis of research findings
concerning the Church proved unacceptable to the Bishop appointed after my
fieldwork had finished. The article in question, *Why Christianity is the 'Religion
of Business'*, the title being a quote from an informant, explored popular perceptions of the Church as an institution held by the rural poor within the diocese
(Green 1995). The main arguments are reiterated, although not without some
soul searching, in this book. It is not surprising that the Church is perceived
as wealthy against the background of chronic poverty in Tanzania. Neither is
it surprising that the Church feels threatened by work which explores these
contradictions, especially since it is so dependent on access to overseas funding
to ensure its institutional survival in a situation where falling rural incomes and
user fees introduced in the aftermath of structural adjustment seem to render
community support if not unsustainable, at least unable to sustain the Church
in its present institutional form. The diocese and other representatives of the
Catholic Church in Tanzania were helpful in the original research, allowing me
access to personnel and to parish records. I am sorry that they are disappointed
by some of the research findings. However, virtually ever resident of the diocese
has an opinion about the Church and a position on Christianity, some of which
do support the kinds of conclusions I reach in this study. Moreover, the strength
of Catholic religiosity within the diocese cannot be understated, albeit in locally articulated forms which on occasion do not meet with the approval of the
orthodox Church. On a more positive note these findings are an indication of the
extent to which Catholic Christianity has become an authentically Tanzanian
religion and an important aspect of personhood in twenty-first-century Tanzania.

Completing this work has taken some twelve years, from initial fieldwork begun in 1989 and completed in 1991, to writing the manuscript in the spring of 2001. An indication of how much issues of inequality and poverty matter in Ulanga and in Tanzania is that in that time period a good many of the people with whom I worked and without whom I could not have produced this book are no longer around to see it or be thanked in person for their help and support, their time and generosity, their hospitality and kindness. One person in particular stands out as friend and confidante, landlord and neighbour, sister and mother. Bernadina Kuoko, thank you for everything. I am grateful to the late Mbui Linkono, to the late Dr Christopher Lwoga, the late Bibi Kalembwana, the late Vicent Kalinjuma of CARITAS, the late Emmanuel Senga of Ulanga District Council, the late Bwire Kaare and the late Bishop of Mahenge diocese, the Most Rev Patrick Iteka, for making the research possible.

I am grateful to the current Mbui Linkono, Mbui Mlali, Mbui Buda, Mbui Matimula, Mama Patia, Mama Asanteni, Tobias Mkamate, Binti Chalala, Mzee Mkwamira, Seraphina Manyenga, Theresia Linkundi, Akina Sangu, Martin Malekero and their families for all their assistance and support, and especially to Paulina Manyenga, Mama Lumeta, and Justin Kuoko for everything. Egen Chalala accompanied me on two visits to Ihowanja and worked as a research assistant in 1996 for a piece of development agency work that we completed together. I would like to thank him for his wisdom and companionship. Thanks too to John Mwanamilembe, Peter Eponda, Leonarda Choma, H. Tendeka, Binti Hakira and Chief Mponda and the staff at Ulanga District Council and to those who work with the Bibi at Ihowanja and Kilosa kwa Mpepo for their hospitality (Hamisa asante!) and assistance. I also thank Hawa, Eki, Dinah, Neema and Talaka for their companionship as children. Everywhere I went in Ulanga district I was met with hospitality and kindness. I particularly wish to thank the people of Mbagula, Nawenge, Makanga, Sangu Sangu, Midindo, Chikuti, Kisewe, Ilonga, Ihowanja, Mwaya, Idunda, Majengo, Chilombola, Mabanda, Msogezi and Mahenge Mjini.

Academic debts are owed to Odhiambo Anacleti and Sam Maghimbi for proposing Mahenge as a site for research, to Aylward Shorter for his advice on researching Catholicism in Tanzania and to Lorne Larson for his generosity in sharing his ideas and his excellent historical research on Ulanga so unselfishly with others. The influence of Maurice Bloch is evident in my work and I acknowledge his contribution to my thinking, in particular for ways of understanding the logic of ritual and for recognising the significance of the persistence of mission. In terms of the development of my work over the past decade I am grateful to colleagues at the London School of Economics, the University of Sussex and the University of Manchester, in particular to Clare Ferguson, Peter Loizos, Chris Fuller, Henrietta Moore, James Woodburn, Jock Stirrat, John Gledhill, Elvira Beaulandes, Sandy Robertson, Todd Sanders and outside these places but within the scholarly community, Katherine Snyder,

Jean Lave and Gillian Feeley Harnik. My work on witchcraft suppression practices owes much to Ray Abrahams of Cambridge and Simeon Mesaki of the University of Dar es Salaam. Thanks also to Terence Ranger for his interest and assistance, especially when this project was at its earliest stages and to Jamie Monson, an historian of Ulanga district. Finally, Paul Baxter kindly read over and commented on the final manuscript, providing sound guidance and advice that is much appreciated.

Other factors have been significant in the completion of this piece of work, factors that are often understated in the production of academic texts – experience and ageing. When I began fieldwork I was a childless twenty-four year-old with little personal experience of life and death or of the emotional importance of kinship. As a mother of two I see life rather differently. This personal experience is reflected in the emphasis given in the text to ageing as a process of becoming and personhood as a dynamic, rather than a static category. Moreover, Ulanga and Tanzania are not simply sites for fieldwork but places where I have now known whole families for one third of my life, and where I strive to maintain personal and professional relationships. Experience of rural living conditions and comparative knowledge gained through academic and practical engagement with social policy issues in east Africa informs my professional priorities which aim to contribute to the development of an anthropology capable of addressing the real world in all its complexity, not merely for intellectual purposes, but to make change for the better possible. The United Republic of Tanzania has embarked on a strategy for achieving its Development Vision by the year 2025. Although this book will not contribute directly towards that vision, it may add to the understanding of rural socialities on which its achievement depends.

The initial research between 1989 and 1991 was supported by the UK's Economic and Social Research Council, with further short visits to Tanzania in 1995 and 1996 funded by the University of Manchester. Additional brief periods of time were spent in Tanzania, and Mahenge, between 1998 and 2001. The original research on which the book is based was approved by the Tanzania Commission for Science and Technology. At the time of the initial fieldwork I was a research associate in the Department of Sociology at the University of Dar es Salaam. I take this opportunity to thank both institutions for their cooperation and support in facilitating the research.

A significant proportion of this book is based on revisions of earlier pieces of work, some of which have been published as articles in journals and as chapters in books. Chapter 4 reiterates some of the ideas expressed in the *Journal of Religion in Africa* piece (1995) 'Why Christianity is the Religion of Business. Perceptions of the Church and Christianity among Pogoro Catholics, Southern Tanzania'. Chapter 6 is informed by an earlier piece entitled 'Medicines and the Embodiment of Substances among Pogoro Catholics, Southern Tanzania' which appeared in the *Journal of the Royal Anthropological Institute* in 1996 and a chapter on descent and kinship which I contributed to a volume edited by Patrick Heady and Peter Loizos in 1999. Some of the arguments expressed in chapters 7 and 8 were initially provisionally worked out in a piece which appeared in the volume edited by Henrietta Moore, Todd Sanders and the late Bwire Kaare in 1999. Finally, chapter 9 on 'Witchcraft Suppression Practices and Movements' first appeared in *Comparative Studies in Society and History* in 1997. Anonymous reviewers and editorial comments from these have contributed enormously towards the production of this piece of work. Josiah Hincks and Karen Egan helped me get the manuscript together at various stages. I could not have finished without their help. Finally, thanks to David, Leah and Saul for being my family, to my parents for living up to the extended obligations of kinship and to Annjoe and Stephen Dickson and Anita Igoe for plugging the gaps.

Map 1 Ulanga district in Tanzania.

Map 2 Catholic parishes and dates of establishment.

1

Global Christianity and the structure of power

Colonial civilisation and the adoption of Christianity

The majority of the world's Christians no longer live in Europe or north America but in the countries of Asia, Latin America and Africa south of the Sahara. Christianities of one sort or another are taken for granted aspects of the lives of billions of people in diverse communities that retain collective memories of non-Christian traditions and, frequently, continue to perform practices associated with them. The present constitution of different local Christianities is highly varied, reflecting in part the different forms and context of its promotion, adoption and ongoing transformation in and through practice. While these Christianities may appear to have very little in common beyond a belief in Jesus Christ they share to an extent a common origin and history. What informed and facilitated the remarkable and comparatively recent globalisation of Christianity was colonialism in its myriad forms (Hefner 1993, Burridge 1991). Colonial *conquest* created the preconditions for the kinds of political and economic contexts with which foreign missionaries could engage relatively unchallenged. Colonial *governance* formalised specific niches for missionary action that complemented the evangelisation endeavour.

Of course, neither colonialism nor missionary evangelisations were unitary projects in any simple sense (Thomas 1994). However, affinities in goal and purpose fostered a synergy that was to enhance the expansionist capabilities of both. Colonialism is essentially concerned with the establishment and consolidation of control over subject populations through their transformation (Comaroff and Comaroff 1992: 235). The aims of evangelical mission were similar. Certain kinds of people needed to be converted from a flawed system of belief to another perfect one if they were to achieve salvation. Evangelical notions of 'salvation' encompassed not only the non-Christian person but the society in which he or she lived. Salvation was not merely a matter of saving 'heathen' souls but amounted to a totalising endeavour in the name of civilisation (Comaroff and Comaroff 1991; Fernandez 1982: 87). For most European missions in the nineteenth and early twentieth centuries conversion to Christianity was viewed as an essential part of a global project of modernisation premised on a particular notion of civilisation as the culmination of an evolutionary progression away from barbarism and savagery. Christian notions of the human body and of perfectible humanity provided the ideological legitimation for widespread mission involvement in service delivery, as did the need for funds (Vaughan 1991). Christian missions in Africa were frequently engaged as contractors to governments for the supply of health and education services, extending the reach and presence of colonial regimes even into remote areas. [1]

Western notions of civilisation, of which missionary constructions were part, held that scientific knowledge was an indicator of intellectual superiority and saw appropriate education as the means to effect a literal transition out of the darkness towards the light. Achieving this transition depended on a critical foundation stone in the form of Christianity, without which there could be no real common ground of trust nor 'civilization', but education was central as the means through which converts could become knowing Christian persons. The primacy of conversion meant that missionary education was generally limited to basic reading and writing so that converts could study Christian texts. Those individuals classified by missions as suitable were permitted to study Christian theology as a basis for entering the ranks of, depending on the denomination, evangelists, catechists or preachers. Nineteenth and twentieth-century missionary imaginations of modernity and the progress with which it was associated imposed a programmatic vision of transition on societies outside Europe which was ultimately premised on difference. Even where missionary orders were committed to the notion of perfectible humanity and, by implication, a belief in the potential inherent equality between themselves and those they intended to convert the achievement of equality necessitated prior Christian status (Thomas 1994: 134). Civilisation as an attribute of humanity and as a basis for equality did not inhere within the non-Christian person. It had to be effected, administered, through the dual strategies of conversion and governance. As in the colonial project more generally different nations, races and classes were to play different roles in the future development of society and economy in the countries in question.

Visions of progress and of civilising mission were influenced by the origins and culture of missionaries (Hasu 1999: 37). In Africa protestant missionaries from England and Scotland promoted a model of the modern for an evangelised community, albeit one which in its rurality bore little relation to the contexts from which many such missionaries had travelled (Comaroff 1985). English Protestant missions gained reputations for introducing what were considered to be progressive scientific farming techniques and technologies, as well as education and ideas which challenged existing hierarchies and inequalities, notably the abolition of slavery (Hastings 1994: 175). The vision of European Catholic orders assumed different forms, ranging from the conquest and conversion model of the Spanish in Latin America and the Philippines (Rafael 1992; Sallnow 1987) to the indigenised conversion strategies of the White Fathers under Lavigerie (Nolan 1977) and the monastic communities of the Benedictines and Franciscans in twentieth-century Africa.[2] These sought, perhaps unwittingly, to recreate the social forms of a pre-industrial Europe, a peasant society of which the Church was patron (Strayer 1978:2). Whichever mission, and irrespective of the kinds of technological innovations they introduced, the certainties of colonial Christianity were arguably antithetical either to the scientific enquiry or epistemological relativism which are today bound up with Western understandings of modernity and the post-modern. In the words of James Fernandez, missionary Christianity was essentially 'pre-enlightenment', obscuring from converts 'what were the essential achievements of Western enlightenment . . . the rational technical, that is positivistic scientific control of the world on the one hand, and the acceptance of diversity of cultural worlds on the other' (1978: 196–7).

The exponential global growth in the number of Christians and in the reach of missionary churches between the second half of the nineteenth and the first half of the twentieth century was not merely a function of the inherent expansionist logic of a religion which promulgates salvation through the medium of conversion. The scale and extent of growth owed its success to the institutional systematisation of evangelisation through the creation of specialist organisations and the infrastructure to support them. Missionary orders dedicated to overseas work multiplied from around the second half of the nineteenth century across the countries of Western Europe (Sundkler 2000: 97–124). Fundraising for overseas missions was an accepted obligation for parishioners and clergy across denominations. Missionary service was romanticised in popular fiction and in Christian ideology as an heroic, but necessary, sacrifice. This historical association of Christianity with colonialism and the foreign has implications for the ways in which ex-missionary Christianity in particular is perceived in post-colonial settings, as well as for the place of Christianity in contemporary discourses about history, transformation and power (Cannell 1999; Fernandez 1982; Comaroff 1985; Stirrat 1992).

The anthropology of Christianity
If Christianity as a global project owes its foundations to colonial conquest and to the development of institutions for evangelisation, what then of anthropology, its Enlightenment alter ego? Although apparent opposites in the sense that

Christian missionaries set out to convert colonial subjects' views of the world and of their place in it while anthropology set out to describe the world views which the missionaries set out to replace, both had a role to play in effecting and, on occasion challenging, colonial rule (Asad 1973). Anthropology is as much a product of colonial mentalities as missionary Christianity and also played a part in the management of colonial occupation. While the respective contributions of missionary Christianities and of anthropology and anthropologists to the colonial endeavour are well documented the relationship between anthropology and Christianity is less so (Van der Geest 1990). At first sight this is perhaps surprising, given the historical congruence of the second wave of colonial mission with the consolidation of colonial anthropology. Anthropologists conducting fieldwork in the very communities which were the targets of missionary activity seem to have paid them very little attention. Christian missions do not inform the backdrop of the bulk of functionalist monographs produced at the height of the colonial period. Their presence is notably absent, for example, in Evans Pritchard's Nuer trilogy (1940, 1951, 1962), even though one book explicitly addresses issues of religion.[3] Where the missionary presence is noted in anthropological accounts, the mission hovers at the margins of the narrative, a peripheral if threatening influence, poised to embark on a devastating assault on what both the anthropologists and their hosts have come to objectify as the domain of authentically 'traditional' culture and custom. A generation of anthropologists who were, if not practising Christians, wholly immersed within a Judaeo-Christian tradition seem to have viewed the Christian future as a foregone conclusion. Where this future seemed dubious, as among the Sudanese Dinka in the 1950s, the anthropologist Godfrey Leinhardt, himself a committed Christian, could only assume it was because of the theological continuities between the 'local' religion and Christianity (1985: 147).

Despite the often aggressive evangelical posturing of colonial missionaries keen to eradicate practices they deemed to be un-Christian and to promote the spread of particular constructions of Christian religion, the practice and assumptions of colonial mission escaped anthropological scrutiny until long after the event. The 1980s saw the publication of two important retrospective studies of the evangelisation process and its cultural legacy in Africa. Jean Comaroff's *Body of Power Spirit of Resistance* (1985) and Beidelman's *Colonial Evangelism* (1982), the latter addressing a more recent historical period and based on fieldwork in a Tanzanian community which perhaps enjoyed a slightly less ambivalent relationship with missionaries than did the anthropologist. These studies exposed the break between the Christian message and evangelical practice through an examination of the kinds of political and economic relationships on which missionary influence depended. They paid less attention to the kinds of ritual and other practices performed by people in those communities who defined themselves as Christian, or in Comaroff's study, to the kinds of practices deriving directly from missionary Christianity. The contemporary legacies of colonial forms of Christianity were not addressed, except in so far as these influenced breakaway Christian movements.

Ethnographic accounts of European and Latin American communities in the 1970s and 1980s gave increasing recognition to Christianity; assisted by the rural focus of Mediterranean anthropology (Pina Cabral 1981; Christian 1972) and the prominent place of Christian derived ritual and syncretistic practice in the Americas. The emphasis of studies of post-colonial Africa was different. Christianity was either ignored altogether or, if mentioned, treated as peripheral, an option made practicable by the fact that in many places members of Christian communities continue to perform non-Christian practices alongside their Christianity.[4] Where Christianity was central, the emphasis was on the Christian derived cults and sects (Peel 1968; Fernandez 1978; Fabian 1971), numerous in some countries, but hardly the exemplar of Christianity throughout the continent. Ethnographic studies of Christian derived sects have tended to focus on syncretism and symbolic meaning, and the practice of adherents interpreted as both derived from, and a critique of, colonial Christianities and their referents (Comaroff 1985; Fernandez 1982). Such groups continue to be popular in many African countries (Hoehler-Fatton 1996; Allen 1991), alongside the persistent expansionism of contemporary Evangelical Christianities as part of an ongoing missionary endeavour driven from the United States of America (Gifford 1991; Hvalkof and Aaby 1981). Despite these efforts, the majority of people who define themselves as Christian in Africa are still likely to be affiliated to the mainstream Catholic or Protestant churches historically associated with colonial conversion. Their significance is increasingly acknowledged in the recent proliferation of anthropological and historical studies of processes of missionisation, indigenisation and identity, of which this book is part (Pels 1999; Hasu 1999; Spear 1997; Bravman 1998).

Mainstream Catholic and Protestant churches have undergone radical change since the formal end of the colonial period. Most have indigenised to some extent, although financial dependence on missionary churches remains. They are less likely to retain previous monopolies in health and educational provision, although they remain engaged in service delivery, often as part of an expanding not for profit sector which may provide an alternative to lower quality state-managed services (Semboja and Therkilsden 1995). And their role is changing. In the aftermath of ongoing economic adjustment programmes and the shifting balance between state and private service provision Christian churches have gained an opportunity for a more formal re-engagement with the state. In many countries ex-mission churches are seeking recognition for themselves as a legitimate component of the kind of civil society promoted in international political discourse as a significant agent in the facilitation of social and economic development and as a potential means through which wider participation in this process can be effected.

Civil society and rural Africa

If the indigenisation and the localisation of ex-missionary churches has to an extent reinforced their claims to be accepted players in the civil society game in Africa it has also transformed the political significance of Christian churches and their personnel. This is particularly evident in countries where churches stand as independent organisations, formally free of government control, but which are strongly associated with particular ethnicities and regions and subject to manipulation by local and national elites (Gifford 1998). Further, in post-colonial Africa, both local and national elites are fostered by and within post-missionary churches (Simpson 1996) which have become power brokers in a translocal political scene claiming to represent specific areas and interests (Bayart 1993: 189). While the political influence and material power of Christian churches has always been substantial in parts of Africa, the gradual erosion of state capacity and control since the 1980s combined with the post-missionary localisation of institutional Christianity has contributed to a situation in which local and national political processes and power struggles continue to be mediated through ex-missionary churches, which retain strong links to international sources of cash and support. Mission agencies and organisations continue to exert enormous influence, often in collaboration with secular development organisations. The institutional structures established by colonial mission perpetuate the consolidation of particular political relations in rural areas. Ironically, the context of apparent post-coloniality is characterised by the persistence of mission. The increased role for missionary Christianities is not confined to Africa. According to one observer, 'The grand era of Western missions was not in the last century or during colonial times. It is now, during the era of development aid in the period after World War 2' (Tvedt 1998: 217).

This perpetuation of foreign influence in many African countries is paralleled by the massive expansion of the Aid industry and the continued importance of foreign donors and multilateral agencies as initiators and underwriters of the policy basis of post adjustment reforms. Liberalisation, a key moment in the reform process, has begun to prise open the stagnant markets long closed off to foreign investment. In countries such as Mozambique and Tanzania, where formal sector companies fear risk, entrepreneurs from other developing nations as well as illegal operators are taking advantage of the free-for-all which characterises sections of the economy, especially in profitable sectors such as mining. Inequality is growing, between rich and poor, rural and urban and between those with access to foreign opportunities and capital and the majority without. Tanzania is no exception. Research conducted by the World Bank and others (Naryan 1997) has shown that the areas with the most poor people are those in marginal rural districts with restricted access to markets and a resource base which does not permit taking advantage of limited agricultural opportunities. These rural districts are precisely the kinds of places where the power of ex-mission churches is strong, and growing. In such places, like the one described in this book, alternative forms of local association may be unable to compete in the struggle for influence. Those opposing church power may resort to the guerrilla tactics of a politics of evasion and, on occasion, resistance to the imposed hegemony of the church through such strategies as participation in witchcraft suppression movements, the formation of independent churches and the perpetuation of explicitly anti-Christian practice. Some of these tactics are explored in detail in the chapters which follow.

The situation in which ex-missionary churches have come to have enormous political significance and power in contemporary rural communities in Africa is the outcome of the kinds of complex social and historical processes which are described in this book. Perhaps the most significant factors contributing to the persistence of mission in the post colony (as both place and representational space, for example the role accorded ex-missionary Christianity in contemporary African fiction) are first, the particular forms of administration which colonial rule imposed and, second, the post-colonial form of governance through, until recently, single party states. Colonial governance in Africa used 'indirect rule' through Native Authorities and the institution of the tribe as a body united through customary law and tenure regimes to ethnicise and localise political control (Mamdami 1996). 'Native' administration over 'tribal' areas combined with the demarcation of missionary spheres of influence created situations in which specific ethnic groups came to be associated with specific Christian identities. This geographical and cultural positioning enabled Christian missions to consolidate themselves as service providers and patrons to specific ethnic groups through various partnerships with those recognised by colonial regimes as 'traditional' authorities. These relationships were often tenuous, breaking down over points of mutual disagreement, as for example the female circumcision controversy in Kenya that lead to the establishment of independent churches (Strayer 1972). Elsewhere, mission churches continued to consolidate themselves, accumulating new members through population growth rather than evangelisation. Evangelical mission does continue to be an important part of the religious scene in Africa, although its focus has shifted. It is now largely the prerogative of Baptist and Fundamentalist churches seeking to convert people who are already Christians from other denominations.

Independence and the transition to single party regimes were accompanied by the outlawing of potential opposition groups and organisations, or their incorporation into the government system. It was not unusual for Christian churches to be left as virtually the only formal organisations with the capacity to mobilise large sections of the population without recourse to government resources or control. The roles assumed by ex-missionary churches in the formal one-party era were varied. In some countries, notably Kenya, Christian churches became, and continue to be, enmeshed in formal sector national politics from an anti-state position, acting as foci for popular opposition to the ruling Kenya African National Union regime. Elsewhere, as in Rwanda, ex-mission churches and their personnel were sometimes so thoroughly co-opted by government or opposition forces that certain sections seem to have become adjuncts to political movements, occasionally indistinguishable from those movements themselves. The formal transition to multi-party politics and the promotion of 'democratisation' have also had an impact on the place and power of ex-missionary churches as they seek to regain legitimacy in the reform context, not merely as the apolitical providers of social services but as an authentic part of 'civil society' with a positive and necessary role in the new national order. Concepts of civil society are problematic to apply in many countries where the institutional separation between family, state and market which would allow the easy identification of the space occupied by civil society does not exist. Politically driven models of civil society intended to promote the kinds of development policies of which the drive to democratisation is part have tended to focus on the formal sector organisations which mirror in their composition and objectives the kinds of organisations that comprise 'civil society' in the West (Tripp 1997: 199; White 1994). Consequently, most of the emerging swathe of what are classified as civil society organisations in Africa are urban in membership and in orientation, with the exception of Christian churches. The implications of this classification are significant, authorising church involvement in politically motivated development, obscuring the political structure of ex-missionary churches as top-down organisations and camouflaging into invisibility alternative forms of political action and modes of engagement in rural areas which do not conform to officially recognised civil society models.

Rural power and modes of domination

The question of what constitutes the nature of political engagement in rural Africa has recently undergone a revival in African studies more generally with the publication of several influential books examining apparent attributes of states, the constitution of civil society and political participation throughout the continent (Bayart 1993; Mamdani 1996; Chabal 1986; 1994; Rothschild and Chazan 1988; Migdal 1988). Despite differing interpretations of the peculiarity, or otherwise, of political processes and institutions, a commonality of themes situates these studies, not merely as part of a particular Western academic discourse on Africa and politics, but as interlocutors of historical processes which seem to recur across several African states. Admittedly, the characterisation of these processes is informed by a particular Eurocentric perspective, on the one hand exoticising Africa and, on the other, viewing political phenomena there as pathological and exceptional (Chabal 1996: 45). Despite these shortcomings, the studies have the advantage of a broad comparative sweep. All remark on the significance of patronage and clientelism as a core idiom through which political relations are conducted and which links effectively rural and urban, the elite and the ordinary. In the views of Bayart (1993) and others, it is this which accounts for the problematic characteristics of African states and modes of governance – weak, patrimonial, unaccountable states dominated by single-party regimes (Callaghy 1987; Hyden 1980).

The significance of patronage and associated relations of dependence has been accentuated by the emphasis of international donors on governance and accountability which dominated the discourse of reform throughout the 1990s. Fundamentally entwined with the extractive state imagined as a peculiarly African phenomenon, patronage is blamed for the misappropriation of public funds through the short-circuiting of formal redistributive mechanisms for the reallocation of public money. Linked with alleged corruption and maladministration, patronage is judged by Western observers, academics and development agents alike, as both bad and pathological: pathological in that it is assumed to be inherently bound up with indigenous systems of kinship and traditional local level politics, and bad because it has supposedly precluded the emergence of the kind of democratic meritocracy which could lead to effective governance and development.

Mahmood Mamdani has forcefully argued against this view of states in Africa as inherently pathological and has challenged the explanation that apparently 'traditional' kinship-based modes of sociality, what Goran Hyden has referred to as the 'economy of affection' (1980), are responsible for the political significance of patronage. He argues that, on the contrary, contemporary forms of political engagement and institutions throughout the continent are not the legacies of *African* cultural forms, but of the specific institutional structures through which colonial governance was affected. In Mamdani's view, systems of dual administration created a split between Native Authorities governed by a codified and rigid customary law and urban centres where civil law was applied to citizens, leading to the constitution of conservative ethnic mini-states controlled by local administrations in the name of custom. The pathological attributes associated with politics in Africa are legacies of this particular institutional form of colonial governance. According to Mamdani such institutional forms persist where dual administration has not been fully dismantled, despite significant changes in legal systems – in countries such as South Africa, Uganda and Tanzania. In such places, rural areas continue to be governed by customary laws, particularly in relation to land tenure, and their access to justice is ultimately mediated by local administrations. In contrast, residents of urban areas have access to national laws and as citizens, the language of rights (1996: 18–22). The problems of politics and administration in Africa will not, Mamdani rightly contends, be resolved unless these structures are replaced with unified national systems of administration.

An enduring legacy of the Native Administration system was the persistence of codified custom and conservatism which consolidated new forms of social relations and property regimes legitimated by customary kinship (cf. Moore 1986). Although it is undoubtedly the case that pre-colonial relations of patronage and clientship *were* significant in informing the future direction of political dependency in Africa, for example through the elaboration of institutions such as pawnship and the incorporation of incomers as dependants of local powers (Douglas 1964; Wright 1993), Mamdani's argument is suggestive. It points to the importance of colonial institutional structures and their persistence, rather than cultural representations, in accounting for the constitution of specific kinds of social relationships in contemporary Africa, in particular for political relations. Rather than posit a radical break between the colonial and the post-colonial, or view the post-colonial in abstract philosophical terms as a kind of conceptual and representational space, perhaps situated outside the post-colony itself (Mbembe 1992), Mamdani's account alerts us to the persistence of colonial institutional forms and their associated power relations well into the post-colonial period. That is, contemporary political relations in Africa are determined not so much by the ideological legacies of colonialism or post-colonial struggles for national sovereignty as they are the outcome of the dynamic of relationships between the specific institutional forms of governance late colonialism introduced and the social contexts of governance. It follows then that there is no absolute or necessary disjuncture between colonial and post-colonial social and political forms (1996: 26).

This line of analysis can apply equally fruitfully to the study of post-missionary Christianities which may reproduce what are essentially the institutional forms of missionary Christianity long after the formal end of colonial mission. This book explores the implications of the persistence of mission for a rural community in Southern Tanzania in the 1990s, at a time when the majority Christian churches were seeking to redefine their role as civil society organisations while at the same time continuing to provide rural populations with basic services and to raise increasing proportions of their funding from local congregations. Some of these costs were determined not so much by the services the Church aspires to provide as by the perpetuation of an image of itself established by European mission. I explore the changing political role of the Roman Catholic Church in the context of the historical constitution of ethnic administration in a part of southern Tanzania long exposed to Christian influence.

The mission quest for the salvation of souls was intrinsically bound up with the establishment of Catholic Christianity as a transformative project which came to have implications for the emergence of inequalities and the distribution of power. My contention is that colonial mission cannot be understood solely as a religious project according to the Western categorisation of religion as the domain of the spiritual, detached from material and economic power (cf. Comaroff 1985; Asad 1993). The expansion of Christianity in Africa, and elsewhere, probably owes as much to politics and economics as to the appeal of a Christian message for colonial subjects. This message was, as Foucault and others have shown, itself made meaningful through the materiality of historically constituted practices oriented towards the discipline of Christian persons and the social control of Christians (1980; Asad 1993). The Catholic Church's desire for control was not always accepted by Catholics, leading to the development of alternative interpretations of Christianity along with widespread participation in practices which the Catholic Church defined, and continues to define as anti-Christian. The dynamics of the political relationship between rural communities and the institutional church in the administrative district of Ulanga is one of the main themes of this book, consideration of which necessitates a re-examination of anthropological assumptions about the nature of religion, the impacts of Christianity and the significance of conversion.

Anthropological accounts of the mass adoption of Christian religious affiliation in Africa, and elsewhere, owe much to the intellectualist paradigm of Robin Horton (1971; 1975), whose influential writings on conversion viewed the adoption of 'world religions', Christianity and Islam, as rational responses to increases in social scale caused by the kinds of social changes which contemporary theorists would call 'globalisation'. Although Horton's explicitly idealist position in which religion functions as an explanatory device for making sense of the world is contradicted by theorists of religion who point out that religion is not an explanatory system (Bloch 1974; Tambiah 1968; Sperber 1975), the tendency to interpret religious transformation primarily as a quest for meaning has continued to inform anthropological accounts of syncretistic Christian practice in Africa, even where theorists have been at pains to adopt approaches which take the materiality of practice as their starting point. More recent accounts of the evolution of Christianity, in Europe and elsewhere, prioritise the political processes through which the categories of Christianity and religion are constituted at particular times and places (Asad 1993; Pels 1999). Mass shifts in religious affiliation cannot be grasped without understanding the historical context of the transition (Fisher 1973), or the materiality both of regimes of power that reinforce the transition and the subjective experience of this power through embodied practice. The image of conversion as a miraculous transformation in the consciousness of an individual is not a sociological account of the historical process of conversion, but a rhetorical device of evangelical Protestantism (cf. Weber 1985: 143; Harding 1987).

This book gives an account of contemporary ritual practice performed by people who define themselves as Catholic in the aftermath of colonial mission. An historical reading of the processes of conversion suggests that the large-scale adoption of Christian religious affiliation over three decades of the twentieth century was essentially a consequence of mission control over schooling and that the appeal of Christianity owed much to local political relations of patronage in the decades of economic impoverishment in the decades following the German suppression of the anti-colonial *maji maji* war. I argue that contemporary ritual practice in Catholic Ulanga plays on the ambiguity of the relationship between an imported Christianity which has become an accepted part of local identities and between political constructions of ethnically based traditional practice legitimated by reference to ancestors as people of the past. Contradictions between institutional Christianity and local practices are articulated in the separation of Christian from non-Christian practice and in the classification processes performed by Church and congregations as they try to demarcate the limits of acceptable Christianity.

The book is divided into two parts. The first part considers the historical establishment of mission Catholicism in Southern Tanzania and the processes through which the institutional Church was able to consolidate itself as an economic and political force in the first half of the twentieth century. This period established the framework for the institutional basis on which post-missionary Catholicism is premised. The second part of the book explores the implications of the persistence of mission for the performance of contemporary Catholic and non-Catholic practice, through an examination of key signifiers of Catholic identity. Changes in Catholic practice and in the relation with the institutional Church in the context of indigenisation and declines in funding are assessed, along with the significance of gender differences in religiosity and personal piety. These issues are elaborated in chapters 6, 7 and 8, which show how constructions of gender as a process of growth and emotional development inform a ritual division of labour in which older women assume specific responsibilities for the management of reproduction and birth. The final chapter returns to the theme of the ambivalent relationship between institutional Christianity and local practice in the context of political control with an examination of the historical significance of witchcraft suppression movements which have characterised Southern Tanzania. The practice of such movements is explained in relation to the constitution of traditional practice centring on ideas about the relation between people and spirits. Their periodic manifestation, on the other hand, can only be explained by the political contexts in which such movements occur and the approaches of the local administrations which make such practices public.

2

Colonial conquest and the consolidation of marginality

Historical geographies

The historical geography of governance in Tanzania fostered the emergence of administrative ethnicities as artefacts of imperial modernity. New relationships between people and places generated by this process were to have implications for the direction of large-scale shifts in religious affiliation in the twentieth century as European missionary orders gained initial rights, and eventual monopolies, in the pursuit of evangelisation strategies in specific areas. The politicised situation of location is manifested in the historical constitution of contemporary cultural identities in Tanzania which continue to be bound up with particular locations, religious affiliations and cultural practices. These processes are clearly evident in the histories of the district of Ulanga and of the Roman Catholic diocese once coterminous with, and now exceeding, its boundaries.[1] In Ulanga, and to an extent outside it, formal affiliation to the Roman Catholic Church is associated with a particular ethnic identity, just as the district, like other 'out of the way' (cf. Tsing 1993: 8–49) districts, is associated in national popular culture with a lack of 'development' (Green 2000a) and is popularly perceived as being so divorced from contemporary political and economic realities as to be legitimately, if jokingly, more properly considered part of Tanganyika – the pre-independence[2] polity.

The district's majority ethnic group, probably numbering around ninety thousand,[3] are people who define themselves, through adherence to a specific language and body of custom (*mila na desturi*) as Pogoro. Most of the Pogoro people who live in the district are, like other rural Tanzanians, small-scale farmers of rice and maize. However, rather in the same way as Maasai people are popularly associated with cattle or Sukuma people with cotton, Pogoro people are associated with a particular kind of Christianity. The fact that the small town of Mahenge, the district capital, is nationally known for its imposing cathedral, equivalent in size and splendour to St Joseph's in the capital city, is enough to associate Pogoro people in the national imagination with Catholicism and, to an extent, with piety.

National stereotypes of Pogoro as predominantly Catholic have some basis in reality. Church records of religious affiliation suggest that a significant proportion of those who define themselves as Pogoro do affiliate themselves with the Roman Catholic Church. Records from the parish of Kwiro in the heart of the Pogoro area and the longest established in the diocese, show that some twelve thousand people out of a population of sixteen thousand were registered as Catholic in 1980. A further two thousand were Muslim and the remainder incomers, probably district staff and shopkeepers, working in the nearby town. Almost twenty years later the diocese as a whole, encompassing the administrative districts of Ulanga and Kilombero, could claim to have almost two hundred and thirty one thousand Catholics out of a population of four hundred and ten thousand.[4] In the strongly Catholic central and northern parts of the district, religious affiliation is a highly visible aspect of personal identity. Men and women wear rosary beads. Large numbers of girls and women wear medallions of the virgin. Schoolgirls pin little paper sacred hearts over their own. Dry and brittle palm fronds are nailed over the doorways of two out of every three village houses. On Sundays and holy days the paths leading to parish churches and far-flung outstations are crammed with brightly clad women scurrying to Mass. In the absence of any architecture of equivalent scale, large and elaborate brick churches and their red tiled outbuildings dominate the villages designated as parish centres (*parokia*).

Patterns of Christian affiliation tend to follow historical patterns of missionisation in the district. Adherence to Islam is a feature of the southern parts of the district and the diocese with which it was once coterminous, while the Lutheran Church has a centre in Malinyi on the margins of the Pogoro area. Religious affiliation is not uniform even amongst Pogoro Catholics in Ulanga. Personal religiosity varies according to a person's age, and life circumstances, as well as where they live in relation to a church or outstation, levels of education and the participation of their immediate family in Church institutions. Gender is also significant.[5] The Roman Catholic Church now has a presence in Ulanga stretching back just over a century. Despite its evident origins in and ongoing relations with an idea of Europe ambivalently associated with both conquest and empowerment, Catholicism is viewed by adherents as authentically *their* religion, as the religion of parents and grandparents.

Ethnicity and inclusion in Ulanga

The present population of Ulanga comprises representatives of diverse ethnic groups, drawn from all parts of the country. Around six in particular consider themselves, irrespective of whether other origins are acknowledged, as truly belonging to the area now encircled by current district boundaries. As well as Pogoro, whose territory of association reaches across the central part of the district, transecting escarpment and plains, peoples identified with the area include N'gindo, Bena, Ndamba, Mbunga and Ngoni. Members of these groups are associated with specific parts of the district, although certain border areas are acknowledged as interstices between population areas. Kilosa kwa Mpepo and Ihowanja, where the shrine of a significant anti-witchcraft practitioner is located, typify such places as cultural apexes of the southern region. Elsewhere, territories of association, including that of the Pogoro, remain virtually unchanged in the popular imagination from the ethnographic maps representing the colonial national order of people and things, despite the realities of incomers, inter marriage and migration.[6]

Cultural differences between those who consider themselves to be distinct peoples on the basis of language (*lugha*) and custom (*mila*) are balanced in practice by similarities in relation to conceptions of kinship and aspects of cultural performance. Like other southern Tanzanians the groups considering themselves to have become indigenous to Ulanga district acknowledge relations of kinship and common origins between them. They share understandings of some of the core rituals which are locally classified as constituting practice which is thought of as being authentically *jadi*, a term which I have glossed as 'traditional' in the sense proposed by Boyer (1990), that is not so much as practice of the past but as practice concerning the relation between people and spirits and, by extension, ancestors as people of the past. This practice is epitomised by the *tambiko* offering as a means through which relations between dead and living are enacted. It centres on the establishment and consolidation of proper relationships with ancestors who, having 'gone before' *(walongulera)*, are appropriate representatives of a particular image of the past while legitimating particular constructions of ethnicity in the present. Similar notions of *jadi* and its performance through *tambiko* offerings are explored in Beidelman's accounts of Kaguru practice (1997; 1986), Pels' recent work on Luguru religious identity (1999) and in Marja Liisa Swantz's (1986) work on Zaramo ritual.

If colonial rule fostered an identification between administration and ethnicity, it failed to promote an essentialist conception of belonging based solely on descent as a biological relationship on the model of Western theories of race. Southern Tanzanian notions of belonging are, and were, informed by the possibility of incorporation. Immigrants, captured slaves and pawns (many of them women) were assimilated across the range of southern societies during the nineteenth century (Wright 1993: 16). Such assimilation was an essential part of the consolidation of local and ethnic power bases, facilitating the geographical expansion and regional domination of groups such as the Ngoni (Gulliver 1955). Less coercive strategies for the incorporation of incomers included marriage alliance and blood brotherhood (Monson 1998: 114). Such practices articulated a theory of kinship as being as much social and contractual as natural and given (Green 1999*b*).[7] Incorporation and the flexibility of kinship continue into the twenty first century. Incomers can, and do, marry in to Ulanga societies, in the process becoming recognised as legitimate members of those societies themselves. Cultural continuities across groups defining themselves as distinct, albeit related, are also explained by the fact that Ulanga's ethnic groups share a tradition of having come into the area from the West and their cultural practice has much in common with that performed by peoples of South Eastern and Central Africa.

The continuity across ethnic boundaries and the fluidity and permeability of these boundaries continues to be characteristic of the constitution of ethnicity in Tanzania (cf. Gulliver 1959: 61–30). Colonial rule and the codification of custom doubtless contributed to the ethnicisation and elaboration of difference amongst the peoples of Southern Tanzania in the twentieth century (cf. Iliffe 1979: 324), but colonial governance in itself does not account for the apparent proliferation of ethnicities in South Central Africa during this period. On the contrary, the process of differentiation and fragmentation seems to have been fairly well established in the thirty years preceding colonial annexation when much of the south and central parts of what was to become Tanganyika were subject to social disruption on an unprecedented scale (Crosse Upcott 1960: 71). Scattered conflicts, the rise and fall of small states and large-scale population movement in response to famine induced by war and locusts characterised popular experience for much of the south, a consequence of the dual impacts of the Zulu/Ngoni expansion from the south west (Iliffe 1979: 56; Gulliver 1955) and, from the east and coast, the catapulting repercussions of rapidly shifting political allegiances and warfare caused by the ongoing trade in guns, ivory and people (Speke 1996).

Colonial conquest did not end instability or conflict. Despite the grand claims of pacification made to justify European involvement in the region, colonial governance in Tanganyika under the German administration fostered violence and disruption in the form of conflict between Germans and locals and between local groups (Kjekshus 1996). Colonial conquest did initiate the stop on movement, in the course of time freezing the association of particular groups of people with specific localities and, through various resettlement programmes in the 1940s, forging new associations between groups and territories (Gulliver 1959: 65). Over five decades colonial administration under first Germany and then Britain was to radically alter the geographical dispersion of populations, particularly in the south, in the process establishing the basis for present-day inequalities between different regions and parts of the country.

Establishing marginality

Ulanga's reputation as an underdeveloped district is largely justified. Tenuously connected to national transport networks and lacking the kind of infrastructure to facilitate economic integration the district is politically and economically marginal to the rest of the country. This marginality is not an inherent attribute of the place or of its population (cf. Tsing 1993) but the direct result of successive policies pursued by colonial and post-colonial administrations. (Kjekshus 1996; Koponen 1994; Seppala 1998). These policies have, over a hundred-year period, denuded southern regions of human, natural and social capital and, by creating barriers to participation in the wider economy, have ensured the economic stagnation of the south western part of the country. The extent of the region's decline is evidenced by its relative position at the start of the German administration. Then the southern region, including the districts of Mahenge, Kilwa, Lindi and Rufiji, was regarded as the economic powerhouse of the colony, not only because of its exports of wild rubber but because of its agricultural production. Prior to 1905 these districts provided over sixty per cent of total hut tax revenue for the colony.[8] Today these districts rank amongst the most impoverished in the country (Lockwood 1998; Seppala 1998).

The present-day district of Ulanga was created in 1974 by the division of the old Mahenge (Ulanga) district, an area corresponding to the present-day districts of Ulanga and Kilombero and to the current boundaries of the Roman Catholic diocese of Mahenge. Whereas the old district encompassed both highlands and the extensive rice-producing flatlands of the Kilombero valley, the amended district comprises mainly highlands which rise to five thousand feet above sea level as well as a range of marginal lowlands to its eastern and western sides.[9] The basis of the district's marginality was established long before the reorganisation of boundaries in the 1970s. Perhaps the most significant determinant of the future direction of the district, and of southern Tanzania as a whole, was an anti-colonial rising which racked vast expanses of the south between 1905 and 1907. It was not so much the rising in itself that caused lasting damage to the south, but the reactions of colonial governments to it that were to exert a malign influence on the direction of development policy in the south for much of the century.

Whether described as a rebellion, revolt, rising or an anti-colonial war, *maji maji* stands as a defining moment in the history of modern Tanzania. Essentially a large-scale rising against German colonial authority and its representatives, what has come to be known as *maji maji*, after the 'water'[10] with special properties distributed by its proponents, consisted of dispersed localised pockets of unrest and successive outbreaks of violence between August 1905 and January 1907, reaching its zenith in the middle of September 1905.[11] Erroneously viewed by the German administration as part of a 'native' conspiracy (Bell 1950: 39), *maji maji* seems to have been not so much a considered response to colonial rule as a spontaneous manifestation of opposition to colonial economic control which had become increasingly dirigiste from 1903. The armed rising became more forceful as news spread of the German incapacity to contain it.[12] The first outbreaks of violence occurred in the Matumbi hills, towards Kilwa, in July 1905 and within two months had spread to Kilosa and Upangwa, on the edge of Lake Nyasa (Iliffe 1967: 496). People perceived to be representatives of German colonialism in general, including missionaries and traders, were targeted by rebel fighters. Despite its extensive geographical spread, *maji maji* was in most respects a low intensity and short-lived war, only resulting in serious violence in a few areas. Its massive impact on the mortality of southern populations was not directly attributable to fighting, but to the means with which the revolt was eventually suppressed. The extended duration of the fighting in the southeast was as much due to the absence of German reinforcements as to the scale of and extent of popular involvement in the revolt, which was highly variable.

Many *maji maji* fighters believed themselves to be under the protection of water (*maji*) taken from a special shrine situated originally in the Matumbi hills, probably near to Ndagala pool some distance north of Liwale (Crosse-Upcott 1960: 71), that would render their bodies invulnerable to enemy bullets and to witchcraft attack.[13] This *maji* was carried throughout the south, along with news of the rising, by messengers called *hongo* (Gwassa 1973). Interpretations of the expansion of the rebellion vary in relation to the causes of the outbreak and the relative importance of the *hongo* and of the *maji* they carried in recruiting people to the cause (see Monson 1998: 99; Iliffe 1967). Irrespective of the purported role of the *hongo* in attracting men willing to fight colonial forces it would seem that, in the south at least, news of unrest and of German weakness would have spread rapidly, fostering enthusiasm for engagement among communities bearing grudges against a violent and extractive military regime. Well-established lines of communication existed along the caravan routes connecting coastal Kilwa to inland Songea. The inner coastal corridor was quite densely populated at the time of the rising, almost, in the exaggerated claims of one contemporary observer, 'like Dar es Salaam'.[14] As to the role of the *maji* in fostering the spread and intensity of the rising, this may be best explained in relation to the symbolic unity which taking the water implied, rather than in terms of its imputed properties, although these were significant.[15] Water shrines associated with ancestral protection and anti-witchcraft powers have long been a feature of the sacred geography of southern Tanzania. And, although people in some places[16] seem to have put more faith in its power than in others, there is no evidence to suggest that the protective properties of the water were the prime motivation for engagement in *maji maji* attacks.

Although *maji maji* can be understood as a general response to colonial rule, and in particular to the oppressive nature of that rule,[17] the specific causes of the outbreak were variable, depending on the area in question. Localised grievances ranged from excessive demands for taxation, forced labour on plantations and compulsory participation in cotton-growing schemes. In parts of the south where Benedictine missions were active, including Mahenge, the forced attendance of children in mission educational facilities was also cited as contributing to popular support for the rising (Hassing 1970: 382). Economic practices that increasingly removed men from agricultural work as well as restrictive hunting laws, including a ban on net hunting, were also significant. The livelihoods of southern Tanzanians were already severely damaged by the combined onslaught of the locusts and smallpox epidemics of the 1890s and the gradual erosion of local economies as indigenous trading systems were suppressed and flooded with manufactured imports from India and Europe (Kjekshus 1996: 81–125; Koponen 1988; 1994: 537).

German colonialism and the East Africa company

Given the historical form of colonial conquest in Tanganyika it was not surprising that outbreaks of opposition to it should assume the very form taken by the conquest itself, that is localised wars between indigenous groupings and the German invaders. *Maji maji* was not the first mass outbreak of opposition to German rule.[18] The first had occurred in the coastal townships of Bagomoyo, Pangani and Tanga in September 1888. It was viciously suppressed by the authorities (Stoecker 1986: 97). The Bagomoyo rising was not technically a response to administration by Germany as a state, but to the inept and brutal regime of the Deutsch-Ostafrikanische Gesellschaft (DOAG), the private German East Africa Company established by Karl Peters which was initially charged with the administration of the area claimed on Germany's behalf. The German government had never intended to become involved in the European competition for colonial territories and, under Bismarck, was at first reluctant to ratify what the mercenary adventurer claimed to be legitimate acquisitions in

East Africa. Bismarck's hand was eventually forced by the wider context of the scramble for Africa and mounting popular pressure at home which viewed the expansion of German influence through colonial acquisitions as integral to the consolidation of a post-unification patriotic national identity. Largely in a bid to restrict British and French influence, Bismarck conceded that involvement in Africa was essential for protecting Germany's position in Europe. Privately acknowledging the fraudulent basis on which Peters' treaties were agreed,[19] he encouraged the Emperor to proclaim a German protectorate over one hundred and forty thousand square kilometres of territory in 1885 (Stoecker 1986: 95) through the granting of an Imperial Letter of Protection (Koponen 1994: 69). That same year Britain and Germany signed an agreement on the boundaries of each other's territories[20] and control over an area running from the coast up to and including present-day Rwanda and Burundi was formally ceded to company control.

The DOAG formally administered Tanganyika between 1885 and 1890, but never managed to establish either effective control over much of the country or the stability which would facilitate the beginnings of a civil administration.[21] Armed force generally preceded the establishment of administrative outposts (Stoecker 1986: 102). Company influence was only extended on the mainland in gradual steps by sequential conquest, starting in the coastal belt with a reach further inland limited in practice to trade routes. The Company lacked both capacity and resources to deal effectively with even routine matters of governance. It could not manage outbreaks of unrest. The end of the DOAG administration was inevitable in the aftermath of the events at the coast. Troops from Germany were sent to quell the coastal rising in 1890, a decision which marked the official beginning of the German colonial state in East Africa (Koponen 1994: 69). The German military formally assumed responsibility for the territory on the 1st September 1891 (Iliffe 1969: 11). A regime of colonial civil servants called *akida* was set in place to manage the day-to-day control of the population in some southern districts including Lindi, Kilwa and Rufiji. Drawn mostly from among the literate Muslim coastal populations the *akida* were responsible for the collection of hut tax introduced in 1898, for labour recruitment and for the day-to-day functions of alien rule. Although the system was not established in all the districts, including Mahenge,[22] the small size of the German presence, even once the government had formally assumed control, meant that the role of the *akida* was pivotal in effecting the gradual dispersal of colonial control throughout the territory. The scope for civilian control was limited by popular unrest, especially in the aftermath of *maji maji*. The military retained direct control over Iringa and Mahenge districts until the end of German colonial rule in the territory (Iliffe 1979: 118).

Impacts of war

In areas where people were known to have taken the *maji* the outbreak simply consisted of dispersed pockets of unrest and attacks on German personnel. Large-scale focused attacks were remarkably rare although the weakness of German forces was reinforced by the vast distances and communication difficulties that obtaining reinforcements entailed.[23] However, such attacks did occur, one of the best-known in Mahenge itself where the partially constructed German military *boma* provided an obvious target. The German military had already established outposts in Iringa in 1896 and Songea in 1897, following the defeat of the Hehe and Ngoni. The area at the top of the Mahenge plateau was next, a site suitable in terms of climate and tactical location (the escarpment heights afforded excellent views across the Kilombero valley) from which they would extend and consolidate their conquest and control of the south western region (Monson 1998: 107). It was also at the centre of a thriving trade in wild rubber that made the collection of hut tax viable. The first wooden fortress was built in 1899 and the stone structure which still stands today started four years later. The German administration initially had grand plans for its southern districts, envisioning a series of prosperous districts linked by rail transport to each other and to the coast.[24] These plans were radically reformulated after the events following 30 August 1905 when several thousand Pogoro and Mbunga fighters, mostly armed with bows and arrows, attacked the *boma* at Mahenge over a period of several days (Iliffe 1967: 495). The assault resulted in a state of siege that effectively confined the German troops, missionaries and administrators to the fortress for almost a month.[25]

Accounts of the attack and the precise details of its organisation differ. What is clear is that those attacking the fort included members of the diverse ethnic groups then resident in the old Ulanga district, and that large numbers of local men were killed by machine-gun fire from the fortress battlements. Despite the fact that few, if any, Germans died in Mahenge, as elsewhere, people accused of participation in the rising were brutally punished.[26] Alleged leaders were publicly hanged while those dwelling in areas believed to have supported the rebels were subjected to the imposition of a scorched earth programme of retaliation. Houses were burned, crops destroyed. Between two and three hundred thousand people died in the resulting food shortage caused by what can only be described as a deliberately induced famine (Stoecker 1986: 214).[27] Some two thirds of the Mbunga population of Ulanga were estimated to have died as a result of the rising and its aftermath (Larson 1976a: 40). Other groups were also affected. Rates of population growth were severely reduced (Culwick and Culwick 1938). This, combined with the large-scale movement of people away from areas hit by famine and German retaliation, left large parts of the area between Songea and the coast either completely uninhabited or far less densely settled than it had been prior to 1905. Hunger, agricultural disruption and the collapse of the wild-rubber economy forced many men into plantation labour in the east. A shift in the orientation of colonial policy in response to German public concerns about the extent of German culpability in provoking the rising led to a formal emphasis on economic and human development through the implementation of what became known, after the Colonial Secretary of the time, as the Dernberg Reforms. Not much changed. The colonial regime under Governor von Rechenberg continued to rely on coercion to achieve its objectives in production and education.[28] Unfortunate southern districts continued to be punished long after formal repression was ended. The decision was taken to reorient the proposed railway away from the south, reorienting investment towards the north of the country (Koponen 1994: 307)[29]. Efforts to develop the local export crop production remained focused firmly on the coast and the north west (Stoecker 1986: 151).

Populations shattered by war regrouped around new patrons and new sources of stability and shelter. In the highlands around Mahenge, Pogoro displaced by war and famine strove to rebuild livelihoods under the patronage of Mlolere Shimata and his successor, Liukawantu, the military and the Catholic mission (cf. Iliffe 1967: 156; Monson 1998: 119). In the longer term, defeat of the anti-colonial forces bolstered the positions of two men who were to have enormous influence on the district, Kiwanga of the Bena in the Kilombero valley and for the Pogoro in the highlands, Mlolere Liukawantu, a leader accelerated to chiefship from an acephalous system by German manoeuvring, and who was to foster the expansion of missionary Catholicism throughout the highlands area (Iliffe 1967: 152–3). An initial attempt by German missionaries to establish a base in the highlands, at Isongo on the outskirts of the present capital, had been thwarted in 1898 when the missionaries were killed and their camp destroyed (Larson 1976: 63). Mlolere's approach was conciliatory. Recognising that the military presence after 1899 made missionary presence inevitable sooner or later Liukawantu offered the Benedictines land to establish a mission station near to his clan territory in 1902, enabling him to embark on a relationship of mutual protection which he was able to exploit, not merely in the immediate aftermath of *maji maji* but well into the period of British administration (Iliffe 1967: 152–4).

Barely eight years after *maji maji* ended, war between European states directly challenged, and later finished, Germany's aspirations to colonial rule in Africa through fighting in Africa itself. Belgian troops occupied Mahenge town in 1917, assuming temporary control over the southern regions. War extracted a heavy burden from local populations forced to provide for the invading armies of

European conscripts and African troops. Food shortage and hardship once again
ensued for the peoples of Ulanga (Crosse-Upcott 1958). The abrupt end of the
German administration did not lead to immediate change in the ways in which
colonialism was implemented and experienced. Interim governance under the
allies ended in 1919 when the British Colonial Office assumed responsibility for
the League of Nations Mandate over Tanganyika territory (Graham 1976: 1).

Indirect rule and the control of nature

Unlike Germany, Britain had embarked on the development of a theory for
the practice of colonial administration based on experience it had gained in
the control of territories designated as colonies in Asia and in other parts of
Africa. This theory was to evolve into Lugard's system of indirect rule, premised
on the creation of parallel systems of administration based on ethnicity and
race which were hierarchically subverted to the directives of colonial authority
(cf. Mamdani 1996). Indirect rule was presented as 'natives' managing their own
affairs according to 'custom', and, as Moore (1986) and Ranger (1983) have
shown, depended on the representation of what was an essentially imaginary
body of 'customary law'.

The successful implementation of Indirect Rule required the existence of
localised polities which could be made to administer themselves according
to custom, or at least foster the illusion of self-administration under the firm
control of colonial officers from Britain. Locating such polities was difficult in
Tanganyika where ethnicity was fluid and centralised polities were few and far
between. This difficulty was recognised by the colonial administration which,
under Governor Cameron, systematically set about transforming pre-existing
ethnicities into tribal identities and, through the realignment of administrative
boundaries, into polities governable by 'chiefs' and 'traditional' (hereditary)
rulers.[30] This process was enthusiastically appropriated by some Tanganyikans,
especially those who stood to gain in power and prestige from the resulting
ethnic reorganisation. In the words of historian John Iliffe, 'Africans wanted
effective units of action just as officials wanted effective units of government.
Europeans believed Africans belonged to tribes; Africans built tribes to belong
to' (Iliffe 1979: 324).

Irrespective of the indigenous initiative in the constitution of ethnically based
polities, the significance of the colonial contribution to their consolidation
should not be understated. In order to realise the congruence between ethnicity
and administration the colonial regime redrew district boundaries and increased
the number of districts (Graham 1976: 1–4). In districts whose mixed populations rendered control by a single group impractical or where small populations
rendered further subdivision undesirable, each ethnicity was made to function

as a chiefdom and territory within the confines of district borders. In Ulanga, the 'sultanates' established by the Germans were able to increase their influence through new positions as native authority chiefs and headmen. The most significant were Ubena under Kiwanga in the Kilombero valley and Upogoro in the highlands under Mlolere.

The 'building of tribes' did not necessarily result in the formation of corporate bodies or identities, especially amongst the peoples of the south with traditions of fragmented political allegiance and acephalous organisation. While a degree of corporate identity may have been represented as existing in the interests of the new native authority elites, social reality was more diffuse. The Pogoro 'tribe' was internally differentiated to such an extent that the highlands and lowlands groups could legitimately have been considered as separate cultural entities (Larson 1976: 30, 118). Chief Mlolere never seems to have acquired a mass following beyond the immediate vicinity of his headquarters at Vigoi, overlooking Mahenge town.[31] The abolition of chiefships in 1962 under the independent government met with little resistance in Ulanga (Mtenga 1971). In contrast to other areas where the position of chief retained a degree of ritual and political significance well into the 1990s, Pogoro chiefs and headmen either faded into political obscurity or sought to convert their status into power through participation in the evolving structures of legitimacy established by the TANU/CCM[32] party machine.[33]

The British colonial administration sought to fix ethnic identity to specific tracts of land and fostered the illusion that Tanganyika comprised distinct ethnic groups with distinct attributes and cultural identities. In seeking to build on what was perceived of as 'traditional', actually a system in flux fixed through codification into customary law, British colonial authorities aimed to preserve what they believed to best suit both 'the native' and his[34] 'natural' environment; 'We are using their own indigenous institutions to promote higher standards of civilisation amongst them', wrote Cameron in 1937[35], obscuring the fact that such institutions were themselves largely the product of colonial history and that, as Kjekshus has shown (1996), what appeared to be the 'natural' environment had itself undergone dramatic transformation as a result of the various onslaughts of the nineteenth century. From the perspective of colonial paternalism 'native' institutions had severe limitations. British administrators, like the Germans who preceded them, felt that the indigenous populations of the territory were inherently incapable of effectively managing and maximising the productive potential of its vast natural resources. Colonial economic policies under both regimes focused on the management of agricultural production and on attempts to enforce the reorientation of farmstead production towards export markets while increasing the production of staples in the misplaced belief that farming households were autonomous units of food production and consumption (Koponen 1994; Iliffe 1979).

Colonial concerns encompassed specific threats posed to and from what was thought of as the 'natural' environment, in particular the threat to people posed by various tropical diseases[36] and the threats to the 'natural' environment seemingly posed by 'native' people rather than European settlers. The two threats were to be addressed jointly in the 1940s through tsetse control strategies which sought to separate game animals permanently from people.

In the first two decades of British administration, effective strategies against tropical disease were limited by low levels of medical knowledge and a basic lack of expertise in rural public health. Efforts were made to encourage basic sanitation in urban centres and to segregate and control those infected with leprosy, generally with the assistance of Christian missions (Turshen 1984). While the attitude of the administration towards the pervasive ill health of its subject population was fatalistic, attitudes towards the preservation of the natural environment were less so, so long as conservation would not interfere with colonial plans for agricultural development. By the 1920s the pattern of future investment and agricultural intensification had been laid over much of the territory, covering the north-eastern and north-western districts, around Kilimanjaro and Lake Victoria, along with other of the higher altitude lands considered suitable for high value cash crops – tea, coffee and pyrethrum. Other areas, if populated, were designated as *de facto* labour reserves of low agricultural potential or, if apparently underpopulated, as potential areas for the conservation of game. The suppression of *maji maji* followed by years of famine in the south had substantially reduced population in the areas between Songea and the coast, and between Mahenge and Liwale. A scattered and defeated population living in dispersed settlements was in no position to oppose the eventual transformation of the land with which they were associated into wilderness from which they would be permanently excluded.

The Germans had initially created small reserves in the area to the north east of Mahenge, in the angle of the Ruaha and Ulanga rivers, and alongside the Matandu river north east of Liwale in a bid to restrict local hunting (Matzke 1976: 37).[37] The need to increase the population's dependence on the market influenced game policy during the early colonial period, along with the desire for the appropriate big game hunting rights for the White invaders. The total area under protection was fairly small, and, being hard to police, would have had a fairly limited effect on local patterns of hunting. Its ideological impact was more considerable, feeding into the resentments which fuelled the *maji maji* war. British policy aimed to conserve game and the natural environment through the extension of controls on hunting and on local populations' rights of access to the environment. The British Game Preservation Ordinance of 1921 brought about the formal establishment of the Selous Game Reserve. Its systematic extension in between 1936 and 1951 was to be a major disruption for the forty thousand N'gindo residents who were forced from their homes (Mackenzie 1988: 251). The successive expansion of the protected area was to have damaging implications not only for the N'gindo, but also for all the peoples of Ulanga, and elsewhere in southern Tanzania.

The initial justification for the establishment of the Selous was the protection of elephants, a justification still used today although the elephant population is widely regarded in the area as a pest damaging to agricultural production. In actuality conservation as an end in itself cannot account for the establishment, and extension of the Selous, which was in effect the key means of making the south marginal, precluding the reintegration of the once wealthy southern regions into a wider economy. From an initial area of two thousand six hundred square miles at the start of the British administration, by 1976, after further expansion under the independent government, the reserve covered over twenty one thousand square miles (55000 km2), the largest area in the country from which human beings had neither rights of access nor residence (Matzke 1976: 37; Mackenzie 1988: 252). The biggest extension occurred between 1936 and 1948 as part of the programme for the elimination of sleeping sickness. Informed by the scientific theories of Swynnerton, the Director of Tsetse Research, British tsetse control programmes in east Africa were based on an understanding of the dynamic relation between the natural environment, host and tsetse fly, the vector responsible for transmitting the sleeping sickness parasite between game, people and cattle. Given the importance of a reservoir of game for the parasite to reproduce itself successfully, combined with the fact that the fly could only traverse a limited distance without bush cover, the creation of a natural barrier between people and game was held to be the most effective way of, if not eliminating, at least containing the disease. This barrier was to be achieved through the creation of cleared areas between animals and people, and through the resettlement of populations to create the kinds of population densities deemed essential for sustaining the requisite levels of clearance.[38]

Tsetse control and resettlement programmes were implemented throughout Tanganyika between 1928 and 1945. Ulanga was no exception. Although residents of the district did not consider themselves to be livestock keepers,[39] with the exception of the Ngoni communities in the west, and sleeping sickness as a disease of people seems not to have attracted the attention of either the German colonial authorities or missionaries, mass resettlement programmes justified by the eradication of the disease took place in virtually all the lowland parts of the district. Around twenty one thousand people were moved into nucleated villages under the policy of population concentration in Mahenge District, from communities at Mahenge, Madaba and Ruaha (Kjekshus 1996: 172). By 1944 all the Pogoro communities in Ulanga were formally living in large villages and the Selous had been significantly extended (Matzke 1976).

Population concentration was not particularly successful in controlling tsetse, or in facilitating the ease of administration and control which the authorities had hoped would constitute an additional benefit of the resettlement programme. Despite the imposition of legal sanctions, punishments and fines, people gradually abandoned the new settlements, eventually returning to old homesteads and farms.[40] But the expansion of the Selous had profound consequences, permanently severing the long-established trade route to the coast and orienting the future direction of the district economy towards the north, to Morogoro and Kilosa, effectively sealing the district's future as an exporter of people, not produce. Bounded on three sides by a designated wilderness the size of a small country, Ulanga had become a *cul de sac* district, the last stop on a road literally going nowhere. The secession of the northern half of the district, comprising fertile river plains rich in fish and high in agricultural potential through the formation of Kilombero district in 1974 and the completion of the Tanzania Zambia railway a year later further accentuated the marginality of the highlands. While Kilombero was now linked by reasonable transport to Dar es Salaam and the expanding regional centres of Iringa and Njombe, Mahenge and villages to the south remained only tenuously connected by seasonal roads to Ifakara, and through it to Dar es Salaam. Until the new pontoon was constructed in the late 1980s transport out of the district to the north via Ifakara was effectively cut off for three months of the year as the Kilombero river flooded.

Independence and socialism. The nationalisation of poverty
Formal independence from Britain came to Tanganyika in 1962, union with Zanzibar and the adoption of 'Tanzania' a year later. The Tanzania African National Union, the political party at the forefront of the nationalist campaign, established a single-party regime and, under the leadership of the charismatic Julius Nyerere, embarked on the implementation of policies designed to bring about a genuinely African socialism (Coulson 1982). Derived from romanticised notions of an authentically African kin based co-operation and inspired by the collectivist vision of peasant transformation from China the ideology of *ujamaa* laid responsibility for development firmly at the feet of the people, and of rural people in particular (Nyerere 1962; Maghimbi 1995; Caplan 1992). Exhortations that 'freedom is work' (*Uhuru ni kazi*) were put into practice in an evolving system which sought to restrict the freedom of non-party bodies while increasing agricultural and industrial output. Under TANU's new incarnation

as the Party of the Revolution, *Chama cha Mapinduzi*, the 1970s witnessed a massive expansion of the public sector, extensive nationalisation and the consolidation of a localised state party bureaucracy which comprised two parallel systems merged under the authority of regional and district commissioners as political appointees (Maghimbi 1992).

Despite the economic failings of *ujamaa* the period *was* revolutionary, in providing a model of a genuinely anti-colonial alternative to western models of how Africa should be managed and in providing formal structures for rural people to participate in politics. It was also revolutionary in its pursual of policies designed to effect a redistribution of wealth away from the rich and urban towards the rural poor. While the successes of the former were to an extent eroded by the increasing strength of the party machine and the assimilation of opposition, the latter policies did have some success at the national level. Reorientation of resources towards rural areas and basic service provision contributed to increased literacy rates and improvements in the health and welfare of Tanzanians, even those in rural areas. These gains were reversed by the 1980s as cuts in social sector spending led to declines in health outcomes and in key poverty and welfare indicators as a consequence of economic collapse and later structural adjustment (Mapolu 1986; Lofchie 1993; Semboja 1995; Lugalla 1995). Collectivisation policies in rural areas damaged agricultural production and reduced incentives and prices for farmers struggling to survive (Collier et al. 1986: 63). Forced collectivisation and the appropriation of assets such as livestock from vulnerable households further weakened subsistence strategies. Perceived as a taking away, rather than as building communal assets, collectivisation, perhaps inevitably in a poor country, 'took from the person with nothing to leave them with less than nothing'. It amounted, in the words of one informant, to the 'nationalisation of poverty' (Green 2000*a*).

Collectivisation entailed the establishment of *ujamaa* villages based on collective cultivation and the implementation of a rural villagisation policy which would ensure that people lived in compact villages as units of production, administration and management (Hyden 1980; Thiele 1984). The villagisation programme was implemented in the Mahenge area in 1976, forcibly bringing scattered populations into the new national system of administration. New villages were not created in Ulanga. Existing settlements were added to, and smaller ones destroyed. The army was brought in to supervise the move, burning houses and demolishing classrooms to prevent people from returning to their old villages. The majority of those who were relocated were moved between five and ten kilometres from their original locations.[41]

The main impact of villagisation in the highlands area has been on farming. Because people moved within walking distance of their original land, and because there was no formal reorganisation of land allocation, most people continued to farm at their pre-villagisation *shamba*. This has resulted in split residence, with people officially living in the village at the same time as they spend much of the agricultural year in temporary houses and shelters at the *shamba*, which may be located in the section of land allocated to another village. Others walk the long distance between village house and *shamba*. The destruction of schools has meant that people with younger children have to live in recognised villages for much of the time because only recognised villages have schools. By the late 1970s people had begun to abandon their new villages and to return, more or less permanently, to their pre-villagisation homesteads, despite strong government opposition. District files show that until 1988 police could be used to recover escapees. By the mid 1980s some 15 per cent had returned (Maghimbi 1990: 258). The exodus continues. Today the figure is probably nearer 25 per cent. Returning is no longer condemned, but tacitly acknowledged by government. Runaway families are easily accommodated into the administrative structure of villages by extending outwards the network of village section leaders to encompass them.[42] In some places, primary schools are being rebuilt as old settlements are given official recognition as villages. The main reason for returning to old settlement sites, and for the establishment of new ones, is the ready availability of good, fertile land away from the immediate vicinity of the villages.

The villagisation policies pursued by the independent socialist administration had distinct echoes of the colonial policy which preceded it some thirty years previously. Not only was it compulsory and explicitly tied in to a desire to increase the effectiveness of rural administration, villagisation was, like population concentration, informed by a rationalistic scientific theory of modernisation and development. Whereas population concentration was justified in relation to public health and rural productivity, villagisation was intended to promote and facilitate rural modernisation through participation in improved agricultural practices and control over villagers as the citizens of a socialist state. Local level participation in decision-making was limited in practice to party members and officials, even in the context of village governments. Although the abolition of the chiefship and the end of indirect rule accompanied the transition to independent government, district political structures in relation to the break between communities and the state remained largely intact in terms of lines of authority and control. District commissioners retained ultimate veto over district decisions and the abolition of local government in 1972 further consolidated state and party power in rural areas (Max 1991: 76). As state resources ebbed in the 1980s and there was less to administer, the power of state and party bureaucrats was increasingly focused on the administration of administration,

administration as an end in itself (Moore 1988). Endless bureaucratic techniques and practices were instituted which required manpower to perform them, and which offered potential opportunities for gate-keeping as the manifestation of power. Local level surveillance through visitors' books, permission for journeys and petty registrations which had to be filled out, created a climate in which people felt that they needed permission to undertake straightforward journeys or to access goods and services, and bestowers of permission gained or retained power as patrons to those dependent on their goodwill and support.

The economic policies pursued by the socialist government failed to resolve adequately issues of supply and demand, doubtless exacerbating some of the main determinants of poverty in rural areas. For much of the socialist period, basic consumer goods were unavailable in Tanzania, and those without access to privileged contacts in the parallel market went without such items as matches, soap, tools, medicines and toothpaste for much of the 1980s. The prices of items such as agricultural implements and corrugated iron were vastly inflated and agricultural prices tightly controlled by government. Small farmers could not afford to buy the goods they needed to improve production or their living conditions, and they were unable to make sufficient money from farming and small-scale off farm income generating activities. People without access to other sources of cash or goods could neither buy nor sell through official channels, giving the impression that rural Tanzanians had 'returned' to 'subsistence' farming (Chabal 1996: 22). Reality was far more complicated than a simple opposition between market participation or withdrawal. The extent and depth of market integration varied considerably in Tanzania even prior to the introduction of *ujamaa* policies.

The kind of integration promoted by colonial and post-colonial governments alike focused heavily on the limited export opportunities for introduced crops, rather than acknowledging the existing production strategies and exchange relations, excluding slavery,[43] which had contributed to making the southern regions relatively affluent in the years preceding the vicious suppression of the *maji maji* war. Many of those who were to become Tanzanians had long been extensively involved in world markets through involvement in long-distance trade. In some parts of the country agricultural surpluses had been sufficient to maintain large groups of people, either as agricultural labourers or domestic slaves for men away earning cash (Iliffe 1979: 73) or as part of strategies to build up networks of dependants and clients around a powerful patron (Monson 1998). Subsistence farming in the sense of agricultural production oriented solely for a household's consumption and utilising that household's labour was not characteristic of either the pre-colonial economy just as it is not characteristic of the contemporary one. And, while colonial officials and their post-colonial counterparts had to struggle to encourage people to produce specific export crops, small farmers did not oppose as a matter of principle but because economic incentives generally favoured alternative, more profitable activities. In Ulanga, the British colonial government resorted to the use of by-laws to force people to grow cotton, despite the fact that rice was more profitable and required less inputs and labour (Larson 1976a; Monson 1995), a strategy pursued by authorities in some parts of the district well into the late 1990s.

Economic collapse amid soaring inflation in the 1980s lead to a change in policy. Government came to an agreement with the International Monetary Fund and accepted at least formally the conditionalities imposed by structural adjustment in 1986 (Cheru 1989: 87; Biermann and Campbell 1989: 82). A gradual process of reform has characterised the 1990s, during which time the country made the formal transition to a multi-party system of government and embarked, if half-heartedly, on the liberalisation process in tacit acknowledgement of de facto changes already initiated from below, especially in urban areas (Tripp 1997). State control over agricultural pricing has officially ended, although competition has yet to make inroads into rural areas and increase farm gate prices dramatically. A mini boom fuelled by foreign aid and investment seems to be underway in cities like Dar es Salaam and Mwanza, symbolised by the pervasiveness of ostentatiously displayed mobile phones. Imported goods are now widely available for those who can afford them. Wages at the top end of the public sector have increased. For those at the bottom of the scale the situation is less promising. Cuts in the public sector have fuelled uncertainty over the future while the low paid must aim to get by on a monthly wage of around $30 US or less, health services remain under-funded and charges of one sort or another are the norm for education and health (Green 2000b). The majority of urban dwellers who are engaged in non-agricultural employment work in the informal sector, which also provides a safety net for those in formal sector employment. Outside urban centres, in places like Ulanga, living standards and modes of livelihood for the majority are not perceived as being vastly changed from the socialist period. Some consider economic conditions to have got worse. Most Tanzanians continue to live in very similar housing to that occupied by parents and grandparents in the 1960s and before. While brick dwellings became popular during the 1970s, few can afford iron roofing or concrete floors, making houses susceptible to weather damage. Hand tools dominate agricultural production. Agricultural technology is little changed because, so long as a hoe blade constitutes a significant proportion of household expenditure, farmers simply cannot afford to invest in new equipment. Although a greater variety of consumer and electronic goods is now available, along with imported new and second-hand clothing, poor rural families cannot afford to purchase these items as long as they have to buy food and pay a range of official and unofficial charges for health care, education and public services (Narayan 1997).

Policy continuity in the post-colonial period

The continuity of colonial and post-colonial policies in Ulanga, and in Tanzania more generally, is striking. In Ulanga the agricultural, economic, resettlement and game protection policies pursued into the 1980s and 1990s were essentially intensifications of the interventions introduced by the British colonial administration, albeit in a changing macroeconomic environment. These policies were to determine or at least constrain the viability of particular subsistence strategies pursued by people in the district into the twenty-first century, through impacts on settlement patterns, agricultural production and expansion. Even the apparently radical reform programmes introduced in the late 1990s in response to international donor pressure were in many respects repetitions of previously implemented colonial policies. Reform programmes in health returned to the colonial mixed economy of service delivery, according bodies such as missions increased autonomy in the running of services. The proposed programme of local government reform, although increasing the potential options of local participation in decision making, retains current district boundaries and aims to introduce a limited decentralisation programme, restoring local autonomy to pre-socialist levels, while the proposed reform of land tenure legislation is at pains to retain the break between customary and civil law.

Although villagisation and game protection policies reduced agricultural production and access to new agricultural land, at the same time as encouraging the massive increase in pest populations, the frailty of the highlands economy was probably well established by the 1940s when the transition away from hardy sorghum towards less predictable, but faster growing, maize as a food staple (Lussy 1953; Culwick and Culwick 1994) combined with dependence on the market and cash to mediate food shortages established the base for longer term future food insecurity and with it, for the possibilities for the perpetuation of patronage which have come to characterise certain political relationships in Ulanga. The disempowerment of the rural poor and the economic vulnerability of some sections of the population has doubtless contributed to the power of the Catholic Church in the district in the 1990s, and to the persistence of mission. This power was not of course uncontested. As we shall see, local political forms of opposition to Church influence were developed through participation in witchcraft suppression practices and in the performance of a Catholicism which could be, if necessary, carried out without recourse to the institutional church.

3

Evangelisation in Ulanga

Post-colonial continuities

Perhaps contrary to initial expectations, there was no immediate break between pre and post-Independence Tanganyika, at least from the perspective of the rural dweller who found that life remained pretty much the same. National policy in the post-independence period merely accentuated colonial techniques for the marginalisation of the south. The TANU regime strove to institutionalise and embed party power across all tiers of Tanzanian society, sometimes by forced nationalisation and confrontation, sometimes by stealth. The result was the gradual conversion of state and economy to an extension of the party machine (Mlimuka and Kabudi 1986; Moore 1988). The aim was to establish new power relations based on a party definition of political legitimacy while eclipsing, if not eliminating, pre-existing positions of political authority.

The impacts of these changes were variable. In some districts apparently 'pre-colonial' positions of 'traditional' authority, in actuality the creations of indirect rule, sustained themselves for a time in parallel to the reformed system (Abrahams 1981: 38; Thiele 1984: 60). Elsewhere, individual holders of power shrewdly strove to build convergence between pre and post-colonial positions through strategic manipulation of the blurred interface between state, party and local level political regimes. Of course, political authority never rested solely with government servants, whether they were chiefs, headmen or representatives of the political party. Power and authority were, and are, fragmented and related to the material and symbolic resources which a person actually had under their control (Lonsdale 1986). Successful families in Ulanga consolidated established chains of influence by seeking new positions within the party and the church, ensuring future influence as self-appointed gatekeepers of the expanding gap between the rural majority and the emerging elite. While ex-chiefs and headmen could convert the advantages of former administrative positions into new bases of power as businessmen and patrons, the new holders of power in the socialist period were the local level administrators from outside the area who were responsible for the different tiers of district infrastructure. With this responsibility came the potential to control the avenues of access to the goods and services now provided by the state. Administrators and district staff were at the same time party staff, constituting a state funded cadre of patrons to the peasant farmer. Their position contrasted with that of the volunteer gatekeepers at lower tiers of administration who formally managed party and village affairs on behalf of the district and region but in practice as clients to their middle tier patrons at district and ward level, and who played an important part as enforcers of state control at the height of the socialist period. This process of public co-option through nationalisation and the creation of a massive public sector has been described in detail elsewhere (Moore 1988).

Despite aspirations to an essentially benign totalitarianism under the single-party regime state control over the population and over the rules of political engagement remained partial, even after the outlawing of what the state had come to view as potential sources of opposition to the party regime: trade and co-operative unions, membership associations and private enterprise (Tripp 1997; Naali 1986). Christian churches, however, retained their independent status, (Westerlund 1980; van Bergen 1981). As state resources ebbed away in the 1980s ex-missionary churches seeped into the ever-widening breach created by the erosion of state power and public services. This expansion took the form of continued engagement in service provision, particularly in education and health (Semboja and Therkilsden 1995; Munishi 1995; Sivalon 1995). It also perpetuated the kind of patronage relations established at the height of colonial mission despite the formal end of the missionary era. The continuities and transformations of colonial and post-colonial governance and its relation with missionary and post-missionary Christianity have implications for the place and perception of popular Christianity amongst Catholics in Ulanga, a perception which encompasses ambivalence *and* ownership, separation *and* inclusion.

Conversion and power: the Benedictine conquest

In Ulanga, as in other colonial situations, widespread 'conversion' to Christianity was not the consequence of the aggregate choices of individuals attracted by the 'message' of Christianity.[1] Actual 'converts', in the sense of adults who had chosen to accept a new religion, were few and far between. Evangelisation was a gradual and contested process that owed much in the short term to the close political relationship between German colonial interests and the Catholic Centre Party and, in the longer term, to the education policies pursued by both the German and British administrations. Catholic missions gained early access to much of Southern Tanzania. Through various agreements with governments, they established an exclusive sphere of influence that effectively excluded missions of other denominations and was to persist in practice long after the old agreements, and the administrations that made them, had ceased to exist.

Like other administrative districts in the southern part of the country, Mahenge was opened up to Roman Catholic influence right at the start of the German military administration. The German missionary order of the Benedictines of St Ottilien was founded in 1884, specifically to fulfil colonial demand for conversion in Germany's new colonies (Smith 1963: 98; Iliffe 1979: 217). The order had close links with the German East Africa Company (DOAG) and with a Centre Party keen, in the aftermath of *kulturkampf*, to be seen to promote colonial acquisition as a means of demonstrating its commitment to the new unified nation state (Koponen 1994: 162). The Centre Party was critical in securing the funding needed to scramble an expeditionary force to suppress anti-colonial resistance in the territory (Larson 1976: 40). It was ultimately this close association between Catholic interests and colonial policy which gave the Benedictines the initial advantage in the south and which, by bringing the Mahenge highlands under military control, made evangelisation possible.

The Benedictines had established a base in Dar es Salaam in 1889 from where they expanded southwards and westwards (Smith 1963: 98) declaring the Vicariate of Dar es Salaam in 1902 (Hassing 1970: 377). The order was involved, together with company troops, in the initial administrative occupation of Iringa in 1896 (Wright 1971: 69), from where they began to consolidate their position in the south. Liaison with the military force facilitated the founding of mission stations at Lindi, on the coast, in 1896 and at Peramiho in Songea in 1898 (Richter 1934: 43). An attempt was also made in 1897 to establish a station in the Mahenge highlands near the present day village of Isongo, at the top of the escarpment. This was unsuccessful (Iliffe 1979: 222). Without military support the missionaries were simply too few in number to establish themselves in hostile territory amongst people who saw no obvious benefit from an alliance. Local people moved away, leaving the camp in flames (Larson 1976: 63–4). It was not until after the establishment of the headquarters of the military administration in 1899 that the Benedictines were able to reconsider the Mahenge highlands as a viable outpost of the Catholic endeavour. What was to be a lasting alliance between the Catholics and the Mlolere family resulted in the allocation of land on which to construct the first mission station at Kwiro, the present-day headquarters of the Roman Catholic diocese, in 1902.

Little is known of what local people first thought of the missionary influx nor of relations with the German military administration whose army, the *Schuztruppe*, comprised both German and African soldiers (Wright 1993: 200–1). Records from the time were mostly written by German administrators or by missionaries. Oral histories collected later tend to privilege the accounts of educated people, many of whom were influential Christians. Evidence from elsewhere in the south, however, suggests that the missionaries were likely to have been viewed, initially at least, with considerable suspicion and hostility.[2] Forced attendance at mission schools, particularly by Benedictines, was cited by southern residents and the German government alike as a contributory factor in the *maji maji* rising (Hassing 1970: 383). Benedictine missions were reputed to underpay labour. The order was generally supportive of the system and methods of colonial administration and on no occasion criticised the more contentious practices of the colonial regime (Koponen 1994: 165). The perceived close association of Benedictine missionaries with the German military administration informed the selection of Bishop Spiss and his party as targets for assassination on the road between Peramiho and Kilwa at the start of the *maji maji* war and for the destruction of mission stations at Peramiho and Lukuledi by *maji maji* fighters (Hassing 1970). In Mahenge itself Catholic missionaries were targeted along with the military during *maji maji* attacks and jointly sought refuge inside the fortified *boma*.

The profound ambivalence with which the missionaries were viewed is further evidenced by the extent and kind of support they managed to attract in the area. A mere 98 people were baptised prior to 1905, of whom the majority were male youth baptised en masse between 1904 and 5 as part of their schooling. The remainder, in what was to become a pattern in baptism which would persist until the 1940s, were baptised in *periculo mortis* (Larson 1976: 182)[3]. Such baptisms were usually performed by other lay people in a strategy common to Catholic missions which initially prioritised numbers of souls over numbers of living Christians.[4]

Distinct trajectories of conversion are discernable from the parish records, trajectories likely to have been replicated throughout the diocese as a whole and which would have had significant implications for the constitution of the Christian community at particular points in time. The baptised can be categorised into three main groups, each corresponding to a distinct phase of colonial conversion: those in *periculo mortis*, schoolchildren and infants. The first two categories predominate up to the 1950s. The first surviving Christians were young men and boys, seeking work or education in the nascent network of bush schools that the Benedictines had founded. Initially they were a minority. Up to 1920, most of those baptised were schoolchildren, among whom the number of girls baptised did not begin to equal the number of boys until the mid 1930s. The majority of adults baptised were on their deathbeds. The remainder were from among the community of lepers, epileptics and paupers who lived under the care of the mission. Adult women do not seem to have been any more attracted to Christianity than their male counterparts. The main motivation underlying the rare conversion of a healthy adult was the marriage to a Christian partner. Infant baptism gradually became the norm once this first generation of school age Christians became parents. As early as 1920, out of 185 baptisms, 137 were of infants born between 1918 and 1920, and, out of the total baptised, 127 had at least one Christian parent. Forty-one of these new Christians died within one month of being baptised.[5] Until the 1950s, perhaps one third of the total number of infant baptisms seem to have been carried out because the infant was thought to be dying. A significant proportion of these children actually died. The total number of baptisms at various points in history then does not give any accurate picture of the actual number of Christians. The lack of any strong centralised political authority, combined with weak and artificial chiefships, meant that adults were not attracted to the Church as a way of challenging the existing political system. Land was plentiful. Situations such as those described by Murphree for the Shona (1969: 9) or by Wilson for the Nyakyusa, in which converts moved to mission lands and the mission came to function as a quasi chiefship, did not arise (1963: 42). Appealing to children and the powerless, the 'expendables' lacking the kinship and other resources to make their own way in the world (Wright 1993), the mission had few local allies before the *maji maji* rising, with the possible exception of the pragmatist Mlolere.

The ambivalent perception of the missionaries was shared to an extent by the German military administration. Aware that missionary education concentrated almost solely on the catechism and that missionary interests prioritised conversion above educational attainment, the administration sought unsuccessfully to gain government support for the establishment of a secular school which could provide an education for non Christian youth and meet the future needs of the administration (Wright 1971: 112). The absence of alternative providers of education combined with the requirement that children receive some basic education gave the administration little choice but to co-operate with the mission. In the years between the end of *maji maji* and the outbreak of World War 1 the administration encouraged, and sometimes enforced, the attendance of children at mission schools (Larson 1976: 163). Hostility from parents was overcome through the provision of incentives such as clothing and the threat of sanctions applied. This period also witnessed a radical shift in the approach to conversion and to education by Catholic missions. In 1912 a meeting of East Africa Bishops agreed to increase the instruction requirement for potential converts from one month, for those resident at mission stations, to three years (Richter 1934: 39), formally making the school the cornerstone of evangelisation policy.

The Benedictines set up a mission station surrounded by farmland on which they grew crops and kept cattle. As a self-sufficient community of priests and brothers, living apart from the people whom they had come to convert, theirs was a semi-monastic lifestyle. Agricultural and technical innovations introduced by the missionaries were oriented towards the establishment and maintenance of the mission and the European lifestyle of the missionaries. Technical schools to train boys in tailoring, carpentry and mechanics were started early. The mission's grandiose building and agricultural programmes demanded semi-skilled artisans and a continual supply of labour, which the mission initially found hard to attract in the face of competition from the wild rubber trade. Even after the system of colonial taxation was sufficiently established to make most adult men into potential payers and rubber prices had collapsed they preferred to work only until they had earned sufficient money for taxes (Mbosa 1988: 90; Larson 1976: 144). Most of these early employees were Christians (Larson 1976: 150). The First World War abruptly ended Benedictine involvement in Mahenge. Shortly after Belgian troops occupied the highland area the Benedictines were deported as German nationals (Larson 1976: 217). The mission was virtually abandoned. A small contingent of White Fathers from the Netherlands assumed a caretaker position for ex-Benedictine stations, but there was no expansion. By 1921, when the Swiss Capuchins, another Franciscan order, arrived the Christian community, consisting as it did of the young, the sick and the dead, was almost non-existent (Larson 1976: 252–4).

Capuchin expansion

Although the Capuchins comprised the second wave of Catholic evangelisation in and around Mahenge their strategy was little different from that of the Benedictines who preceded them. Trade schools, bush schools, hospitals and mission stations were expanded and extended, the boundaries of Kwiro parish shrinking as new parishes were demarcated within the old Ulanga district. The last mission stations to be built were those at Malinyi and Ngoheranga in 1954 (Kilumanga 1990: 50–1), in the plains to the west of the Mahenge highlands, on the very margins of the area associated with the Pogoro. The Pogoro heartlands had been effectively incorporated into the network of mission centres and outstations some twenty years previously. No other mission gained access to the Pogoro area until Lutherans from Denmark established their small church in Mahenge town in the late 1940s.[6] By this time the whole of the old Ulanga District was, in any case, officially designated as a Capuchin 'sphere of influence' under the order of the Apostolic Delegate of 1932.[7] Initially,

Catholic missions had been hostile to spheres of influence, advocating freedom of religious movement in opposition to the demands of the Protestant missions for discrete mission territories (Wright 1971: 120). Increasing competition with Protestant missions and the attitude of the British administration resulted in a change of policy. Even without the sphere of influence, the Lutherans would have found it difficult to attract converts in Ulanga where, because of the crucial role of the school, the Capuchins had effectively made competing evangelisation impossible. Situated at the edge of a housing estate constructed for the temporary occupation of public sector workers from all over the country the Lutheran church was, and is, primarily intended to serve a congregation of already Lutheran outsiders. In 1991 the pastor estimated that 'less than five' out of a regular congregation of sixty were Pogoro from Mahenge. Colonial resettlement policies had advantages for the mission, creating nucleated communities near to which mission stations could be established and schools accessed. Although the Capuchins were not slow to respond to the opportunities created by concentration, moving their mission station from Ketaketa, in the N'gindo area, some ten miles east to a new settlement at Luhombero in 1938, they never succeeded in attracting the already Muslim N'gindo.

The Swiss Capuchins were inexperienced in the field of missionary work. Tanganyika was their first overseas venture. Correspondence in the colonial files of the time suggests that the Capuchins lacked the political skills necessary for dealing with the secular officials of the British district administration. The mission was frequently in conflict with the authorities over land for mission stations, the payment of its labour in goods rather than cash and, in the 1940s, over the administration's use of a witchcraft eradicator in 'Christian' villages.[8] More threatening for the evangelisation strategy was the Government's 1925 report on the state of education in the territory. This was highly critical of the poor standards of education in the Capuchins' schools, which concentrated on religious education (Larson 1976: 35–6). The introduction of government grants in aid to approved mission schools over the next three years (Thompson 1976: 35–6) meant that the Capuchins had to improve their schools or lose influence. They chose to upgrade. By 1945 there were 44 church run primary schools in the old Ulanga District as opposed to only seven run by native authorities, which took mainly the relatives of colonial appointed native authority 'chiefs' and headmen. A further 4,000 pupils were enrolled in 'bush schools' and catechetical centres (Larson 1976: 314), which, under the 1927 Education Ordinance, were exempt from government regulation (Thompson 1976: 47). In the Mahenge highlands occupied in the main by Pogoro communities there was only one native authority school. All the rest, bush, grant aided and the Central School at the mission centre itself were directly under mission control.

Promoting natural increase: the 'matrimonial agency business'
The mission did not confine its involvement with young people to strictly educational matters. The practice of secluding girls (*wali* – literally 'maidens') between puberty and marriage was appropriated by the mission, which, under the authority of missionary sisters,[9] assumed responsibility for the daughters of Christians from throughout the area and kept them 'inside' on behalf of their parents.[10] An elderly Capuchin missionary informed me that this was necessary to allow the girls to attend church services, as had they remained at home they would not have been permitted to leave their houses. There had been debate in educational and colonial circles during the 1930s about the widespread practice of secluding girls in southern Tanzania and elsewhere, and the need to replace this with what was then considered to be a 'modern' domestic education in a boarding context.[11] Girls, under the care of the sisters, were taught the skills that their contemporaries in Europe would have learned at home, knitting, sewing and cooking.[12] In reality neither 'modern' education nor attending services underlay the church's attempt to appropriate the seclusion of the *wali*. What was at stake was more fundamental – the very future of the Christian community to be achieved through the 'Christian family' and the possibility for its creation through ensuring that young women had Christian marriages. The mission appropriated the seclusion of the girls because it gave the mission an element of control over marriage, or at least over the marriage of the girls under its control, which it was hoped would promote the expansion of Christianity through the Christian family.

Older women who recalled being kept 'inside' by the mission told of happy times in a boarding setting where they were well fed but taught tasks of total pointlessness, such as how to knit socks, while being forbidden by the Sisters to wear shoes lest they become 'big headed'. These girls became known locally as the *wakubwa*, the 'big ones', to differentiate them from younger female primary school boarders. The mission, acting in *loco parentis*, not only sought to arrange marriages for the *wakubwa* with Christian men but also even received bridewealth for them on occasion, as it was happy to do for young pagan divorcees. These practices were viewed with disapproval and incredulity by the colonial authorities. As one District Officer informed his successor in 1934, 'It sometimes happens that the mission, when anxious to convert a Pagan wife who is already married, actually advance money to her father so that he can pay back the brideprice to the Pagan husband, and the girl is then taken into the mission and after a probation period married to a Christian. I think that this matrimonial agency business is not within the strict sphere of missionary operations, and is really the result of overzealousness . . . I have warned (them) . . . that divorces are . . . the affair of the local native courts.'[13]

Mission involvement in this 'matrimonial agency business' continued at least into the 1940s. In some instances the mission paid over bridewealth to the father of the girl even before a suitor had been found. The groom would then reimburse the amount either to the mission or to the father of the girl who would reimburse the mission. In 1937 Daudi Liambandowe of Kwiro parish received fifty shillings from the mission as bridewealth for his daughter Afra, which he undertook to repay should he receive bridewealth directly from a Christian groom.[14] Some young men appear to have performed what was in effect brideservice to the mission, in order to pay off bridewealth debt transacted through the mission rather than paid over to the relatives of the girl. Thomas bin Sauli signed a *mapatano* agreement with the mission at Kwiro in June 1936. Translated from the Kiswahili the document reads 'I agree that I have a debt of twenty-eight shillings and twenty five cents to the Kwiro mission that is bridewealth which is owed on my betrothed Lucia daughter of Limpeta. I shall pay this debt while doing work at the mission.'[15] Of course, not all the *wakubwa* had Christian marriages and only a minority of Christian girls were ever secluded at the mission. That minority was, however, significant, for they comprise today much of the core group of devout Catholic women, women who are virtual specialists in the recitation of prayer and song and Christian procedure. National Independence in 1961, heralding at least officially the end of the missionary era, brought the seclusion to an end although it continues in modified form as a fee-paying domestic science school for girls, run by the indigenous sisters of the Diocese. The domestic science school continues to be popularly associated with seclusion and, amongst older generations, with ideals of if not pre-marital chastity, some element of control over young women's sexuality.

The economics of mission
The Capuchins control over the education of the district's children served to establish and eventually institutionalise an association between schooling and Catholic Christianity and between economic power and Christian mission. Baptism, followed by first communion and confirmation, if the child remained in the system long enough, was an integral part of the educational process, associated with an individual's progression through primary school. For much of the missionary period, children who had not been baptised as infants were baptised as a matter of routine when they reached the third standard. The education in 'bush schools' was basic; reading, writing, arithmetic, song and prayer, limiting the aspirations of most children to local concerns (Zanolli 1971). For a select few boys, performance at school was rewarded with the prospect of proceeding to secondary school or seminary, with a view to either securing a

place in government service or in the Church itself. For others, a short-term incentive was a position as a catechist on whom the main burden of teaching fell in the bush school system. The mission Central School at Kwiro, established in 1928, provided a higher level of education for those who were to become trained teachers or priests. In 1950 the junior seminary at Kasita was begun, to accelerate the production of an indigenous clergy. This seminary takes students from all over the country and functions in effect as a private secondary school for boys. Of these only a minority, between two and six per cent, will ever proceed to ordination. Perhaps surprisingly, the nationalisation of schools in 1969 (Westerlund 1980: 221) had remarkably little impact on the access of the Church to primary schools, even though it no longer controls them. Catechists have virtually unrestricted access to the classroom, where they teach several periods of religion a week. Church involvement in education is increasing as private provision becomes politically acceptable in post-liberalisation Tanzania (Sivalon 1995). The diocese has recently established a secondary school for girls and is involved in the delivery of pre-primary education.

The expansion of Catholic influence in the highlands was not confined to transformations in ritual practice or religious affiliation, which were to remain partial. The economic influence of the mission itself was substantial. Its growth was directly associated with the expansion of the colonial economy and systems of administration. Even in the years preceding *maji maji* the mission provided opportunities for employment for those needing to amass cash for tax. It also provided food and shelter for labourers and the vulnerable who comprised the first generation of Christians. As the mission consolidated itself through the establishment of the farms and workshops it required skilled and semi skilled craftsmen, as well as increasing numbers of catechist-teachers to provide the elementary education offered in its multiplying bush schools. Up to the 1940s porters were regularly employed to transport the imported goods the missionaries required between Mahenge and the coast and as escorts. The scale of the mission economy is indicated by Bishop Maranta in a letter to the District Office written in 1936. 'An average of more than one thousand men are daily employed in our missions in the Ulanga District...A high percentage of tax money collected in this district is from mission sources.'[16] By the mid 1930s the mission stations were, in the absence of any similar institutions in the area outside the administrative centre of Mahenge town, 'important socio-economic centres (functioning) as bank, post office, medical dispensary, market and employer' (Larson 1976: 313).

Initial participation in education was viewed with suspicion by local people, as an indicator of subjection and conquest. As the opportunities associated with education became better known and educated status accepted as a means of achicving wealth and power, attitudes shifted. Families encouraged children to become educated in order to obtain employment, rather than for its own sake, fostering a perception of education as an attribute of schooling, rather than of culture or society. The fetishisation of education as an attribute measured in quantity not quality persists today in popular attitudes that lay sole responsibility for educational outcomes on schools and teachers rather than families and students. Under the colonial and post-colonial welfare regimes, educated people generally left the district, often posted away on government service, contributing to the formation of an urban middle class in Dar es Salaam and leaving poorer relatives in the rural districts of the south for whom education continues to be viewed as a responsibility of failing external institutions. The result is a resident rural community in which the vast majority have low levels of education and income in contrast to an urban diaspora who are reluctant to return and invest in an isolated district with few economic and other opportunities.

The break between resident poor and absent rich is manifested in rural attitudes towards towns which extend to those in salaried employment. Such persons, optimistically viewed, are moneyed sources of potential support. Pessimistically viewed they are fickle and subject to the demands of favourites. Expectations of patronage persist, despite the experience of rejection for all but the closest kin, while those defining themselves as elite may be at pains not to be exposed as lacking the resources to effect lasting bonds of dependence and mutuality. The injunction to '*Gwizi shirau*', (come tomorrow) preserves both the pride of the potential patron and the hope of the person seeking short-term economic assistance. Unlike salaried employees in the public and private sectors whose power and resources are increasingly threatened by a competitive environment and new regulatory frameworks, priests continue to retain privileged access to the material and symbolic resources which constitute power through a network of transnational patron–client relationships with 'benefactors' in Europe. Whereas missionary priests across all denominations generally came from backgrounds in which ordination was viewed as a sacrifice into a life of poverty, ordination in Tanzania is perceived as entry into the kind of life which missionary priests were perceived by the missionised as living; a life of this worldly privilege and power, a life in which one has the power to command others and receive tribute in turn, in short as an increase, rather than a dissolution, of status (cf. Pels 1999: 111).

The economic significance of the Catholic Church in the new Ulanga district remains considerable some forty years after independence.[17] Outside Mahenge town, with its government offices, bank and police station, there is no postal service, nor any regular transport to the villages to the south. In the early 1990s, prior to a major donor funded project in support of the district council, the Church had more vehicles than all the public sector offices in Mahenge combined, along with substantial commercial ventures in the form of large-scale mechanised farms and grinding mills. At parish level mission stations provide an unofficial transport service, selling rides and renting out vehicles and tractors,[18] as well as access to radio communications via the diocese network in the absence of a viable telecommunications facility in the district. The Church continues to be a significant source of permanent and casual employment, both administrative and agricultural.[19] It distributes relief in times of flood and famine, such as after the El Nino induced food shortages in 1999. First communion and confirmation continue to have their place as markers of a child's progression through the seven years of primary school. Becoming a 'full' Catholic is still associated with schooling. Religion and education continue to be valued as attributes of identity in the post-colonial nation state.

4

The persistence of mission

Along with Independence and the end of colonial rule the 1960s saw the official end of the missionary era in much of Africa, including Tanzania, and the formal transfer of power to a new generation of African clergy. Not so much in anticipation of this as the perceived need for more priests as their Christian communities expanded the Capuchins had begun to train local men for ordination relatively early. The first priest from within the diocese was ordained in 1948, but it was not until the late 1970s that over 75 per cent of priests working in the diocese were Tanzanian. Prior to 1960 a mere five indigenous clergy had been ordained. Ordinations increased in the 1960s and 1970s, with a further twenty-eight ordinations. In 1988 the staff of the diocese comprised forty-one indigenous priests and nine missionary fathers,[1] not all of whom were in residence. A decade later the diocese had a mere five Capuchin priests, two mission brothers and two mission sisters, as opposed to fifty-eight diocesan priests, four indigenous Capuchin priests, three indigenous brothers and two hundred and fifteen Diocesan sisters of St Francis of Assisi.[2] On the face of it the Church in Mahenge is no longer a missionary church. This is not in fact the case. The diocese remains heavily dependent on external funds and, at least up to the early 1990s, received the bulk of this either from or through the missionary orders which were the agents of evangelisation in the diocese. During this period less than 20 per cent of Church funds were obtained from local revenue, the remainder coming in the form of grants from Rome and from the Swiss Capuchins.[3] This estimate does not include donations of machinery and vehicles or gifts to individual clergy from benefactors in Europe, some of which are substantial.[4] The continuing dependence on Europe and on European Christian charities to finance mission services ensures that the institutional presence of mission remains strong along with missionary influence, perpetuating the close personal and financial connections between the personnel of the diocese and their

European patrons. This perpetuation of mission is recognised by Pogoro Catholics, for whom *missien* refers to both the buildings and personnel of the diocese, in fact to anything and anyone associated it, in contrast to *kanisa* (church), which is used to refer only to actual church buildings.

The price of self reliance

This perception of the Church as a unitary institution is to an extent reinforced by the fact that the surface structure of the diocese appears virtually unchanged since the height of colonial mission. The Church remains organised on the mission outstation model. Ecclesiastical hierarchies between bishop, priests and sisters are self evident even to non Catholic outsiders who witness the daily performance of power between the Church personnel occupying different tiers in the hierarchy and between Church personnel and parishioners, ritualised in the style of greeting as an index of submission, from the merest stoop of respect to kneeling and prostration. However, the inevitable fragmentation that follows expansion and diversification lurks beneath the façade of institutional unity in the post missionary context. Catholic dioceses in Tanzania are now semi-autonomous units under the Bishop's jurisdiction, formally separate from the missionary orders which once controlled them. The Capuchin Friars are now incorporated within a wider east African brotherhood whose headquarters are situated within the boundaries of the diocese. What people think of as 'mission' in actuality comprises a number of semi-autonomous institutions. These include the seminary, the friary, the congregation of sisters, the diocese headquarters and the constituent parishes, all of which are responsible, as far as possible, for their own financing. The diocese had failed to meet the initial deadlines for financial sustainability set by the Capuchins in the early 1990s. This was not surprising given the enormous costs involved in maintaining the infrastructure of land and buildings set up by the missionaries.[5] In addition, the growth in the number of clergy and sisters, and in the scale and scope of church activities had imposed additional costs. Religious personnel alone exceed around three hundred priests and sisters, but the diocese also supports numerous other workers who administer its parishes and enterprises, as well as the labourers who work on church farms, the house servants of priests and the guards of parish houses.

The Church no longer prioritises evangelisation at any cost. Charges are levied for church-managed health and education services and, more con-tentiously, for access to some key sacraments around which the religion is struc-tured. The leper colony, once an apparent symbol of missionary generosity, has been wound down and many of those previously in the care of the mission have been returned to the community. The leper colony was, throughout the colonial period,[6] a joint venture between the local administration and the mission, assisted by grants from government which, under the British, assumed financial responsibility for the destitute, including the relatively large numbers of people with the chronic epilepsy that is prevalent in the district (Jilek-Aal 1976; 1979).[7] Shifting social policy priorities implemented in the drive for structural adjustment have led to reduced spending for the vulnerable. Local government has cut its assistance to Church social services although the mission hospital at Ifakara receives ministry of health funding to function as the Kilombero district hospital. The Church continues to provide other services that are appreciated in the absence of alternatives, particularly in more remote parts of the district. Educational facilities, particularly trade schools and the seminary, are oversubscribed, attracting a diverse national body of students. More locally oriented services operated by the diocesan welfare office under the auspices of Caritas or by individual parishes include grinding mills and dispensaries.

Annual fees, *zaka*, payable by Christians to the Church were introduced as early as 1947 (Larson 1976: 346) when the missionaries realised that the Church was unsustainable if it continued to give as a way of attracting converts. Willingness to support the Church materially was, and is, regarded as an index of Christian commitment. People then (Larsen 1976: 347), as now, were reluctant to pay. Only a minority, perhaps 20 per cent, now contribute *zaka*.[8] Sanctions in the form of prohibitions (*kizuizi*) on accessing certain sacraments are commonly imposed on non-payers in order to encourage them to pay. In 1991 *zaka* was 225 shillings for a farmer, having increased from 80 shillings in 1989, a sum roughly equivalent to two days' casual labour. According to the parish clerk responsible for accounting and overall collections, people tended to underpay if they paid at all, even though the actual amount requested was probably affordable for the majority of parishioners. Attitudes to payment of *zaka* in Ulanga are not dissimilar to attitudes towards the payment of local taxes and the user fees introduced during the 1990s for health and education services. Opposition to these charges is not based so much on a perception of cost as a rejection of the social relations of coercion implied by the compulsory nature of the transaction (Green 2000b). Unlike tribute gifts as a voluntary indication of respect or payments to healers and diviners working in what is locally defined as the 'traditional' medical sector which are determined only after drawn out negotiations between healer and client *zaka*, like colonial 'head tax' and its contemporary successor,[9] is widely perceived as being extractive, exploitative and inherently unjust. Demands on congregations for material support are not restricted to *zaka*. Congregations are expected to support the church with food and to respond generously to requests for special collections, often to support church celebrations. The annual request for contributions of food, especially maize, after the harvest to 'feed the priests', was resented by many as seemingly inappropriate in the aftermath of continued mission involvement in the distribution of food aid. 'What do priests eat? Rice! But they ask us for maize', an old woman muttered as she recounted the incongruity of the parish demands on her household from the doorway of her ramshackle house. Rice, as a higher status food than maize, is the preferred food at feasts and celebrations. Some priests are rumoured to participate in the food trade and to sell donated maize back to people at shortage times for a profit. Allegations like this, combined with the various income generating enterprises of the Church, contribute to a widespread perception of Catholic Christianity as '*dini ya biashara*', 'the religion of business'.[10]

The 'religion of business'
Perhaps the majority of highlands Catholics who depend on farming as their main source of income live in poor conditions, regularly experience chronic food insecurity and have to struggle to meet basic needs and state expenses (Green 2000*b*). Unable to afford road transport and living in a district where roads to rural holdings are simply non-existent they walk many miles every day between village home and *shamba*, as well as to hospital, market, primary school and church. Around them they see well-dressed priests and government officials driving around in large comfortable vehicles and the flaunting of priests' apparent wealth every time they walk past another house under construction for the relative of a priest.[11] The physical stature of priests, who get little exercise and eat well, is viewed as further evidence not merely of wealth but of indulgence in uncontrolled appetites. Against this background it is perhaps to be expected that the fees levied for utilisation of church managed services and the contributions demanded from the parishioners are not popular with many people.

Government dispensaries in the rural areas could have provided an alternative to those run by the Church but post adjustment drug shortages have thrown people back on the mission, in effect forcing people to use Church dispensaries for which they must pay higher fees. Patients presenting themselves at government clinics may find themselves referred on to mission dispensaries where drugs are available. Some patients prefer to do this anyway because they think that the state will cheat them, providing 'weak' medicine manufactured in low status countries like China. The drugs available in mission dispensaries are popularly believed to be superior because they come from '*Ulaya*', usually translated as 'Europe', a category that includes the people and products of what are thought of as Western countries, and which has been extended to encompass such places as Thailand and Japan. Paradoxically, the state's failure in the provision of health services reinforces the perception of the Church as a business venture. It is widely believed that the drugs in mission dispensaries are donated as charity from abroad and the Church is, once again, seen to be making a profit. The Church denies this, saying that it buys the drugs for its dispensaries and charges only to recoup its costs. The truth is probably somewhere in the middle. Drugs and medicines are donated and then sold on within the Catholic network, making donations of medicines a source of revenue for the church. Many of these goods have 'gift of the . . .' stamped in large letters on the packaging.

The price of 'self reliance' demanded by Church and state alike seems high. Almost everybody thinks that they are being cheated by the state, and when the Church asks for money, by the Church too. 'Now we give to the Church, not get from it', I was told, which seems unreasonable to many. The Church still presents itself as a wealthy organisation, not merely enmeshed in land and buildings (Tanner 1967: 200), but in vehicles, business ventures and lucrative contacts with Europe. It represents a stark contrast in terms of wealth and resources with dilapidated government facilities and the basic living conditions of the poor. Church buildings had electricity and piped water long before the district hospital and do so even in remote parishes. Most priests and the parishes with which they are associated have at least one four-wheel drive vehicle, in addition to enterprises such as shops, grinding mills and farms.

The lifestyle and expectations of the current generation of priests are, like their surroundings, informed by a missionary model which replicated the domestic conditions of rural Western Europe in the economic wasteland of Southern Tanzania. What must have seemed to the rural observer as conspicuous consumption in the form of electric appliances, gas cookers, motor vehicles and imported food characterised mission lifestyles, even at the height of Tanzania's economic austerity. It continues to do so, along with what are locally viewed as lavish and frequent meals, served thrice daily and, supposedly, always with fish or meat. Such assertions may seem trivial but are highly significant when considered in relation to the idioms of food and eating around which Ulanga social life is structured and in relation to the daily eating habits and seasonal food shortages prevalent in most parishioner homes (Green 1999c). An extended period of *njala* (hunger) is experienced by many highlands people in the wet pre-harvest season when food stores have run out, as has the money with which to purchase maize in the market. Even in the immediate post-harvest period the majority of households cook and eat only two meals a day. Meat, fish and rice are the stuff of prestige meals not everyday food, which generally consists of coarse once ground maize meal (*dona*), cheaper to produce than fine ground which requires two grindings,[12] and a vegetable side dish.

The Church continues to enjoy good relationships with Catholic donor agencies in Europe, although it has yet to adopt more contemporary participatory approaches to 'development'. Community-based projects were certainly unusual in the 1990s and service provision tended to be determined by the interests of clergy, often via ex-missionary priests. The primary objective of most projects was not community development, but the sustainability of the Church as an institution, either ensuring revenue is raised for parishes or providing church institutions with items of capital expenditure. The diocese is trying to sustain itself as it is by presenting its future plans in terms of 'development' and 'local sustainability'. What this obscures is that 'development' refers in practice solely to the development of the infrastructure of the diocese and that local sustainability will come, not from local support, but from profits made locally. The Church justifies this position with reference to the organisation of the Catholic Church in Europe and the example set by the Swiss missionary orders with their large farms and substantial properties. 'You can't draw a line between the Church and business anywhere in the world', I was informed by the priest responsible for diocesan funding in 1991. For the Church to continue to support its mission derived infrastructure and the lifestyle of its personnel, it has no option but to function as a business. The alternative option of reliance on local support would change the whole nature of the organisation. The latter vision of a community church, a locally funded church, a *poor* church seems less than appealing to Catholic clergy, although it has support amongst lay people in European countries influenced by liberation theology and ideas of the small Christian community.

While the engagement of the Church in the material world of enterprise and commerce is essential for its survival, it contradicts the image of itself that the Church tries to present as a 'religion' concerned with the soul. People other than Catholics notice this merging of 'religion' and 'business'. An Assemblies of God pastor intent on securing my miraculous conversion was at pains to point out the difference between his kind of Christianity and the Catholic Church. 'The Assemblies of God is *not* religion', he stated emphatically, in contrast to Catholic Christianity. 'The person is not given the Holy Spirit, it chooses them. Unlike religion, we have no *miradi* (referring to "projects", such as grinding mills and so on). Our project is the spirit.'[13]

Not all money transactions involving the Church are viewed as commercial. Contributions made at services are seen to be or are represented by the church as being *sadaka*, that is an offering to God. Even then, totals for contributions at Masses remain low, individuals giving on average less than the price of one egg. The same word, *sadaka*,[14] is also used, but not by clergy, to refer to offerings to the dead with which Masses have come, on some occasions, to be equated. Although Masses, costing around the equivalent of one day's *kibarua* (casual labour), represent a significant source of income for many parish churches, Catholics generally underplay the economic aspects of the transaction, emphasising that *sadaka* are not for the church but for the dead, and it is the dead and their descendants who can expect to receive the benefits deriving from the expenditure.

Legacies of mission

Although some charge was made for mission-controlled services even in missionary days and the Church was always involved in business and trade, the financial demands of the mission were somewhat diluted by the behaviour of individual missionaries who helped many with medicine, clothing and school fees. It would probably be difficult to find a single family in the parish of Kwiro who had not received help of this kind in the past. Mission control of schooling meant that the missionaries could supply students with clothing and uniforms, paper, pencils and food. In so doing they set up a large network of clients who came to expect missionary support and assistance in the provision of material goods. There is now considerable resentment among the younger priests about the attitude of missionaries who criticise them for not 'helping people'. Elderly missionaries may unintentionally subvert the work of the diocesan priests by distributing assistance in the form of cash and clothing, in the process rebuilding old client groups dependent on the mission, a practice perpetuated by the European lay workers in church projects who are viewed as virtually indistinguishable from missionaries. The criticism of 'not helping' is echoed by members of Catholic congregations whose expectation of priests and the mission in general is based on their experience of the past. The gift giving of the missionaries has another legacy in the way in which the divine figures of the Church are conceptualised. The human divine beings of the Church are popularly imagined as Europeans, an image reinforced by the painted representations which the missionaries placed in their churches and which remain there to this day. Mary and a few select saints are approached through prayer for assistance. This is usually material and is often for basic goods and food. Votive offerings are not made. There is no notion of debt with Christian divine beings. Rather, they are potentially capable of procuring, as did the missionaries, a semi-miraculous supply of cargo.

Priests: businessmen or ritual specialists?

In Mahenge, as elsewhere in Africa, there is a relative shortage of priests and high priest to congregation ratios (Hastings 1978:35). This constrains the organisation of the Church which cannot abandon the missionary framework of parish centres, where one or two priests reside, and outstations managed by catechists that are visited perhaps once a month for Mass. Catechists are more numerous than priests and undertake much of the day-to-day work of the church in the parish, providing religious education in primary schools, conducting preparation for marriage, confirmation and first communion, and taking routine services in the absence of ordained clergy. Drawn from among the mass of ordinary Catholics, catechists are likely to have some secondary education but to make their living from agriculture and to live in houses little different from those of the majority of villagers. Whereas the colonial position of catechist was something to aspire to for economic reward and as a potential avenue to formal sector employment, the contemporary position is voluntary and, though respected, conveys little status. Until the mid 1990s catechists were treated as church employees, but without the benefits of housing loans or accommodation. Despite opposition to the decision to end catechist salaries their commitment to a different and community-based version of Christianity has ensured that catechists have not abandoned their posts and they continue to represent Christianity in outlying villages on the periphery of parishes.

Women can become catechists, but the majority are male. They are not regarded as being of a special status by the people, beyond that of teachers. They 'are able to bury people', and to pray and sing. These skills are no different from those of some ordinary people who have reputations for being good at prayer or knowing Christian procedure at funeral events. Priests are seen somewhat differently. They have more status in the community than catechists because they can 'read Mass' and give communion. In general, priests have status as ritual specialists. They are reputed to be able to drive out spirits and to 'see', thus potentially destroy, witches.[15] The Diocese discourages the involvement of its priests in healing and exorcism. In this it is consistent with the post-Vatican 2 attitude of the Bishops' Conference in Tanzania and in the wider east African context.[16] Another consequence of Vatican 2 is the prevailing consensus of a liberal, individualistic and rationalistic approach to religious practice among the clergy and hierarchy, not only in Tanzania (cf. Christian 1989: 182–5), which demands that Catholics 'understand' Catholicism as an intellectual system as opposed to a system of practices through which the person can experience God. This attitude informs many of the post-Vatican 2 innovations which, in general, have served to undermine the supernatural authority of Catholicism, which by being changed, is exposed as something manufactured, an artefact of humanity. Mahenge priests do not involve themselves in healing or in driving out spirits, although people want them to, and their refusal is interpreted as selfishness.

The present generation of priests are mainly from within the diocese. They have their own obligations to the kin who have contributed to their education. They also have less money than the missionary priests who retain the support of Catholic communities in their home countries as well as access to the resources of the order. Because the priest is the parish, income-generating projects aimed at the support of the parish are seen to be supporting the priest and what is perceived, accurately or not, as his personal fortune – his vehicles, houses and grinding mills. The priests, living apart from the community, better educated, driving cars and wearing good clothing are regarded as rich. The position of priests as patrons to a rural community, which continues to depend on them for access to transport, medicine, emergency assistance and credit, puts the priests in a very real position of power over poor communities. People who see that their chances of assistance in the future depend on the maintenance of a good relationship with the priests strive to be seen to be good Christians, volunteering for the lay committee and contributing towards the costs of ordinations and Church celebrations.

In Ulanga, as in other poor rural communities, the desire for patrons far exceeds the capacities of such individuals to deliver benefits in kind. There are always more clients in search of a patron than there are patrons searching for clients (cf. Haugerud 1996: 48). The mere presence of a priest in such circumstances is a position of latent, if ambivalent, influences and power. At parish level priests continue to wield influence and control over what have become, in the absence of alternatives, significant community resources and expect to be treated with the respect and deference which they regard as due to important people in the community. Wealth and education as two attributes of priestly status reinforce this perception. As levels of education are still correlated with expectations of wealth and power associated with the kinds of public sector positions which sixth-form leavers and university graduates were allocated under the socialist system, priests' years of education implicate them in expectations of patronage, irrespective of their personal circumstances. The priests acknowledged as most powerful are those who have obvious influence above the parish level and evidence of whose personal power is manifested materially in the spacious dwellings scattered throughout the diocese constructed on their behalf for members of their families.

In a small community where the Church is powerful and where the personnel of the Church are either local or have lived in the area for many years, what the Church does is seen to be the result of decisions by these individuals. No distinction is made between changes instituted by the diocese and changes initiated by bodies external to the diocese. Unpopular policies are blamed on the individual priests thought to be responsible for their introduction. Consequently, demands for contributions from congregations are often seen to reflect the greed of individual priests and what are in effect national decisions of the Bishops' Conference in Tanzania, with regard to such issues as *zaka*, marriage or baptism, are held to show the insensitivity or downright pigheadedness of priests. The younger priests are not widely respected in a society that prioritises the status of elder. Older people dislike addressing them as 'father' (Baba), preferring instead to use '*padre*' which is not loaded with reference to kinship and authority.

The fact that they live apart from the community and have little experience or understanding of its problems and priorities, combined with years of seminary education, distances the priests further from their congregations. In the seminary, priests have been taught to regard much of traditional practice with contempt. There is no doubt that this is how the missionary priests perceived it.[17] The following quote is taken from an announcement (*tangazo*) written by a missionary and posted outside the cathedral in 1958.[18]

We are losing the blessing of God here in our country for three things.1. Our faith is being lost by following the bad things of Paganism, witchcraft and divination. 2. We are missing to make the day of God holy by dancing in the night on Saturday. 3. And those who are . . . refusing to marry are they who are refusing the blessing of God

(and are by implication responsible for the bad state of things in the country). Although the priests of today are local, the *tangazo* are virtually unchanged. The attitude of condemnation prevails. It comes across most forcefully in the Sunday sermons that are inevitably about people's failure to lead a 'Christian life'. As a parish priest told the congregation on Easter, 'Christ is the light of the world, but we are still looking to the darkness'.

Catholicism depends on priests, whose ordination conveys on them the ability to administer the sacraments on which the theological structure of the religion is premised. The only sacrament, which a non-priest can bestow, is that of baptism. The core Catholic sacrament is communion when priests feed their congregations a wafer and wine that are thought to have, through a process of Divine substantiation, become transformed into the body and blood of Christ. For the priests, this is the miracle of Mass. A person wanting to 'receive the Host' should be in a state of grace. This is achieved through the confession of sin, the doing of penance and absolution. Only priests may take confession, and convey God's absolution to the person. They cannot only transform the offerings of the congregation into the Host but the congregation into a state of fitness to receive it. Priests insist that their role is to say Mass and, as the only people able to do this, they deserve the financial support of their congregations. There is a strong degree of ambivalence in the perception of the Church as a bureaucratic organisation, which is reinforced by the Church's attempt to recoup more costs from its congregations in the drive to become self-financing. Priests seem to have lost, or to be losing fast, what supernatural power they were once credited with. They are still asked to guard newly dug graves in churchyards to prevent the entry of witches. Everybody believes that priests still keep watch over graves as a matter of course in this way, but they are no longer thought able to curse entire villages or to know a person's doings or whereabouts from a distance.[19] These kinds of powers were associated with the early missionary priests who seem to have deliberately exaggerated their ritual powers, both within and beyond the context of services. Reading Mass in Latin, a language only they understood, dressing at all times in the habits and robes of the Capuchin Fathers, living in special communities set apart from interpersonal relationships with local people, missionary priests strove to differentiate themselves from both local communities and the secular staff of colonial administrations (cf. Strayer 1978: 87–90; Carmody 1988).

Priests, like church buildings, statues and artefacts can become like ritual objects as points for the diffusion of Christian powers. This role is most pronounced when they are performing services and reading Mass, dressed in special clothes and reading the word of God (cf. Campbell-Jones 1980). At other times, the personality of the priest transcends the office of priesthood, and priests behave as individuals enmeshed in local struggles for influence and power, often refusing to distribute the powers of priesthood, excluding people from blessings and, occasionally, it is alleged, indulging in the practice of witchcraft. The ambiguity of priests is not, of course, confined to African contexts (cf. Christian 1972; 1989; Pina Cabral 1986). A similar situation is described for Ireland by Taylor, in which priests are viewed either as malevolent drunks with magical powers or sacred heroes who make perilous journeys across difficult terrain to give the last rites to the dying. The hero priests are associated with eighteenth century fathers, valorised as part of the historical struggle for Irish Catholicism in the face of British colonialism and Protestant encroachment (1995: chs 5 and 6).

While the attributes of priesthood are imagined rather differently in Ireland and Ulanga, Taylor's analysis is suggestive. In Ulanga hero priests are now part of a Catholic tradition, associated with missionary fathers who were said to have made spectacular efforts to reach the dying in remote areas and administer the sacraments. This devotion is contrasted with the present day situation in which indigenous fathers are said to refuse to visit the deathbeds of people whom they define as 'public sinners', and are reluctant to leave parish houses to visit parishioners at all, preferring to leave the administration of day-to-day Catholicism to catechists, who have no ritual powers. There is a degree of truth in such stories, although, as in Ireland, the ultimate intention of narratives on priesthood is to make explicit contrasting political relationships, between people and the institutional Church, between missionaries and indigenous clergy, and between independent and colonial Tanzania. Old people tell stories about the miraculous doings of these priests, which often reveal competition between the priests and indigenous ritual specialists in terms of access to powers associated with spirits, both Christian and local. Not surprisingly, in these tales, the local powers win the struggle because being foreign, the priests lacked the vitally important close association with place. These missionaries were thought to be able to make medicines and talk with the dead. The fact that they were Europeans enhanced both their mystique and the degree of ambivalence with which they were regarded.

'African Europeans': the Africanisation of the clergy

At one level *wazungu*, 'Europeans', is a general descriptive category, conveying the physical and cultural attributes of a kind of people, like 'Africans' or 'Indians' or 'Arabs'. In the popular stereotype, 'Europeans' are wealthy and have a cunning manipulative cleverness that always puts them ahead of the African peasant. Things 'European' are similarly mysteriously powerful and clever, linked inextricably to the amoral and exploitative world of market relations transacted through the medium of cash. This attitude informs the widespread belief in *wamumiani*,[20] 'bloodsuckers', people so corrupted that they steal other people's blood and then sell it to 'Europeans' who export it for profit.[21] As a category, Europeans stand opposed to Africans, and exploit them. For some people, Africans will always lose out to Europeans. One woman told me that this was because in the beginning, the forefather of the Africans was drunk and laughed at the nakedness of his father. As punishment, the father created a division between his sons. The disrespectful one became poor and black, while the one who fled in shame became white and rich. Similar tales are told all over Africa (Leinhardt 1970: 283; Fernandez 1982: 69–70). Being a certain kind of person is not, however, merely an attribute of race but depends on behaving in ways thought appropriate to the category. People who behave in 'European ways' are mockingly called 'Europeans', which in this context has strictly negative connotations. Those who eat 'alone' from their own plates are similarly dismissed. Because these people are *not wazungu*, this way of behaving is inappropriate.

The indigenous priests are equated with the negative aspects of Europeanness. They are said to be behaving like foreigners, turning their backs on traditional culture and ignoring obligations to assist kin and neighbours. They are frequently accused of greed and selfishness, attributes given a wholly negative image and strongly associated with witchcraft. The Africanisation of the clergy has, paradoxically, done little for the image of the Church. It is still regarded as foreign, and Christianity as the 'European religion'. Christianity is seen to be at moments powerful and at others inappropriate for precisely this reason. Having a 'religion', especially Christianity, can make people less what they should be, and more something else which they should not. A middle-aged client at a diviner's put it this way: 'We Africans we don't have religion, only tradition. Priests, even the Bishop, they are just following money. If they have problems they come here...If they say they are Christians it is lies – they don't have belief.' On another occasion, a male elder gave this account of Christianity. 'Christianity and Islam have no origins in Africa. The Arabs brought Islam and business – they sold people for salt. The Europeans brought the Christian religion and Jesus and Mary. Jesus and Mary were of the Jewish tribe, which was their tribe. They are not close. We did not choose this religion. They, the missionaries, baptised the small children.'

The issue of celibacy is often invoked by people living in Catholic communities as a commentary on the moral status of priests.[22] It seems to be a common expression of hostility to priests in situations where they are powerful to allege that they do not keep to their vows on this point.[23] Tanzania is no exception. Missionary fathers were accused of sexual abuse and alleged to have lovers in villages while contemporary priests are said to have lovers and children, and to roam the villages in search of casual sex. In contrast, it is said that if the *wambui*, the diviners of the shrines of the spirits associated with territory, broke the proscriptions surrounding sex and pollution prior to entering the sacred area of the shrine they would be punished by the spirits with death or other calamity. Adultery has similar consequences for these diviners. Both offences can result in the loss of their powers, as the spirits will withdraw their co-operation from them. That priests can break the law of the Church without anything happening to them serves only to expose priests as servants of an organisation, not servants of God. Ideas about purity in ritual contexts add to the revulsion people feel at the thought of priests going direct from bed to altar to read morning Mass because, as many people expressed it, 'It's not clean.'

In the popular view, priests set an example that proves that there is no mystical sanction on those who break the law of the Church. The concept of sin (*dhambi*), as presented by the Church, is seen for what it is, as 'breaking the laws of the Church'. Everybody who I asked explained to me in these terms. That there is no mystical sanction on those who break the laws of the Church suggests a fundamental weakness in Christianity, confirming the view that the Church is essentially an organisation run and manipulated by people. Changes in Church ritual, which, in the aftermath of Vatican 2, were intended to make the church truly 'local', and of which the most visible is in the language of Mass, have also reduced its mystical authority. In the Pogoro conception of *jadi* or 'tradition', what gives something mystical sanction is its very unchangeability and the fact that in the ideal these things are not open to manipulation by humanity, unless, of course, authority for innovation is seen to come from elsewhere, from the spirits themselves (cf. Boyer, 1990: 60). This attitude probably explains why the notion of 'calling' is so popular with priests, sisters and catechists, making an individual's choice of career look as if it is the result of some higher authority than simple material self-interest.

The current status of priests is ambiguous. On the one hand they are people who have a privileged access to both divine and material power. On the other, they are the self-interested representatives of an institution which is foreign because it was brought by foreigners and because it stands, at moments, in opposition to local practice. Priests are, however, frequently equated with other ritual specialists and, as such, they are thought to have the potential to do the same kinds of things. The Christian Church and its personnel, both human and divine, is merely one avenue of access to the supernatural in a landscape which has many routes of access to the supernatural and many ritual specialists. The tradition within which a specialist is working does not render him or her unable to treat people coming from different traditions or with different ethnic and religious affiliations. All share equivalence, and each has its moments of greater usefulness or validity. Pogoro Catholics frequently seek the assistance of an Islamic *shehe* who uses Islamic texts and writing for the making of medicines and divination.[24]

The post-missionary position

The Catholic Church in Ulanga finds itself in an ambiguous situation, at the same time a twenty-first century diocese within a well-established and fairly autonomous East African ecclesiastical structure, yet still firmly on a trajectory established by the Capuchin fathers and perceived as essentially a missionary church by its own congregations who continue to differentiate and demarcate between objects and practices which they categorise as Christian and those which they categorise as indigenous and in accordance with custom (*kimila, jadi*). The formal structure of the diocese and the hierarchy of parishes and outstations seem to rural Christians to be little changed from that which was established by the missionaries. The reality is of course different. But despite the increased autonomy of the diocese, the indigenisation of the clergy and the partial transition from an evangelising mission to a community church, the fundamental relations of power between population and clergy established by the missionaries remain essentially unaltered, founded on inequality and un-equal access to resources, consolidating the position of the clergy as mediators and gatekeepers between rural communities and the structures of power.

5

Popular Christianity

Successive post-missionary ecclesiastical regimes in the diocese have continued to emphasise the importance of sustaining a clear break between what is categorised as Christianity and non-Christian practice, a situation mirrored by clergy in other post-mission contexts in Africa and Asia (Mosse 1996; Stirrat 1992; Bond 1987; Wijsen 1993). The result, at least in Ulanga's Catholic communities, has been a perpetuation of practices that the Church defines as non-Christian outside the boundaries of the Church. This separation between church defined Christianity and apparently 'un-Christian' practice is not manifested in a separation between Christians and non Christians, but in the lives and practice of people who, while they define themselves as Christian, continue to perform what is classified by the Church as 'un-Christian'. The majority of such practice concerns the relations between predecessors and descendants and is glossed in some contexts as belonging to the category of tradition or custom (*kimila/jadi*) (Green 1994).

Practice defined as 'traditional' is not unchanging (cf. Boyer 1990). It can incorporate change as long as change is initiated on the authority of the dead and the spirits associated with the specific territories in which Pogoro people reside, facilitating the inclusion of distinctly Christian elements into contemporary strategies for maintaining relationships with ancestors. Masses for the dead have come to be regarded by some families as equivalents to offerings of beer and food to remember the dead. But, because the spirits of the dead, as people who were alive in the past, occupy an essentially non-Christian domain there are distinct limits on the extent of this incorporation and Christian practice can only supplement, not supersede, other avenues through which relations with predecessors are established and maintained.

Formal Christianity

Formal membership of the Church-defined Christian community is viewed locally as distinct from an individual's relations with Christian divinities and
sources of power. People's self definition of themselves as Christian differs
from that imposed by the Church, which requires minimally that a person be
baptised and, for full Catholic status, that they are confirmed and in a moral
position to receive the sacraments. The conjunction of global Catholic practice
regarding contraventions of canon law with policies specific to the diocese has
created a situation in which this is often not possible in practice for ordinary
Christians who may find their access to sacraments restricted for contraventions
of diocesan regulations regarding payment of *zaka* as well as for breaches of
Canon law. Those in breach of the latter are classified as 'public sinners', a
category that includes those who live together without marrying in church and
anyone who engages in practice defined by the Church as anti-Christian.

Public sinners are denied any sacraments except that of penance, which is
of course the precondition for readmission into the Christian community of
the Church. Most short-term excommunications (*kizuizi*) concern marriage and
participation in practices directed against witchcraft which are viewed by the
Church as the paradigmatic anti-Christian activity. Although exclusions relating to breaches of diocesan regulations are reversible bureaucratically, without
recourse to penance, they nevertheless impact on the accessibility of certain
sacraments. Those excluded for the non-payment of *zaka*, for example, can
receive communion, but are denied baptism or confirmation for their children,
a marriage service and burial in a Church plot. While exclusion from Christian
burials and church graveyards was resented by some, the potentiality of penance
was recognised as an option by those who believed that they could secure the
presence of a priest at their funeral by such radical strategies as renouncing a
polygamous spouse. In such instances the second wife, assuming that the first
wife was married in church, is viewed by the Church as illegitimate, therefore
expendable, leaving the first wife as the recognised Christian partner. Despite
the technicalities surrounding definitions of Christian status and its sacramen-
tal entitlements, the burials of people recognised as Christians are popularly
viewed as Christian burials, whether or not a priest or catechist is present and
wherever they take place, at homesteads or within the consecrated grounds of a
churchyard. For the many who are unaware of the subtle distinctions between
breaches of Canon law and breaches of diocesan regulations, and of the impacts of Church policy on priestly practice, the range and extent of exclusions
are taken as further evidence that Church is now wholly self-interested. 'The
mission', a man of sixty complained, 'no longer does anything out of love. Now

if a person is dying and you ask for a priest, he doesn't come. Instead he asks the chairman of religion, what kind of Christian is this? Has he married in Church? Are his children baptised? You wait and wait . . . He doesn't come.'

Giving a name

The diocese, in line with global Catholic policy, regards baptism as the minimum condition for defining Christian status. While not viewed as essential by a congregation from whom it can be withheld and for whom the religious affiliation of one's parents and grandparents ultimately determines one's Christianity, baptised or not, both congregation and Church agree in general terms on the significance of baptism as an attribute of Christian status. While the Church views baptism theologically, as the precondition for eventual salvation, others perceive baptism in more immediate terms as the act through which a person's latent Christian substance and identity are confirmed through the giving of a name and the bodily incorporation of substances with transformative potential locally classified as 'medicines' (Green 1996). In contrast to the missionary emphasis on the baptism of infants and the sense of urgency conveyed by the drive to baptise in *periculo mortis* this sacrament is no longer performed for individual children, but for groups of children three or four times a year, often coinciding with annual festivals such as Christmas and Easter. The average age of candidates for infant baptism is between about eighteen months and two years. Other children wait until they take communion for the first time. The timing of baptism is the outcome of a compromise between parental desires and what the Church allows. It may be delayed until the parents of the child can afford to put on a feast with beer and dancing. More usual reasons for delay are the impacts of diocesan policy with regard to the non-payment of *zaka* and people living together without marrying in church.

Parents wishing to have a child baptised may have to wait until *zaka* has been paid and they have married in church, which also means saving money for the Christian wedding celebration. As we shall see in the following chapter, Church definitions of the Christian family and of Christian marriage are at odds with indigenous conceptions of kinship understood in performative and processual terms. Moreover, Christian weddings, like other Christian festivals, have become occasions for the ostentatious display of wealth and Christian status – that is status associated with Christianity as an index of education, wealth, consumption and 'modernity' in the sense of imported practices which are the antithesis of the *kienyeji*, the local, the rural. Public and personal Christian festivals provide opportunities for the rich to hold lavish formal parties, which in the utilisation of space and seating, the food and drink on offer and their exclusivity are intended to contrast with 'local' ways of doing things. Such parties tend to be by invitation only (guests are presented with cards), food is served to individual guests seated at tables, rather than served to a group seated on mats and the food is served on individual plates. Christian parties are occasions for serving high-prestige manufactured drinks, in contrast to local beer and *ulanzi* (Green 1999c). And, as with food, drinks are served in individual vessels rather than a collective cup. Occasionally, differentiation is dramatised by the separation of guests into two groups, a seated elite served in the contemporary '*kisasa*' (literally 'now-ish') style, influenced by urban western and missionary conventions, and the remainder allocated a drum of maize beer and cheap everyday food served from communal dishes.

Wanting to have children baptised was the reason most frequently cited for having a Christian marriage. The children of married people are baptised together on the most special day of the festival while those viewed by the Church as being born out of wedlock, but whose parents are not living together, are baptised as a separate group, usually as part of a regular Sunday service. Baptism provides another opportunity for the dramatisation of social differentiation between the Christian elite and others in the selection of sponsors for the children baptised. '*Wasimamizi*', literally overseers, adopt a limited godparent role with a formal emphasis on the supervision of the child's parents' own attempts to lead a Christian life. They play similar roles at first communions and weddings. Both overseers and parents attend some hours of Christian instruction prior to the baptism; a strategy intended to increase their consciousness as Christians. Sponsors are generally selected by parents but, as they must be people viewed as good Christians by the Church, those selected often have some close association with it, as employees, descendants of mission employees or relatives of clergy. This positioning adds to their appeal for parents, as potential patrons. It is not unusual for the same people to have 'overseen' as many as thirty or forty children. However, no long-term relation of obligation is implied between 'overseer' and the child's parents, or with the child itself.

It seems likely that the group baptism policy has, along with the imposition of exclusions and the move away from the baptism of infants, contributed to a stated shift in the perception of baptism from a ritual which informed the social constitution of Christian persons to a naming ceremony which, while it bestows a Christian identity through the transmission of Christian substance, is not perceived to be an essential precondition for the growth and development of children. That it was thought so in the past is suggested by the evident popularity of infant and deathbed baptisms and the fact that a significant proportion of these were carried out by laity. Infant baptism remained the norm for children of Christian parents until the early 1970s when parish records show that the average age at baptism was less than two months. Babies born at home were taken to be baptised at mission stations when they 'came out' of the house in which they had been secluded with their mothers until after the tied end of the umbilical cord had dropped away. 'Coming out' involved, and continues to entail, the administration of a medicine called *shirala* which, through the transmission of substance from father to child, creates paternity as a social relationship and ensures the future growth and fertility of children. Children born in mission dispensaries were baptised before returning to their homes. Older people's accounts of baptism during the missionary period make an explicit comparison between the giving of *shirala* and the baptism of babies, which many Christians seem to have preceived as equally necessary for the development of children. Both practices involved anointing the child's body with substances thought of as having the transformative properties of 'medicine'[1] and both were associated with the specific gendered practices that characterise the end of seclusion periods following the key life crisis rituals described in more detail in the following chapters. The change in the age of baptism and the fact that the Church no longer insists on baptising all children confirms for people that baptism is not something essential for the child's future. Unlike *shirala* medicine which ensures the growth of children and the fertility of women[2], baptism is not essential for the reproduction of society, only for the reproduction of the Catholic congregation. Although the Church tries to use the *kizuizi* as a means of making Christians conform to the demands of orthodox Catholic practice people know that if it delays baptism for too long it will soon run out of Christians: 'They will refuse until when? If they don't baptise them, how will the religion continue?'

Baptism continues to be important as an occasion at which substances with the power of Christianity can be incorporated into a person's body, fixing their latent Christianity as an aspect of the person. The water and oils used in the rite of baptism are sometimes referred to as 'medicines of the Church' or 'Christian medicines' *(dawa ya kikristo)* and baptism as an occasion when religion finally adheres to a person. Observing a group baptism of children at the cathedral my companion turned to me and remarked approvingly, 'Look! They are completely Christian now.' Baptism also marks the formal transmission of *dini* (religion), with the giving of a 'Christian' *(jina la kikristo)* or 'baptism name'. 'Having a name' is a way of talking about being Christian. A person 'without a name' has no 'religion', in the sense of affiliation to expansionist religions such as Christianity or Islam which people can have or not as the case may be. Christian names, like other aspects of Christianity, are differentiated from non-Christian names by Christians and clergy. Mahenge priests, indigenous and missionary, refuse to baptise children with Tanzanian names, insisting on appropriate 'Christian' names, which are, in the main, Germanic versions of the Saints' names introduced by the missionaries. That the Christian names are foreign and, unlike local names, have no meaning, perpetuates the association of Catholicism with its origins in Europe and the outside. Christian names are used only in the most official contexts, for example when registering for school, for a court case or for employment. Teknonyms are the norm for adults and most children are known by 'home names' relating to the circumstances of their conception and birth. Individuals are known by different names in different contexts, by a nickname, by the name of their father and by the names of their children. Christian names associated with aspirations of education and a mission inspired vision of modernity allow for the presentation of an 'official' self in the contexts of the state nationalist project, still in thrall to what are essentially colonialist ideological legacies of 'development' and 'civilisation' in which world religions have a role to play as a catalyst of progress. Educated people are expected, and expect, to have associations with religious organisations. In Tanzania lacking religion is negatively regarded as a descent into a devalued paganism, rather than an attribute of global post-modernity.

Being Christian
People who define themselves as Christian attend services periodically, depending on how far they live from a church. Those who live in villages designated as outstations may attend services taken by a catechist or the monthly Mass. As in Catholic communities the world over devotion is periodic and varies with the life cycle and generation of the individual in question. School age children and young people are regular participants in church services and choirs largely because of the prevalence of Church sponsored youth organisations and the influence of catechists in the primary classroom. Gender is also significant. Church attendance in general is highest amongst older women[3] and is highest for both sexes at the main Catholic festivals, and highest of all at Easter. Baptisms and the first communions of children also attract large congregations. Although going to church is described as 'going to pray', people also pray at home, often with the rosary. Going to pray is one among several ways of becoming closer to God. For ordinary Christians this is achieved not so much through participation in the formal sacraments of the Church as through participation in a range of practices which have come to have status as informal sacraments, centring on accessing the power of blessing (*baraka*) and on the establishment of social relationships between people and the divine beings of Christianity.

Primarily, people go to church because, as the most public Christian activity, it is what Christians do. It has become, like other Christian celebrations, an occasion for personal displays of wealth and status. For the poor this means dressing up in good clothing in contrast to ragged everyday farm clothes – shirts and trousers for the men and newer *kanga* or *kitenge* for the women, often worn over western style dresses. Men and women sit on separate sides of the church, replicating the domestic and ritual separation between male and female space. Services last a couple of hours following a standard format, comprising readings from the Old and New Testaments and the *mafundisho* or sermon, interspersed with hymns and prayers. A choir leads the singing of Christian hymns. In a community where most people have been attending church services since they were children, the words and tunes are as familiar as the structure of prayer. Sermons, often delivered in the style of an authoritarian teacher instructing a class of disobedient children, frequently strive to establish coevalness between the bad practices described in the past world of the scriptures and the apparently un-Christian practices performed in the present within the diocese, situating Christian Tanzania within a timeless New Testament world. Avoiding Christian marriage and visiting diviners and anti-witchcraft specialists are common targets for condemnation, as is the reluctance of Christians to support the church financially. Services culminate in the distribution of communion to those who are in a position to receive it after the tinkling of bells has signified the miracle of transubstantiation.

Confession and communion are underplayed in popular Catholic practice. Even at Easter, the most important of all Catholic festivals, only about one third of adults present in church receives communion. Parish priests reckoned that fewer than one fifth of Christians made regular annual confessions. The lack of emphasis on confession rests partly on popular definitions of sin (*dhambi*) as either breaking the rules of the Church as an institution or, alternatively, as the practice of witchcraft and adultery. The former may lead to temporary excommunication and the exclusion of the public sinner from the Church-defined Christian community. The latter are activities that are locally condemned but which are not thought to alter the individual's moral fabric to such an extent that their destination on death will be affected. All dead people, whether witches or Christian sinners, become spirits who walk the forest paths at night. As one woman explained, 'Heaven is for saints. We go to the forest.'

Perhaps more importantly, confession is not elaborated in local Catholic practice because of fundamental ideas about the relationship between people and Catholic divinities and an understanding of the process of mediation in which the priest is merely a channel of Christian power rather than a node in a reciprocal communication process between people and divinities. Pogoro Catholics do not view confession in terms of a kind of reciprocity in which the person transforms sins into words to be exchanged via the mediation of the priest for the sacrament of communion as reported, for example, in Ireland (Taylor 1995) or among the Tagalog communities of the Philippine lowlands (Rafael 1992).

On the contrary, mediation is conceptualised as a process through which the Christian person is able to incorporate Christian substances and objects into themselves and, in so doing, to embody a particular relationship between themselves and Catholic divinities. This relationship hinges, not on the incorporation of a *deity* as Leach understood it in his essay on mediation as a means of access to the divine (1983), but on the incorporation of Christian powers, just as kinship in Ulanga, as elsewhere in Southern Tanzania, is constituted through the incorporation of substances through the ingestion and sharing of food, drink and medicines (Green 1996; Wilson 1957). The person of the priest is central to the process, not as a mediator between people and divinities, but as a distributor of Christian powers and substances.

Blessings and powers

The person of the priest is merely one among many sources of access to Catholic artefacts and substances, which, like the priest himself and the words he reads in Mass, have the potential to contain and condense the power of Christianity, which can then be appropriated by Christians. This power, described as *baraka*, 'blessing', is diffuse, but assumes material form through concentration in objects – in garments, ritual paraphernalia, buildings, texts, holy water, images and statues (cf. Gray 1990: 103). *Baraka* is also inherent in the language of prayer when words assume the status and properties of ritual artefacts (cf. Bloch 1974). The power of *baraka* can be transferred via objects and substances, including communion wafers, ashes, holy water, oils, medals, rosaries and Catholic words, printed on paper or read aloud in the form of Mass and prayers (Sangree 1966: 202). This kind of understanding of *baraka* is of course not confined to Christianity. Nor is *baraka*, whatever its source, only available to Christians. Similar powers deriving from Islam can be disseminated through texts, amulets and incantations, and accessed by Christians who go to seek the healing and divination services of Islamic ritual specialists or *shehes* who practise what is known throughout Tanzania as *dawa ya kitabu*, 'book medicine' (Swantz 1990).

The Church is well aware of the importance of *baraka* to local Christians and ensures that opportunities exist within the annual ritual calendar for its dissemination. Easter, the key event in the Catholic cycle, provides various formal and informal means through which relations with Christian beings and Christian powers can be effected. In addition to practices aimed at 'remembering' Christ, more personal blessings can be obtained through participating in the ritual of ash on Ash Wednesday, kissing the effigy of the Crucified Christ placed at the front of the church on Good Friday and by obtaining palm leaves blessed with Holy Water on Palm Sunday. The blessed palm leaves placed over the main doorways of houses are, like rosaries, said to discourage the entry of witches and to protect the occupants of the house. An annual procession to 'respect' a cross – placed on a hillside near the Cathedral by missionary Fathers usually attracts a substantial following of women. Held in September, shortly before the start of the rains, the occasion provides an opportunity to pray for rain and to obtain *baraka* from the cross which people kiss and touch before they return to their houses. This hillside, which some people say Mary once visited, is situated close to a territorial shrine on an adjacent summit, continuing to dramatise the latent conflict between their assumed and indigenous powers over fertility and rain as the missionaries must have intended.[4]

Occasions involving the scattering of holy water are also special.[5] A woman describing in mime a priest's action at a Mass on All Souls said, spreading her arms in a rising arc over an imaginary congregation before her, 'You see. The blessing goes everywhere.' Water is recognised as a medium of blessing. Its use in Church contexts is equated with its use by shrine diviners and by ordinary people 'to cool things down'; a medium of transformation between the ritual states of heat and cool sought and brought about through life crisis events that are explored in the following chapters. The use of incense is similarly perceived. Incense is used by *waganga*[6] to drive out *mashetani*, the troublesome foreign spirits that recurrently possess people, especially women. The use of these ritual artefacts in church enhances the authority of some aspects of Christian ritual and confirms that the Church is indeed concerned with the same sorts of things as some aspects of what is locally defined as 'traditional' practice. There is no doubt that the special dress of priests and catechists on occasion does too. It sets them apart from ordinary people as ritual specialists. Now only Brothers and Sisters wear special dress all of the time. Priests dress casually and, while several favour collars some of the time, most are indistinguishable from government officials and traders. Of course, nobody thinks that Christian amulets and substances can totally protect the Christian person from witchcraft, sickness, or possession by spirits. What Christian power does is to provide the person with an additional armoury of protective substances (cf. Sangree 1966: 206) and the sense that, by 'having religion' they have access to an additional range of relationships with Christian divinities. These relationships place the residents of Ulanga district within the sacred geography of the Catholic Church making Pogoro Catholics part of a global Christian community, in which even the poor and marginal are equal before God.

Son, mother and spirits

Tanzania's population is roughly equally divided between adherence to Islam and Christianity, as it has been for much of the past fifty years. Popular conceptions of God informed by Islamic and Christian traditions are shared to an extent by people of all religious traditions including those adhering to what they regard as traditional non Christian religion and which the Catholic Church, like other Christian churches, would classify as 'paganism' (cf. Horton 1993: 175). Pogoro conceptualisations of divinity, in line with other African representations, emphasise a pervasive power rather than a personified deity. This power is manifested in various ways through various phenomena (Leinhardt 1961: 28–9; Culwick 1935: 99–101). Rain is a manifestation of divinity, as is the fruition of crops and the powers embodied by diverse diviners when they connect with spirits of various kinds. Although different in some respects from formal Christian representations of a personified God, this conception of divine power can accommodate formal Catholic notions of mediation in which God the Father is accessed through intermediaries. Consequently, human relationships with God are articulated through relationships with the dead and other spirits, as well as through their relationships with the Catholic divine beings, of whom the most important are Jesus and his mother Mary.

The Catholic divine beings, saints, angels and spirits, have much in common with the different kinds of spirits (*pepo, laika*) who are present in the lives of people in Ulanga. Some of these spirits are specifically local, such as the spirits of the dead and those associated with particular tracts of land that reside in the pools of still water which constitute their shrines. Both spirits of the dead and territorial spirits are referred to as *mahoka* (sing. *lihoka*). Some belong to wider spirit traditions in Tanzania and beyond. Territorial spirits and those associated with regional cults such as Songo, have specific locations where they may be accessed via the mediation of diviners. Others are conceptualised as foreign, as in the case of *mashetani* appropriated from Arab and Swahili possession cults, and may access the living periodically, without respect for time or place. Spirits occupy a contiguous domain to that occupied by living people (cf. Boddy 1989: 3). In the case of the *mahoka*, the territorial spirits and the spirits of the dead, this domain is defined in opposition to where the living are. The dead stay in the forest while the living are at home, but come into their own at night while the living sleep. They occasionally cross over into the space occupied by living people through possession or appear in dreams. Spirits are not, however, inhuman, although they are differentiated from the living people with whom they share different dimensions of both space and time. They talk, desire food, beer and cloth, and crave attention and respect.

The destination of the dead is an essentially un-Christian domain, locally defined as 'traditional' in self-conscious opposition to Christian and imported practices. Offerings of beer and food for the dead are served in what are considered to be traditional vessels, made of bamboo and clay, rather than the manufactured items of glass, plastic and metal of everyday use. Beer for the spirits is made from sorghum, the crop of the past rather than the present day staple, maize. Diviners of the shrines associated with the spirit territories into which Ulanga is divided, and their male descendants, may not be buried in Christian coffins, nor in Christian dress, emphasising the point that Christianity is imported, not indigenous, a religion of the present that cannot incorporate the past.

As spirits are fundamentally social, their existence is constituted through their relationships with living people, with whom they share different dimensions of the same space (cf. Lambek 1981). With the partial exception of Mary, the Christian divine beings occupy the different space of the Christian heaven, *mbinguni*, literally 'in the sky', which serves to separate them from and constrain the kinds of interaction which can occur between themselves and people. The Christian heaven is imagined in theocentric terms (McDannell and Lang 1988: 178). As the place where the Catholic divine beings reside, it is an opposite of the earth and everything with which it is associated. Far from the earth and the daily lives of people, heaven is not a place where the spirits of local dead are found. Its population comprises the divinities and the religious dead – missionaries, nuns, priests, angels and saints.

While God has a presence in the world through other spirits as manifestations of divinity, he is largely absent from social relationships with people on their own terms, a situation quite different from that of some of the Protestant and independent churches popular in Africa which privilege the subsumation of the person by the Holy Spirit (Comaroff 1985). Jesus, as part person, part divinity and part spirit – whose proper domain is the Christian heaven – is similarly distant. Described by many informants as the child of God, several insisted that this did not imply Christ's literal filiation, but a conceptualisation of his closeness to divinity in kinship terms. Jesus as a 'person of many wonders', empowered by God to heal and perform miracles, is imagined as a kind of super diviner (cf. Sundkler 1961: 284–7). During his lifetime Christ had a special relationship with his followers and clients. This relation is fundamentally transformed, despite its short-lived restoration after the resurrection, by his death and ultimate ascension to assume his rightful place in the Christian heaven.

It is Christ's death as much as his resurrection that transforms the position of his mother from ordinary woman, albeit one selected by God, to the prime intermediary in Mahenge Catholic experience. As will become clear in the following chapters, it is this conceptualisation of Mary as a bereaved mother with whom a relation of compassionate empathy is possible which is fundamental to the gendered experience of Christianity in Ulanga. Imagined as the mother blessed by God to bear and lose a special child, Mary is valued for her maternity, rather than her virginity (Bloch 1993), and treated with compassion as a suffering mother (Walker-Bynam 1987: 269). Her presence on the earth is confirmed through the well-publicised sightings of the Virgin, who periodically appears to people in various parts of the world, including Tanzania. Stories are even told in some parts of the diocese of a visitation by Mary, which are vehemently denied by priests and the church authorities. Mary's annual ascension to Heaven is widely celebrated. As in other Catholic communities this liminality makes her a key point of contact between Jesus and living people (cf. Warner 1976; Christian 1972; Pina Cabral 1980). The Legion of Mary is popular among older women in particular, who share and hoard glossy devotional literature with its colourful images of weeping statues, tales of visitations and special rosary prayers. Parish records of Masses ordered suggest that devotion to Mary became widely popular in the diocese during the 1960s. In the early 1990s the diocese was once again promoting Mary, through the introduction of all night services in Marian months and encouraging people to use the rosary. Whatever the origins of Mary's introduction into the lives of ordinary Catholics, she is thought to have a real and powerful presence on earth and a place in heaven.

Remembering Christ

Christ's death and ascension into Heaven establishes a permanent separation from the daily lives of human beings but at the same time provides an opportunity for the establishment of a new relationship between himself and people. This relationship assumes the same form as relationships between dead and living and is effected through acts of remembering. The most important of these is in the annual re-enactment of his funeral inside the church on Good Friday, during which time songs associated with funerals are sung and the crucified Christ brought before the altar to be kissed by mourners.[7] More routinely, Masses are a daily means of ensuring that Christ is remembered. Only the religious participate on a daily basis, remembering on behalf of the ordinary people who also participate directly in remembering Christ from time to time through the institution of communion. As with 'remembering' the dead what matters in remembering Christ is that the act is routinely performed by others. The ultimate responsibility for remembering Christ lies with the religious and in particular with priests. While ordering the reading of Masses achieves the remembrance of Christ in a general sense, receiving communion and placing it in one's mouth is an act through which the individual 'remembers' Jesus, at the same time as it transforms the recipients' bodies, making them feel 'holy' and 'clean' (cf. Mitchell 1997: 90).

Communion is an appropriate way to remember Christ because it is the act that Christ specifically requested his followers to perform in his memory. What people 'remember' in Ulanga is Christ's own 'offering' of blood, described as his '*sadaka*'. This is not conceptualised in the sacrificial terms of Christ exchanging his blood for people's sins but as an offering of his life to God. Just as descendants make offerings to related dead in the acknowledgement of their existence in the present, not in the expectation of future returns *Sadaka* offerings do not imply reciprocity in the immediate sense but are, rather, acknowledgements of what has been received in the past. Christ's *sadaka* is an acknowledgement of what already belongs to God, and which he has already received through his life. In contrast to the experience of communion described for some European settings (Camporesi 1989; Mitchell 1997; Campbell-Jones 1980) communion is not thought of as a meal, and so lacks the connotations of eating together which are prioritised by both traditional practice and formal Catholic theology. That it is taken inside the body is important. Blessing given by the diviners of the shrines of the spirits associated with territory, the *wambui*, involves the use of 'medicine' and this, as is all medicine, is both applied to the body and placed in the mouth. Some spoke of communion, like baptism, as the 'medicine' of Christians and the Church (Green 1996).

Embodying Christianity
Pogoro Catholics prioritise the human body as a site for mediation with the divine. This mediation is not effected through the third party of the priest, nor through the Christian divine beings, but through the incorporation and embodiment of substances and words with Christian powers. Through the physical processes of eating, wearing, touching, speaking and listening, a person's body becomes their own point of contact with divine power, as substances and objects are incorporated by it. This process is similar to that described by Camporesi for the experience of communion in European Catholicism in the eighteenth century, in which the person's body was thought to be transformed by the absorption of the holy wafer into it. For these communicants, as for the Maltese Catholics described by Mitchell (1997) and the Franciscan nuns of Campbell-Jones's study (1980), the reality of their own physical transformation ultimately rests on their understanding that the communion wafer actually embodies Christ, hence their obsessive concern with the establishment of a degree of internal cleanliness through the avoidance of food prior to receiving the Host. On ingestion, the communicant's body merged with Christ's body, transforming the communicant into the limbs of Christ and believers into the body of the Church (Camporesi 1989: 229). There is a significant difference, however, between this experience of communion and the experience of the incorporation of Christian medicines that I have described for Pogoro Catholics. This difference hinges on what is actually thought to be embodied in the communion

wafer, which, in orthodox Catholicism differentiates it from other substances with Christian power. For Pogoro Catholics, communion is not differentiated from other Christian substances because it does not literally embody Christ, only Christian power. Communion is not then experienced as the ingestion of Christ's body, nor as a merging of person and Christ, human body and Holy Ghost. Communion understood as the ingestion of *dawa ya Kikristo* (Christian medicines) has a place in this process, not because it is thought to be Christ's body, but because it embodies Christian power. There is no notion of people literally consuming Christ's body, nor of the wine which priests consume turning into Christ's blood. Communion is understood in essentially symbolic terms; that is, as a self-conscious representation of Christ's body and blood.

As Feeley-Harnik points out, with reference to early Christian sects and to the Judaism from which they developed, the food symbolism of Christianity was not self-evident even to early Christians. Its meanings had to be explicitly spelled out, to such an extent that the symbolic significance of meals depended on their translation and on the acceptance of specific Judaic conventions in which the food embodied the textual laws of the Torah (1994: 144). This point is significant, for it suggests that we should not assume *a priori* the translations people chose to accept concerning the core symbols of Christian practice which, despite claims for universality, are not universally interpreted. Luise White is possibly misled by just such assumptions when attempting to account for the association of Catholic missionaries with tales of vampire-like blood thieves in colonial Zambia. She suggests that Zambians implicated foreign missionaries in the blood trade because of their participation in non-reciprocal labour practices, and the fact that priests could have been thought actually to consume flesh and blood as part of their ritual obligations. I suggest that the symbolism of communion and what White refers to as 'the literal interpretation of the Mass' (1993: 759) has little to do with blood stealing accusations, common throughout the region, which are premised on local idioms of exploitation concerning power over people and human bodies. The origins of tales of blood stealing for sale lie in the legacy of the slave trade rather than Catholic ritual, hence the widespread association of blood thieves with 'Arabs' as stereotypical representatives of the trade in people (Baker 1941). If rural Zambians really thought that Catholicism was about eating flesh and blood they would not have been so keen to associate themselves with missionary Christianity nor to avail themselves of Christian powers.

Catholic ritual in sub-Saharan Africa seems to be generally understood in symbolic terms rather than as a magical transubstantiation of food into flesh.Catholicism, and indeed, Christianities in general, are premised on a reading of scripture which privileges the construction of a 'limitless unity' between categories which are self evidently separate, between self and other, between life and death and between Christ and living Christians (Feeley-Harnik 1994: 153). This unity is achieved theologically through the dislocation of natural laws caused by the magnitude of Christ's sacrifice (Camporesi 1989: 226). It is not accepted by Pogoro Catholics, for whom the body of Christ can only *represent* the body of the Church and be resurrected and made to appear from nothing in a symbolic sense. Their interpretation of Catholic ritual is not surprising when considered in relation to the historical specificity of Christian practice and symbolism as it developed in Europe (cf. Asad 1993), and in relation to Pogoro, and indeed, east and central African notions of what anthropologists would refer to as 'symbolism' and 'interpretation' more generally. These centre on an acknowledgement that ritual practices and substances have an intrinsic efficacy which is not derived only from what they represent, but from what are culturally defined as their inherent capacities to transform the person (cf. Kratz 1994: 130). These capacities are not determined solely by representation. Ritual practice in sub-Saharan Africa, and very probably elsewhere, is thought to actually bring about real transformations in the physical bodies of participants (cf. Bloch 1992). Such understandings are central to the constitution of kinship which is explored more fully in the following chapters.

6

Kinship and the creation of relationship

Kinship relationships are not conceptualised as given. Biological relatedness merely creates the potentiality for kinship qualitatively defined. Consequently, claims to kinship and the quality of the content of relationships with kin are potentially negotiable in the public fora where kinship is performatively constituted through ritual and exchange. Decades of migration mean that those to whom a person is related (*walongu*) are widely dispersed throughout the country. Beyond the idiomatic kinship that characterises neighbourly sociality, the formalisation of kinship relations and their association with specific locales is now a transient artefact of life-crisis rituals. Kinship is dramatised at events associated with marriage and at funerals, where relationships are displayed by such actions as shaving, marking the faces of the relatives of the deceased with flour, the transaction of token payments and the inheritance of property and names. Participation matters, as 'evidence of kinship' (Wilson 1957: 200). Payments at funerals and those that make up the marriage process are transacted in cash and are thus highly divisible among those who can present a claim to receiving a portion of them. The sum of money a person receives is less important than the fact that by receiving it they have a legitimate claim to the relationship which receiving a portion of the payment implies. Actual sums obtained by those at the margins of kinship transactions are so small as to be of little economic significance, even to poor households. The value of relationship, however, cannot be overstated. Social relations in general, and kinship relations in particular, have enormous worth as indices of belonging and status, as entry points to wider social networks and as potential avenues to support in times of crisis. Kin are represented as assets and relationships as wealth, despite the more ambiguous social reality of kinship.[1]

The flexibility and performativity of kinship has implications not only for the social construction of descent but for the potentiality of female agency in the

75

context of kinship, a factor systematically underplayed in anthropological accounts of kinship (cf. Molyneaux 1977; Harris 1981; Parkin and Nyamwaya 1987: 4–5). Marriage, though a desirable goal for young women, is neither essential for adult status nor for the constitution of kinship relations. Pogoro kinship recognises potential rights of filiation through the paternal or the maternal line. Women have strong and complementary relationships with men as brothers and as husbands. A woman's loyalties between her husband and her brothers have to be constantly negotiated (cf. Beidelman 1986: 12–18). A man can claim rights of paternal affiliation with his children, whether or not he is the husband of their mother through specific payments for rights in his offspring and the provision of medicines from his own place of origin. Unclaimed children remain affiliated to the family of their mother's father or if she has no 'father', in the social sense of *pater*, her mother's brothers. A substantial proportion of households are female headed, as they have been in fact, if not *de jure*, for much of the twentieth century.[2] And, as in other communities characterised by recognition of some degree of matrilineal succession, brother–sister bonds continue to influence patterns of residence and the experience of descent not so much as a relation between ancestors and descendants, but as a relation between adjacent generations.

Gender and female autonomy

Widowhood, divorce and labour migration all contribute to the number of female-headed households, as they do in other parts of Morogoro region (Ministry of Health 1997) and indeed elsewhere in coastal and southern Tanzania (Lockwood 1998). The choices of individual women are also significant. Women, unlike men, can establish their own households without recourse to marriage because of a domestic division of labour that assigns to girls and women the essential tasks of fetching water, food preparation and cooking and the fact that for women having children confers adult status. Agricultural work is divided between men and women, according to the quality of the relationship between co-operating individuals. Some couples farm shared land together. Others maintain separate plots tended by each partner. Although clearing fields is said to be men's work, women participate in heavy agricultural labour, often as casual workers, and both men and women plant, weed and harvest.

A woman does not need a man to secure her livelihood. She can access land via village governments or male kin and can perform agricultural tasks alone or hire in male labour where necessary. As her children grow they can assume increasing responsibility for domestic and agricultural chores. Women also trade in the domestic skills that they have practised since childhood, making money from brewing, food processing and preparation (Green 1999c). Men, in contrast, need wives to establish their own households and to provide the hospitality that signifies adult status, but they do not need wives to obtain status as fathers or formally to establish recognition of their paternal relations to offspring. Not only are men more likely than women to remarry in the event of a wife's death or separation, they are also more likely than women to marry. A woman should cook and prepare food for her husband, should wash his clothes and should sleep with him. He in turn has a duty to provide her with clothing, soap, cosmetics and cash. He should also provide for his children. If a man fails to provide a woman with 'clothing' (in the sense not only of clothes to wear but purchased goods more generally) she has sufficient justification for leaving him and returning home.[3]

Conventions regarding the sexual division of labour mean that women bear the brunt of domestic chores. Fetching water, food processing, preparation and childcare all fall on the shoulders of women and girls. Only very young boys are expected to assist in what are locally constituted as female tasks. Beyond infancy, boys and girls are encouraged to behave in what are considered to be gender appropriate ways and to learn and acquire the skills and styles of behaviour associated with adult men and women. Girls spend time helping female relatives in domestic and agricultural chores, looking after younger siblings and, once they reach puberty, must ostentatiously display 'shame' (*soni*) in the presence of male seniors. Boys are encouraged to spend time with men, to participate in hunting and house building and to spend time alone on their own enterprises developing a strong sense of autonomy. The emphasis on female sociability and male autonomy persists throughout adulthood. Women's association with the responsibilities of tending home, men, guests and children directly involves them in duties of emotional and physical care, which are regarded as essential attributes of being female. These duties include tending the sick, mourning the dead and praying for others, dead and living. Women are involved in caring for others and collective activities to the extent that they are said to have a natural capacity for 'love' (*upendo*) and pity (*huruma, lusungu*). Men of all ages expect to be recipients of this care, at the same time as their capacity for emotional self-containment is a source of strength both for themselves and their dependants. The separation of the sexes is especially marked on public occasions where autonomous but interdependent spheres of male and female influence are demarcated, and is most pronounced at funerals.

The Christian family
Being unmarried and having children with different men is not considered shameful, despite the Church's systematic condemnation of 'highway children' as evidence of the community's failure to live the Christian life. What is

considered shameful by and for women is to be 'rotten', childless and barren. Evidence of fertility is valued by those women who want to establish their own families, with or without a husband. This is sometimes given expression in a child's name such as Bahati Njiani, literally 'Luck on the Path', pathways (*njia*) connoting a socially valued connectedness between people and places as opposed to the more ambivalent 'highways' and 'roads' (*barabara*) invoked by church discourse on what it defines as moral laxity (Hasu 2000: 243–308). For others, evidence of fertility is more ambivalently received. Delays in starting primary school and a tendency by some young women to seek out relationships with men as a means of accessing basic goods like soap and clothing independently from parents contribute to less desirable pregnancies amongst schoolgirls and women in their teenage years, removing the opportunity to complete their education and increasing the risk of maternal mortality (cf. Puja et al. 1994). Young women recognise the downside of unintended pregnancies. It is common knowledge that deaths from illegal abortions and accidental overdoses of chloroquine are not infrequent occurrences. After the initial onslaught of the disease in the Western parts of the country AIDS is slowly tightening its grip on rural communities in Southern Tanzania, its spread facilitated by the dispersal of social relationships entailed by post-liberalisation reintegration into the regional and international economy. The Catholic Church in Tanzania maintains its global silence on issues around HIV and contraception, averting its gaze from the complex realities in which people struggle to maintain an existence of sorts in the communities further marginalised through the geopolitics of adjustment and globalisation. Sermons on 'living a Christian life' and forming 'Christian families' entreat Christians to avert the risk of HIV and AIDS and to reduce the number of 'highway children'.

Forming families, Christian or otherwise, is not in any case a straightforward matter of following the directives of clergy. Conjugal relationships are worked out in progressive stages over an extended time frame which may, or may not, include an official ceremony of church or state. In Kipogoro, there are no words referring specifically to 'husband' or 'wife'. There are only *mdala*, woman, and *mpalu*, man, which are used with a personal possessive pronoun to indicate a conjugal relationship. Kiswahili, the language of the nation state, has a more specific vocabulary, differentiating between man (*mwanaume*) and husband (*mume*), woman (*mwanamke*) and wife (*mke*), and lover (*mchumba*). Kiswahili also has terms referring specifically to marriage (*ndoa*), and *harusi*, from the Arabic, for wedding. These words comprise the core vocabulary around marriage for the Catholic Church which privileges the wedding as a significant event which transforms the status of the man and woman who undergo the ceremony into husband and wife. For Pogoro Christians, *harusi* refers only to the wedding ceremony, and in particular to the events of the church wedding, while *ndoa* refers to 'official' marriage as a written contract between individuals recognised by the Church or the state. Marriage is not thought of as a single event but as a process which is talked about in the corporate terms of 'taking' the woman. Unlike Church or state marriage, which it precedes, it explicitly involves the creation and recognition of a relationship between groups of people who are related to the bride and groom. Marriage is constituted practically through the payment of bridewealth, or a portion of it, at a public ceremony and the 'taking' of the bride, irrespective of whether the bridewealth is eventually completed or the couple marry in church. Formal polygyny is understated when it occurs because of its association with Islam. Some single women are in effect unofficial second wives to men with whom they have long-term relationships, although living in separate households. This is a private arrangement between the man and the woman. It does not entail the transaction of bridewealth. The few Christian men who are openly polygynous have taken another wife because their first wife was infertile and they did not wish to abandon her. In these cases the first wife, if they have married in church, is recognised by the Church as the 'wife of marriage' *mke wa ndoa*.

Church weddings, if they happen at all, take place long after a couple has been practically married, often in response to a desire on behalf of parents to have children baptised. The reduction in missionary support, and its change of emphasis, has altered the significance of Church marriage which has become, as in other parts of Tanzania, essentially a matter for the elite (Hastings 1979: 243). The conspicuous consumption associated with Christian weddings means that Christian marriage is now perceieved as far beyond the reach of those without access to non-agricultural employment. At the height of the Capuchin mission the Church not only arranged the marriages of Christians, it provided them with material incentives to marry in church. Older people recalled being given clothing for church weddings, in the thirties and forties a *kanzu* for the man and a *kitenge* for the woman, and later, as conventions of dress changed in the 1950s and sixties, the *kanzu* becoming associated with Islam, grooms were provided with suits and the women patterned dresses in western style doubtless donated from Europe for the 'poor African Christians'. People are still entreated to marry in church as the way of achieving the 'Christian family'. There are now few incentives to do so. This may have contributed to a sharp decline in Christian marriage which began in the 1970s and which coincides with the decline in Capuchin control. In the 1950s, at the height of Capuchin mission, it was not unusual to have in excess of one hundred church weddings in Kwiro parish. Twenty-six church weddings were held in 1988. An average of only thirteen were held annually between 1975 and 1985. Those intending to marry in church have to attend a *semina* (seminar) given by a priest, together with their sponsors before the wedding, aimed at instructing people in matters pertaining to the Christian family. The seminars are necessary, a diocesan parish priest told me, 'Because our people are ignorant. They do not know how to live.'

The marriage process

Individuals are more or less free, in theory, to marry whomsoever they choose. Cash bridewealth at comparatively low levels means that all but the least able young men can theoretically amass sufficient resources to complete at least the first transactions of marriage exchange and set up homes with their brides independently of kin groups. In practice the potential opportunities to engage in the politics of alliance and the receipt of cash as an index of relationship ensures that kin groups struggle to retain a hold over marriage transactions and strive to resist wholly autonomous unions. Although the 1971 Marriage Act made the payment of bridewealth optional and parental consent unnecessary (Westerlund 1980: 162; Coulson 1982: 205) so-called customary law takes precedence in rural areas where many people are unaware of their rights as defined by the state legal system. Bridewealth exchanges, in Ulanga at any rate, are not primarily a matter of men exchanging wealth between themselves for rights men hold in women. Rather, the range of symbolic payments made to both male and female relatives of the bride and the subtleties of allocation suggest that bridewealth is as much about the recognition of influences on the bride as it is about the establishment of descent relations for the groom's family.

Bridewealth, *maheto*,[4] is not a single payment. The term refers to a series of named payments made in instalments by relatives of the groom to the relatives of the bride over an extended time frame and which continue to bear reference to either the objects or the labour which were previously exchanged. Brideservice was a routine part of marriage exchange until some fifty years ago when the groom was expected to assist the bride's parents with agricultural work. Older informants reckoned that the material wealth exchanged in those days comprised around ten hoes (*mahuka*) and one or two goats, in addition to the brideservice. Both the mother and father's sisters of the bride continue to receive payments in recognition of their contribution to her upbringing and development, much as their equivalents did among the Nuer of the 1940s, described without elaboration by the anthropologist Evans Pritchard (1951). This reallocation of the wealth transacted extends to the bride herself, who receives what can legitimately be interpreted as a portion of bridewealth in the form of household goods and gifts provided by her family as trousseau with which to establish her new home. These items remain her property which she can remove in the event of separation or the death of her husband. As so many families regard the provision of trousseau as a marriage expense which justifies asking for increased bridewealth payments from the groom's family as well as cash for 'moving' the bride the final steps to the groom's house, trousseaux cannot be considered apart from the total context of the marriage exchange (cf. Bloch 1978). The bride also receives a personal and private gift called *shibani*, with connotations of agreement, from the groom as a token signifying her consent to the betrothal. Acceptance of *shibani* is a precursor to the negotiation of bridewealth proper, the first payment of which is known as *barua*[5] and representing around five per cent of the total is in effect a down payment on the bride which is made after the parties have agreed on what the total amount of *maheto* should be. *Barua* is publicly handed over at an elaborate ceremony during which the bride herself is made to re-enact temporarily her seclusion inside the house as an initiate, and which up to the 1950s would have lasted from the day of her first menstruation to the day of her marriage itself.[6] If the relationship between the parties is good the girl's parents might agree to her being 'taken' by the groom once the *barua* is paid. A trial period for a young couple is thought prudent as, in the event of a separation, returning only *barua* is less of a problem than returning the full amount handed over as *maheto*, which may have taken several years to accumulate (cf. Parkin 1980: 207).

Maheto is calculated and divided on the basis of its component parts, *barua* between the bride's fathers, her mother and mother's brothers. Of the remainder, the bridewealth proper, the bulk goes to the bride's father who may then, if he so wishes, further divide it among his brothers and sons. A token payment is set aside for the *shangazi* (FZ) of the bride, representing the chickens to which she was previously entitled. The bride's mother receives a similar amount in recognition of the care she gave to her daughter. This payment is called *shibebeo*, after the carrying cloth in which infants are carried, for 'did she not carry her on her back?' The brideservice component, *matemeko*[7], around ten per cent of the total, goes to the parents of the bride as those who would have benefited from the groom's labour in the past. A payment called *shilemba* (headcloth), between ten and twenty per cent of the total, is set aside for the *mjomba* (MB) of the bride, standing in for the 'cloth' which he would have previously received when men's, as well as women's cloths, were a store of value and a signifier of wealth. As with all the payments, they may be further divided between those who have a claim to them, *shilemba* among the mother's brothers and so on. If a girl has 'no father', real or classificatory, or has spent most of her childhood at the home of her mother's brother, it is he who is entitled to receive the bulk of the bridewealth payment.

A married woman is usually buried at her husband's place, but never loses her connection with her natal family to which she may well return in the event of his death or a separation. And, while the bridewealth payment recognises the bride's mother, compensates her parents for the loss of her labour and for her removal, and gives her husband legal rights to her offspring, these are by no means absolute. The consent of a woman's brothers is needed prior to the marriage of her children and a child may choose where to make his or her home, settling more or less permanently at the place of his father's or mother's relatives. An individual's choice of residence ultimately depends not on some fixed principle of kinship, but on the quality of the relationship between all the parties concerned (cf. Gluckman 1950: 171). Formally at least, divorce is relatively straightforward. Practical divorce entails the reversal of practical marriage, the woman returning to her place and to her natal kin. A couple's separation does not end the relationship between parents and children. Nor does it terminate obligations between spouses. Even those who have divorced officially shave at each other's funerals. What has popular recognition as official divorce *talaka* is an artefact of the state's recognition of customary law derived from Islamic practice and is spoken of in terms of being 'given' to the woman by the man. Most separations do not involve Church or state. People who separate say simply, 'We left each other', a more accurate reflection of the situation in which it is often women who take the initiative in leaving. In the case of a separation where bridewealth has been completed and the woman has borne children, the husband has legal rights to the children who may or may not remain living with him.

Descent and the matrilineal opportunity

Relative ease of separation, like the option for women to establish their own matrifocal households, seems to have characterised southern Tanzanian kinship for much of the twentieth century. District records from the 1930s remark on the prevalence of female-headed households and the fact that a substantial proportion of marriages terminated prior to the completion of bridewealth.[8] Where a woman became pregnant prior to betrothal or marriage her children remained with her and were the legal responsibility of her fathers and brothers.[9] Similar arrangements were made by other groups occupying the area between South Western Tanzania and the Coast, at least from the late nineteenth century (Beidelman 1967). Such practices, where they occurred, were usually interpreted by colonial officials and anthropologists as evidence of the negative impacts of social transformation and the inevitable decline of systems of 'matrilineal descent' in the onslaught of modernity, (Swantz 1970: 88; Beidelman 1967: xiv; Richards 1950; Poewe 1978). Rereading colonial ethnography and accounts of the matrilineal 'puzzle' in the light of contemporary sensibilities which emphasise the processual aspects of kinship (Carsten 1997) permits a reappraisal of the situation. What seemed to previous generations of kinship theorists to be a matrilineal *problem* can in fact be viewed as a matrilineal *opportunity*, an inherent attribute of flexible kinship systems premised on the social construction of reproductive relationships through spouses *or* siblings. In reality, the majority of these peoples seem to have recognised what appeared to be matrilineal and patrilineal descent as alternative succession options, and different attributes and kinds of property were passed along relatively shallow patrilineal and matrilineal lines. Of course, attitudes towards property or the social construction of property relations have implications for the extent to which any one ideology of descent is realised in social practice (cf. Bloch 1975). But the attitudes of anthropologists (and other outsiders) towards descent were equally, if not more, significant in privileging a particular perspective on social practice not only in Southern Tanzania but in Africa and within anthropology more generally.

It was the ideological emphasis on descent within anthropology as a discipline, rather than ethnographic accounts of practice, which predisposed anthropologists to write about unilineal descent as the key organising principle of society in Africa, casting into the shadows the non descent basis of sociality around which daily life was managed. Monica Wilson noted this disjunction in her study of apparently 'patrilineal' Nyakyusa communities in the 1940s. She remarked that ties through women were recognised and 'groups of cognates with a patrilineal bias . . . cooperate' (1950: 117). The main significance of the patrilineal 'lineage', for which there was no local term, was in the contexts of inheritance and bridewealth that involved the transfer of cattle and rights in them (Wilson 1950: 117).

Names, statuses, offices and ritual prohibitions, which are only partially constituted as 'property' in that their alienability is limited (Strathern 1985) can also constitute the assets on which complex descent systems are sustained. Among Pogoro communities ideologies of descent continue to legitimate the succession of names and statuses in ritual contexts where recognition of descent from *both* the mother's and father's side ascribes positions of relative importance to one side *or* the other and hence to either the father or maternal uncle. Like the Nyakyusa communities described by Wilson, Pogoro people differentiate between practical kinship and the formal ideologies of descent which are articulated and enacted in formal contexts such as the giving and receiving of bridewealth, matters of inheritance and rituals surrounding the processes associated with reproduction and death. On these occasions descent is made explicit as the basis of certain rights and obligations between people standing for each side of a family, and the acknowledgement of certain symmetries between these two sides. A person traces descent from both their mother's (*washimau*) and their father's people (*washitati*). Recognition of both the father's people and the mother's people is not an indication of double descent. Rather, the inclusion of the mother's brothers is a logical consequence of adelphic succession in which younger brothers succeed elder brothers and an elder son inherits the position of his father, dividing same generation siblings across generations by transforming elder brothers into fathers. Pogoro kinship is classificatory. The brothers of one's father are one's fathers, and the sisters of one's mothers one's mothers, differentiated by seniority usually based on birth order but also determined by whether the individual in question is the offspring of a junior or senior wife. In the context of *tambiko* offerings to 'remember' the dead their eldest living descendant (cf. Beidelman 1986: 111) sets out identical offerings for deceased members of both patrilineages, the 'father' and his 'fathers' and the mother and her 'fathers', practically enacting descent within the same generation, not between them. While this construction of descent privileges the mother's patrilineal kin, it permits recognition of what appears as a limited matrilineal option across adjacent generations from mother's brother to sister's son, facilitating the transfer of paternity, as a social relationship, to the matrilineal line. This is possible because a brother and his sister are equally related, whether descent is reckoned patrilineally or matrilineally. The inheritance of names and statuses can, and did, pass either from father to son or from maternal uncle to nephew.

Up to the early years of the twentieth century the mother's brother had extensive rights over his sister's offspring, at least some of whom could expect to benefit from his inheritance. The maternal uncle had the right to sell at least one of his sister's children into slavery, without the consent of the child's father. 'We were', several elders remarked, 'like the Luguru, and we congratulate them on sticking to their customs.'[10] The possibility of alternative reckonings of descent in matters of inheritance and marriage transactions certainly confused the colonial authorities which attempted to make patrilineal descent legally binding in January 1935.[11] The debate over the relative positions of fathers and maternal uncles now has limited practical significance.[12] Succession to positions of shrine mediumship passes from maternal uncle to nephew (*mpwa*), but the inheritance of immovable property such as brick houses passes, where a paternal relationship is recognised, from fathers to sons. Formal kinship transactions and the etiquette of avoidance and respect stress the potential equivalence and practical asymmetry of maternal uncles and fathers. The two positions are not conceptualised as equal, but as alternatives. One position or the other must be emphasised. This asymmetry is dramatised in the etiquette of respect and in funeral and marriage payments. The degree of respect demonstrated towards the *mjomba* (MB) is somewhat greater than that shown towards the father. It is, at any rate, more dramatic and elaborated. According to older informants, until the 1960s, this entailed kneeling before them, sitting lower than them and, for women, virtual avoidance. Neither sex could enter into the house of a mother's brother. Some older women still kneel and look away on greeting, and ensure that appropriate distance is maintained. Marriage and funeral payments are unequally divided among specific categories of kin on both sides of a person's family. The side receiving the bulk of the payment is not determined by principles of descent, but by the proportionality of the social relationship between them and the person in question. Thus for example the bulk of the bridewealth payments received on behalf of a woman living with her father's kin is handed over to those standing in the social position of father, while the male representatives of the mother's family receive only token payments. If a woman lived with her mother's kin the pattern is reversed, and the bulk of the payment goes to a mother's brother or, if he is alive, her mother's father.

The asymmetrical equivalence of mother's brothers and fathers is further justified by notions of relatedness, conceptualised in terms of degrees and kinds of closeness premised on the sharing and embodiment of different kinds of substance. Although a person's mother's sisters and father's brothers are also classified as mothers and fathers, birth parents are differentiated from their siblings. Similarly, siblings related only through one parent are differentiated from those born of the same parents (cf. Wilson 1950: 114). Siblings born of the same father and mother are especially close, and the 'one father, one mother' nature of their relationship is emphasised. Those related only through the same father are somewhat less so, although this is played down in formal contexts such as the handing over or receiving of bridewealth. Offspring of the same father have a different kind of closeness than offspring of the same mother, who are said to have been 'born from the same belly' or 'suckled at the same breast'. This gives them a kind of 'natural' closeness, an idea of maternally related kin that extends to encompass all those related on the mother's side. Ordeal medicine had to be taken not only by a man accused of witchcraft, but also by his sisters' sons. Those related through the mother are differentiated from those related through the father's side as *walokolu* as opposed to merely *walongu*. This difference stems from the fact that maternity as a social relationship is regarded as uncontestable and given, at least in its residuality (cf. Astuti 1992). In contrast, paternity is conceptualised as a social relationship that has to be created through the transmission of substance via the medium of kinship medicines as well as payments for rights in the child.

Constituting paternity
In discussions about reproduction adult men and women maintained that it is the man's 'blood' (*mwazi*) or 'seed' that forms the foetus. The woman is merely a belly, a vessel, analogous to the soil in which a seed is planted. Young people

gave greater weight to a woman's role in reproduction, talking of the woman as being like a hen with eggs inside its body. An older woman said that eggs were lined up inside a woman like bullets in a gun. Opinions differed slightly as to what extent the woman's blood enters into the substance of a foetus. Some men eventually conceded that it must all get mixed together when the child is in the womb, but others firmly maintained that the foetus is formed solely from the 'blood' of the man. This insistence makes sense when we consider the significance of notions of 'blood' in Pogoro constructions of kinship. 'Blood' is an idiomatic reference to the biological contribution a man makes to a child, but it also refers to family, to those to whom one is related.[13] The former understanding of blood informs the cultural epidemiology of a disease known as *mapinga*, to which women who conceive after sex with more than one man in fairly close succession are said to fall victim. *Mapinga* is, I was informed, caused by the mixing up of the 'blood' of all the men with whom she has been sleeping inside the woman's body. The symptoms of this disease are claimed to resemble epilepsy (*kifafa*), which is highly visible in the area (Jilek-Aaal 1979: 616). Seeing the colour white triggers a victim's fits or dazzling reflections of the sun on water because her eyes are clogged with mixed-up blood. The foetus is also affected. Such pregnancies, it is said, never come to term, or if they do, the mother never survives the delivery.

Under the British administration, the symptoms of *mapinga* were taken as evidence in native courts that a woman was committing adultery, for which her husband could claim compensation.[14] Although younger women now dismiss the risk of *mapinga* as non-existent, it still haunts the imagination of older women who are keen to encourage female kin whom they suspect of sleeping around to seek medicine from specialist healers to prevent the onset of the disease. The ideas underlying *mapinga* suggest that 'blood' should not be mixed up and should go only one way, from men to women. Thus not only is it considered unclean for a man to sleep with a woman during her period (and what women stress about the instruction of girls during their seclusion on puberty is their duty to avoid men while menstruating), it can make him sick because her blood gets into his body, causing his genitals to swell. These ideas are consistent with the statement that the blood which makes the foetus comes from the father, and the woman is nothing but a vessel. However, the implications of these notions are not pushed to the limits of the logic behind them in the justification of categories of marriageable kin. People say that not only did they marry cross cousins (*binamu*) in the past, but also that this was a preferred union. A man could marry either his fathers' sisters' daughter (FZD) or his mothers' brothers' daughter (MBD). Despite the fact that notions about blood would seem to imply that the offspring of the mother's sister are of the same degree of unrelatedness as either cross cousin, the marriage of parallel cousins, as classificatory brothers and sisters, was prohibited. Such notions about 'blood' as constituting kinship demonstrate that kinship is not solely about blood in any inherent 'biological' sense, even if we take into account notions of folk biology (Carsten 1992: 45). The two aspects of 'blood', as common substance and as a symbol of social relations, are present in the idea of blood brotherhood, which was, according to the older generation, previously practised (cf. Monson 1998). It involved making incisions in the skin so that the blood of the new kinsmen could be mixed in their bodies. When people say 'this child is his blood', pointing to a child's father, they also say 'this child is his wealth'. The two expressions are used interchangeably. They can also refer to a pregnancy. The woman 'has' (is with) the foetus (*kana inda*), but the *inda* itself belongs to the man who has responsibility towards it. Mothers of teenage pregnant daughters try to make their daughters tell them who the father is, 'because then if we know, we can go to him and say (pointing to the girl's belly), "This is your *inda*. Look after it."'

Children are a person's 'wealth'. This is especially emphasised for men who are more associated than women with formal rights over children. Social relations and obligations are still regarded as assets. Although people in their twenties and thirties are beginning to see children as a cost, as rural living standards plummet and the price of education rises, the pauper remains the person without kin, rather than the person without property. In a practical sense children are wealth because they are labour and because they increase a person's network of kin, but children are a man's 'blood' and a man's 'wealth' because the man has given wealth over for the child. This is either as bridewealth for the child's mother, or as a one off payment to her relatives for rights in the child. It is this payment that makes the child formally the child of that man and his fathers. Yet this payment itself, like conception and birth, is insufficient to create paternity as a social relationship between a man and his children without the giving of medicine after the child is born.[15]

Like other agricultural peoples Pogoro communities make explicit comparisons between the fertility of plants, animals and people. A newborn's umbilical cord is planted like a banana sucker in a clump of banana trees by an old woman who is past childbearing age. This is done in secret, to prevent others from displacing the cord and stealing the fertility of the mother. The cords of baby girls are planted at *ndala* 'female' banana trees, which produce many small fruits and reproduce quickly. Those of boys are buried at banana trees considered 'male', yielding big, heavy fruits with fewer bananas to a head.[16] Plant-like natural fecundity in itself is an insufficient basis for the reproduction of people. A man as a person has 'no root of the family', so he has to create it with medicine made from roots.[17] Babies are given a medicine called *shirala* before they can be taken out of the house inside which they have been secluded with their mothers until the tied end of the umbilical cord drops away. This medicine ensures that a man's children will 'grow' and become fertile adults. It also ensures the fertility of his daughters. This medicine should be provided by the child's father and is made from the ground roots of a tree, which, in the ideal, come from his ultimate place of origin and have been handed down for generations. If a family has no *shirala* medicine, it can be bought from a specialist who knows where in the forest to collect it. This medicine is applied to specific places on the child's body. A small quantity is put into the child's mouth. Although each family has slightly different ways of applying the medicine, what is important is that the medicine is rubbed on the child's body and consumed by the child. The child thus incorporates the medicine, just as the child itself, through the consumption of the medicine, is incorporated into its father's side.

If a child has 'no father', that is nobody claiming the social position of father, the medicine comes from the side of the mother's father. The medicine for babies is ground by both the child's parents, the father and mother from two pieces of root. One of these is big and fat, and is called *mdala*, 'woman'. The other, small and thin, is *mpalu*, 'man'. The symbolism here relates to sexual intercourse, with which grinding and pounding are associated (cf. Beidelman 1964:370). Each parent grinds his or her own root into a powder which is mixed with water to make a paste that adheres to the child's body. A man should not see his first child of each sex of a particular union until he, together with the child's mother, has put the medicine on the child's body that he should do with his eyes closed. 'Seeing' is a way of talking about knowledge, particularly knowledge of the relationships between things, events and people. Only after the father has given the child *shirala* can the father see his first child of each sex of that particular union, and only after the child has been given the medicine can the child 'come outside' of the house. The connection between paternity, as the child's relationship with the father's side, and the coming out of the house is explicit. *Shirala* here transforms the baby into a socially recognisable being, as the child of somebody, who can come out of the house and into the wider society. Like the '*ikipiki*' medicine of the Nyakyusa, it not only marks the relationship between the child and the father's side but *creates* it. As one of Monica Wilson's informants explained, 'They say of the medicine it is our kinship, it is our blood...The medicine is to create relationship' (1957: 105).

While boys receive *shirala* medicine only once in their lifetimes, girls are given another dose when they reach puberty. The complex series of ceremonies and rituals which comprise the girls' rites known as *unyago*, described more fully in the next chapter, have two main objectives. The first is to 'teach'

(*kufunda*) the girls and mark their transformation from maidens (*wali*) to potential wives, as others have remarked on for the similar rites performed for girls
throughout East and Central Africa (e.g. Richards 1939; 1982; Swantz 1966;
1970; Turner 1968; Caplan 1976; Brain 1978; Beidelman 1964). Secondly, and
more importantly, the rites aim to make the girls fertile in a direct and immediate
way. Without their proper completion girls will either be infertile, as among the
Zaramo (Swantz 1970: 365) and Nyakyusa (Wilson 1957: 101), or, as among
the Bemba (Richards 1982: 124) and Ndembu (Turner 1968: 200), they will
have difficulty in reproducing. While a range of practices performed as part of
the *unyago* help to ensure the fertility of women, the contribution of *shirala* is
paramount. If a child dies while its mother is still living the mother should have
another dose otherwise her fertility will be impaired forever.

Gender and power

Pogoro ritual practices centring on fertility and kinship emphasise the social
construction of paternity, while formal kinship occasions stress the role and
position of the father. Despite the seemingly 'natural' connection with maternal
kin, the asymmetrical opposition between father and mother's brother generally
privileges the father on occasions when formal kinship is enacted, except in
cases where a person has 'no father' and is thus only matrilineally related.
Human reproduction is conceptualised as involving a complex sequence of
social and biological relationships in which the successful development of a
child in the woman's womb and outside it depends on her relationship with two
men in different generations, her father and her sexual partner, who may or may
not become her husband or the social father of her child. The provision of *shirala*
for a child by a man creates paternity as a social relationship between father
and child, assigning the child to its father's family and to their place of origin. It
ensures that children grow and that girls will be fertile, sustaining the fiction that
without the tangible contribution of substance from the father's side the child
would be weak, and that the fertility of women depends, in part, on socially
recognised relationships through men. Paternity is represented in ritual contexts
as *the* pivotal relationship on which social reproduction depends, in contrast to
the reality in which many children 'have no fathers' and many women establish
autonomous households relatively free from male control. Because paternity is
a social relationship premised on the incorporation of land substance rather than
semen, and on rights over persons rather than on impregnation, it follows that
the mother's brother can assume the social position of the father, merging with
it and subsuming it through the ritual acceptance of social responsibility for the
sister's offspring and the provision of *shirala* medicine from her father's place of
origin. Paternity conceptualised in this way can, and does, skip generations, and

the role of father and the substance he provides can be assumed by a woman's father or brothers.

The emphasis on paternity and on male authority is not realised in practical social relations in which women are autonomous agents who can effect kinship decisions and operate independently in terms of access to land and livelihoods. Indeed, while the sexual division of labour retains the status of an ideological ideal it can be argued that this ideal, like paternal substance, probably never amounted to a description of historical practice. Gender relations at the level of the household and conjugal partnerships were characterised by flexibility even in the 1930s, and the sexual division of agricultural labour allowed women to maintain independent households. However, gender complementarity at a more cosmological level is central to the constitution of gendered personhood and social reproduction. The significance of a ritual division of gendered labour for local Catholic practice and for anthropological approaches to understanding the ritual roles of women in Africa are explored in the following two chapters.

7

Engendering power

In Africa, as elsewhere in the world, gender is experienced as a process of gradual transformation in a person's physical and emotional being. Bodies matter,
and are made to matter through the repetitions and reiterations which performatively effect gendered personhood (Butler 1993: 9). For Pogoro Catholics,
bodies are given meaning at the level of experience through a twofold process
of incorporation. Symbolic constructions of gender are embodied and incorporated into male and female persons through rituals that establish and consolidate
gendered identities by the manipulation of both physical substances *and* cosmological powers capable of affecting the body. Participation in such rituals is
not merely experienced in the symbolic terms of representations, but as progressively emotionally affecting those who participate. Representations of gender
are not confined to the abstract level of symbolic discourse, but are enacted
and experienced through specific ritual roles of gendered interdependencies
(cf. Kratz 1994). These roles centre on a division of labour between men and
certain categories of women who assume responsibility for dealing with the
potentially dangerous powers generated through fertility and death.

I argue that women's experience of loving and caring for others, and of
managing death and sorrow, underlies a distinctly female religiosity premised
on the remembrance of the crucified Christ through compassion for his bereaved mother, Mary. The specific content of the religiosity associated with
older Catholic women with its emphasis on love and mourning is informed by
their particular experience of gender and age, through which the female person
is progressively transformed from a mere girl into a fertile mother and, ultimately, into a woman who has 'dried out', past childbearing years. This process
inevitably brings a woman into intimate contact with the physical and emotional
aspects of reproduction and death, which are conceptualised as so fundamentally affecting those closely associated with them as to effect transformations

in the very substance of a person's physical and emotional being. These changes ultimately empower a person to assume specific ritual roles on future occasions at which reproduction and death are central.

Gender as process

Gender and personhood are imagined and experienced in processual terms, effected through the dynamic of ageing as it is culturally constituted (cf. Beidelman 1997: 3; Lutkehaus 1995). A person moves from the raw physicality of the neonate through the sequence of growth, adulthood and death to become, ultimately, a spirit. Time alone is insufficient to effect this transformation. Ageing entails growth, literally 'becoming'. This is not viewed as a natural process. It must be mediated by rituals which effect the physical transformation of people's bodies in gender appropriate ways, through contact with the cosmological powers generated by life and death and the ingestion and incorporation of substances endowed with power as 'medicines'. The successful completion of the life course is facilitated by the gendered interdependency of male and female persons in the enactment of the specific life-crisis rituals on which the process of becoming depends. Male and female are differentiated through rituals that effect the constitution of their physical substance, facilitating a cumulative gender differentiation on which the ritual division of labour, premised on age and sex, is founded. This process begins with a rite of female initiation (*unyago*) in which pubescent girls are endowed with the capacity to reproduce themselves and sustain the growth and development of offspring.

The capacity for human reproduction entails inevitable physical transformations in women's bodies contingent on motherhood and menstruation, which are imagined as ultimately empowering them to assume ritual responsibilities for dealing with the cosmological powers generated by the reproduction of others. The physical changes in female substance engendered by reproduction are paralleled by equivalent changes in both male and female bodies affected through close contact with death. Bereavement fundamentally alters the state of the person, lessening their vulnerability to the powers released by the deaths of others, thereby enabling them to undertake specific duties at funeral events. The embodiment of power leads to ritual empowerment, determining future roles in life-crisis rituals. Because the powers generated by human reproductive capacity and death are released through life processes there is a fundamental identity between them (cf. Bloch 1992; Douglas 1966). This identity has implications for constructions of gender and the kinds of ritual obligations women are accorded. A particular construction of the female body as the locus of reproductive potential implies that women's bodies have a greater capacity to be affected by participation in life processes than male bodies are. As women age they assume increasing ritual responsibilities at life-crisis rituals concerned with the management of reproduction and death. The changes in a person's substance brought about by close contact with reproduction and mourning are not confined to a person's physical body. They also affect a person's emotional and affective development, augmenting their ability to love and feel pity. Older women have special obligations to mourn the dead, as well as dealing with the more ambiguous powers generated by death and decomposition.

Heat and life

Just as paternal kinship is created in the present through the transmission of *shirala* from a father to his children, incorporating substance from his place of origin into his children's bodies (Green 1993; 1996; cf. Wilson 1957: 105), relations between generations on which future fertility depends are effected through co-residence and the sharing of food and substance (cf. Lan 1985). These relations transcend death, creating chains of continuity between living people and those from whom they are descended (Middleton 1982; Beidelman 1986, 1997; Wilson 1957; Fernandez 1982; Boyer 1990). Relations between people and spirits are effected through offerings of food and beer that help ensure the fertility, in the widest sense (Bloch 1982: 212), of land, crops and people. What matters is the possibility of continuity, of ensuring that humans can reproduce themselves and perpetuate relationships between themselves, land and spirits through time. This rests in turn on the management of human reproductive capacities through the careful manipulation of the cosmological powers generated by the life process as a transition between person and spirit. The relational existence of the spirit community expresses the fundamental dynamism of the dialectic between life and death. People die and become spirits, just as settlements are abandoned and return to bush, day follows night, and waking follows sleeping. Occasions when domains merge are sought periodically by either party, either through possession when spirits take hold of living people's bodies or appear in dreams, or when living people make offerings and invoke spirits to receive them.

 Spirits, having abandoned their physical bodies in the earth, are far removed from the biological processes of living. Their state, like the places and times with which they are associated, is one of essential cold. Territorial spirits reside in the pools of still water that constitute their shrines, deep in sections of unviolated forest. Human habitation is forbidden and people may only enter the area in the company of a male shrine diviner (*mbui*). Spirits demand that those seeking to approach them avoid close contact with processes and people who have become implicated in activities concerning reproduction and death. These processes, centring on sex, birth and death, are said to make a person hot and dirty, as well as generating cosmological powers that can be transmitted to others thereby affecting their fertility and mortality. Prior to making offerings or entering shrine forests both men and women must abstain from sexual intercourse to ensure that their bodies are sufficiently cool so as not to pollute the shrine area. Women who are menstruating, have recently given birth, or are wearing the shroudcloth neckbands on their bodies, which indicate a state of mourning, are not permitted to enter the forest area surrounding territorial shrines. The contrast between heat and cold, human and spirit, underlies the idiom of blessing as a relation between spirits and people. Its ultimate objective is *shimba izizimiri*, that 'the body be cool', and it is often carried out by the application of water to a person's body. While the idiom of cooling connotes association with spirits, as well as good health and emotional calm (cf. Jakobson-Widding 1987), the request that the body be cool is not merely concerned with the temporary achievement of wellbeing, but with the proper completion of the life course as a process of gradual reduction in the 'heat' of biological activity. Consequently, cooling down is a key element of life-crisis rituals (cf. Beidelman 1997: 175; Jakobson Widding 1987: 1), which seek to deal appropriately with the physical changes brought about in persons through participation in the biological processes of living and dying. These centre on reducing and removing some of the heat and 'dirt' which inevitably accumulate in people's bodies through being alive and growing older.

As the existence and attributes of spirits are defined in terms of what living people are not, ideas about the human body and the processes with which it is associated come to assume cosmological significance. The processes of birth and death, which ultimately engender spirithood, have the capacity to release dynamic powers necessary for human development, but which must be carefully controlled and allowed to dissipate lest they jeopardise the life process itself. These powers are conceptualised as forces that inhere in the bodies of people. They centre on two contrasting notions, on the one hand the power of death and, on the other, the power of life experienced as the capacity for human fertility. Neither the subject of explicit discourse on the nature of life and death, nor abstracted as concepts, powers are given reality through being experienced as immaterial essences which have material effects. They can be transmitted to others through vectors having properties analogous to the powers themselves (cf. Herbert 1993: 226). The most usual vectors are fire and water, which are incorporated into food and ultimately into the bodies of others. Certain actions can also transmit power, in particular sexual intercourse, symbolically associated in East and Central Africa with heat and fire making (Herbert 1993; Richards 1982; Beidelman 1997).

Managing power

A person's death generates a potential power to transmit death to all those who have been in contact with it. The contagiousness of death is carefully managed by ensuring that those leaving a burial are adequately cleansed, washing their faces, hands and feet in water, and by restrictions on who may handle the corpse and its belongings so that only those who have acquired some immunity to death power through previous close association with death come into immediate contact with them. The power of death is not only transmissible between persons. It can alter their very substance and, if properly managed, enhance their capacity to deal with the deaths of others. Post-burial practices, some of which are explored in the next chapter, aim to contain death power within the bodies of close relatives of the dead, thereby short-circuiting its transmissibility. The power of life generated through the processes associated with birth and the emergence of female reproductive potential is similarly transmissible but, because of the construction of female fertility as essentially tenuous, affects men and women in different ways. This power is intimately associated with female fertility and conveys the capacity for human reproduction. While both men and women can pass on this power to others, only women are affected by its transmission, either as beneficiaries of other's fertility or as those from whom fertility can be taken away. The transmissibility of the power of life has implications for the ritual management of female fertility and for the particular roles of older women who have a duty to contain it, thereby protecting a woman's capacity to give birth.

Because the powers generated by life and death epitomise excessive physicality in contrast with the state of the spirits there is an identity between them (Bloch 1992; Douglas 1966). This identity is expressed through the idiom of 'dirt' generated by life processes and which adheres to the bodies of those affected by them. They are not in themselves polluting, in the sense that contact with them does not imply the social devaluation of the person, nor is 'dirt' inevitably regarded as something that must be removed. The notion of 'dirt' is context dependent, a ritual state, which enables the symbolic representation of its antithesis, the state of the spirits. Identity in one context can become incompatibility in another. On occasions where life and death are in obvious contradiction the powers associated with each must be kept separate or they will cancel each other out, hence the incompatibility of pregnant women and burials.[1] Fire and water are vectors for the transmission of powers and, on occasion, opposing forces capable of reversing the effects of the other (cf. Jacobson-Widding 1987: 1).

Water applied to the body is used to purify and reverse states of excessive heat through cooling, while ideas about the life process itself acknowledge the interdependency and necessity of access to both heat and wetness to the generation and regeneration of life. The life course is conceptualised as a process of gradual drying out, a transition from fertile wetness to brittle old age effected through implication in heat. Women and men experience this transition differently and at different rates. Although men gradually lose their vitality, they never totally lose their capacity for fertility and sex. Women, wetter to begin with, dry out more quickly. Older women, fertile no longer, are said to have 'left off things of reproduction'. The supposed non-involvement of older women in sexual activity has implications for their capacity to act as containers of cosmological powers, which they will not transmit to others. As the power released by reproduction is identical in some contexts to that released by death, older women whose bodies have already been altered by engagement in reproductive processes have a special capacity to deal with the powers of death and decomposition. The category of women with the greatest burden of ritual responsibilities are *wamakolu*, older women who have themselves embodied the powers of birth and death can embody the powers generated by other's involvement in these processes with impunity. The fact that having 'dried out' they are no longer engaged in reproductive processes means that they will not become vectors for the transmission of power to others, either draining away the fertility of others or passing on the contagiousness of death.

Unyago and the fertility of women

The specific duties and obligations accorded older women in the management of life processes stem, in part, from ideas about human reproduction which accord men and women different capacities for fertility. Neither men nor women are inherently capable of successful reproduction. A person's capacity to reproduce ultimately depends, as we have seen, on the establishment of paternal kinship via the transmission of *shirala* medicines to babies of either sex shortly after birth. Boys receive *shirala* medicine only once in their lifetimes. Girls receive another dose on the occasion of their first period and if one of their children dies before them. *Shirala* in itself is insufficient to ensure female fertility. Although in the local idiom of conception, a woman is merely a vessel for the man's seed, the ground must be properly prepared through performance of a series of rituals called *unyago* aimed at establishing and safeguarding female fertility. The series of ceremonies which comprise the *unyago* are similar in orientation and content to the girls' puberty rites performed throughout South East and Central Africa (Swantz 1966, 1970; Richards 1982; Turner 1968; Beidelman 1964, 1997; Wilson 1957; Brain 1978; Caplan 1976). In contrast to the female initiation rituals, which seek to transform cohorts of girls into generations of marriageable women, the concern of *unyago* and related rites is with the reproductive potential of individual maidens. Without them girls will be infertile, as among the Zaramo (Swantz 1970: 365) and Nyakyusa (Wilson 1957: 101), or, as among the Bemba (Richards 1982: 124) and Ndembu (Turner 1968: 200), they will have difficulty in reproducing. The practices associated with the puberty of girls in Ulanga are not primarily concerned with nubility as a precursor to fertility, as Richards described for the Bemba *chisungu* and related rites among Lunda peoples in Central Africa (1982: 170–86), but with the establishment and protection of fertility itself through the administration of medicines and the containment of the excess potency entailed by the onset of menstruation so that it is unable to escape and be lost for ever. There are no equivalent ceremonies for boys who are circumcised in hospital when they are small.[2]

The orientation of girls' puberty rites in Africa has altered along with attitudes and expectations around marriage, fertility and gender through the twentieth century. Ulanga is no exception. The kinds of rites for girls performed by Pogoro communities up to the middle of the twentieth century were, like those performed by other central and east African peoples, intimately connected with those associated with marriage and the birth of a first child. I do not know enough about the constitution of practices from the nineteenth century and earlier to speculate about their content or transformation. However, folk memory and historical records would seem to indicate that prior to the 1930s seclusion as a key signifier of the transition between maiden and mother lasted from the onset of a girl's first period until she was formally 'taken' by the man she was to marry, which was often several years later. Indeed, extended seclusion remained unexceptional for some communities and families in Tanzania until well into the 1960s, although the gradual erosion of the practice had begun with the missionary onslaught in the German period. Despite sustained missionary opposition and mission initiated reforms such as the establishment of girls boarding schools, Tanzanian communities did not abandon the *unyago* or the series of rites which would ensure the fertility of their women. They adapted them; in Pogoro communities reformatting and compressing the components of the *unyago* to focus on what were defined as essentials within a shorter time frame. A perceived equivalence between the school as a place of teaching and the instructive purpose of the *unyago* means that the average time a girl is actually inside has been reduced to around one week. Links with marriage are maintained through the manipulation of the symbolism of coming out of seclusion at bridewealthing ceremonies (Green 1993). Despite curtailment, *unyago* matters, as an occasion for wider community celebration and as a life changing event for young women and their families. Similar processes of collapsing girls' puberty rites have occurred throughout the region (Swantz 1970: 363, Richards 1982: 55, Turner 1968: 200).

Maiden of the inside

Unyago marks the beginning of real womanhood and is a prerequisite for having the children on which female identity depends. Age brings increasing and gender specific responsibilities for female children that are nevertheless eagerly anticipated. Small girls, when they are not otherwise engaged in household chores for their mothers, relatives or neighbours, play at being grown up for much of the time, carrying banana stalk and maize cob babies on their backs, which they pretend to suckle and nurse. Maize cob babies are gradually replaced by real siblings whom they must tend and carry. By the time girls are eleven or so, they are tall enough and strong enough to perform the heavy work of pounding grain with a long pestle in a full-sized mortar, and to help their mothers with agricultural tasks in the fields and gardens. A girl between childhood proper and puberty is a *muhinga* or *kigoli*, a transient status that comes to an abrupt end with the onset of menstruation. A girl between puberty and motherhood is a *mwali*. As such she is expected to behave like an adult woman and to stop playing games with other children in the evenings. She must also display a consciousness about her body and behaviour lest she be accused of having no shame, especially when around men and boys. Any conversation with boys is now looked upon suspiciously by adults, and, a child no longer, the *mwali* is expected to be sedately subservient to her elders in a way in which small children are not. While young girls may feel some ambivalence about the abrupt change of status that becoming a *mwali* entails, their older female relatives seem not to, commenting endlessly on the visible changes in a girl's physique and remarking in particular on how her breasts have grown.[3] Girls are encouraged to work hard at the tasks of adult women, often rebuked for not making the kind of effort expected from somebody about to cross the threshold of childhood. 'You! You're almost a *mwali*. Work!'

The *mwali* ceremonies are initiated by physiological puberty, as evidenced by the onset of menstruation, although the actual 'coming out' can be delayed and held when convenient. Keeping a close eye on the physical development of their daughters,[4] mothers put aside some of the seasonal items that the *unyago* ceremonies require; a quantity of some of the dried cucumber seeds (*ntanga*) around which the rites are structured and some millet with which to make the *ubaga*[5] for the special meal with which the cucumber seeds will be eaten. When a girl realises that her first period has started she is expected to inform her mother who explains about 'cleanliness'. The older women with whom I spoke placed great emphasis on this aspect of 'instructing' a *mwali*, which any older female relative or even non-relative may do, if it is thought that the girl would be ashamed to discuss such things with her mother. They stress that the girl must wash herself well, and must never sleep with men while she is menstruating. The onset of physiological puberty has made the girl into a *mwali kam numba*, a maiden of inside the house. She should not go outside unless she is completely covered with cloth, and only then if there is special reason. She should not see any men, not even her own father. Only women and children may sit in the room with her. She should sit in silence. She may do inside work, but no cooking. If she has to say something she should gesture and 'talk with her hands'. Word is passed on to neighbours and female kin living in other villages that the girl has begun to menstruate, '*kalama*'. Arrangements are made to shave the *mwali* and eat the first lot of *ntanga*.

During the girl's first period and initial seclusion a range of restrictions are imposed on all the residents of her household. They must abstain from sex. Fire and water cannot be given to people from other households, nor can fire be taken from neighbours' hearths. The novice herself must not eat food that has been cooked on other people's fires, and food cooked on her fire can only be given to older women past childbearing age. Even they, however, should not be given fire from the house of the *mwali*, lest they pass it on to others who are sexually active, and with it the young woman's fertility. This is talked about in terms of 'depriving her of giving birth'. Not only could people use the fire, water and food to pass harmful medicine to the girl, the restriction on fire is crucial in that it prevents the *mwali* from 'drying out'. Fire is a potential vector of the girl's fertility, which could be dissipated further if those who receive it have sexual relations. The restrictions on food, fire and water apply only while the girl is actually bleeding. Only cooked food is involved, because its preparation involves fire. After the first, and sometimes the second period, apart from a prohibition on intercourse, no other domestic prohibitions apply to menstruating women or their households, although certain restrictions apply with regard to access to territorial shrines and participation in ritual occasions which seek to establish contact with spirits of the dead and those associated with territory. Protection of female reproductive power is insufficient in itself to ensure the future reproductive capacity of the novice. This capacity must first be established through the incorporation of *shirala* medicine into the young woman's body. While the transmission of *shirala* medicine through paternal kinship is seen to endow female reproductive capacity, its establishment generates a volatile power that could be lost to others if not carefully controlled. This is achieved through its incorporation into the bodies of older non-sexually active women through the manipulation of another medicine made from ground cucumber seeds (*ntanga*).

The first cucumber seeds
At some point during the girl's first period she is taken outside by older women who are a mixture of female kin and neighbours, under the leadership of a woman recognised as a specialist in *unyago* matters, and who would at one

time have had special duties regarding the delivery of children. The *mnyagu* receives token payments for her part in the rites which are handed over by both sides of the girl's family as each stage of the ritual is completed. Covered completely in two pieces of *kanga* or *kitenge* the girl is made to stand with her arms over the shoulders of one of the women, as if she is being carried on her back like a baby. She is taken to the front of the house and made to reach up to the central pole supporting the ridgepole of the house which in turn supports the roof. While holding the pole, she is made to 'step on'[6] a hen, which becomes her responsibility. She must let it lay and not kill it, because, 'This hen is her child.' She may also be given 'responsibility' for a much younger sibling and told the same thing: 'This is your child. Don't deprive him of anything!' According to the older women, when they were young, this child would have been the *mwali*'s main companion inside, fetching the water with which she washed and helping her to scrub her back. Girls are also 'taught' not to refuse their husbands anything.[7] Feeding others is the duty of women and inhospitality with food (*upati*) a uniquely female trait. Either on this day or the next, the girl's head is shaved by one of the older women with a razor blade and water while she sits passively in the lap of the woman who 'carried' her from the house. Shaving is, as we shall see, a critical medium of transition in life-crisis rituals, and recurs in all pollution contacts, whether relating to birth, death or witchcraft. The hair is collected by one of the *wamakolu* and put aside until the girl has had her second period, or until after she has been washed, when it is taken in the morning or evening to be 'buried by water', in the muddy banks of one of the many all-year rivers in the area. If this is not done, some women explained, the girl will stop 'growing' and will not develop into a mother as she should. After being shaved, the *mwali* is taken back inside the house. Before going in, she is fed a piece of millet *ubaga* dipped in a rough paste made from the finely ground cucumber seeds. Throughout she sits passively in the lap of the woman who holds her. Her eyes are shut, her head down. The *ntanga* are prepared, ground and cooked into a paste by one of the women. Only a small quantity of seeds is prepared, for only a restricted circle of people can eat them. Apart from the *mwali* herself, who is fed the *ntanga* like a baby, the eaters of the first lot of *ntanga* are the *wamakolu* themselves. For other women and men to eat them would be, 'Completely taboo. Younger women are unable because some of them wander about.[8] If they were to eat the *ntanga* this *mwali* would get problems, that is to say she can't give birth ... They would deprive her of giving birth.'

Bathing the *mwali*

After being shaved, girls remain inside for a week or so, depending on the time of year and parental attitudes, before the ceremony that will end their seclusion is held. The bathing of the *mwali* comprises a day-long sequence of singing and dancing around the theme of awakening the sleeping novice who is prepared for marriage in a highly evocative series of ritual scenarios that equate the girl with infant, bride and morsel literally ripe for consumption. The day's events are organised and conducted by women under the leadership of the *mnyagu*, who determines in which order things are done and the accompanying song and dances. Men may attend the day's events but are more likely to join in later in the evening for a general celebration, rather than be seen to participate in what is explicitly viewed as the height of specialist female ritual activity. Two dances in particular are associated with mwali events, the *libantha*, a dance held at weddings and festivals and the *shinyago*. According to informants, this was formerly a key element in the ceremonies that were also known, as among the Bemba (Richards 1982: 54), as the 'dancing of the girls'.

The day begins with the preparation of another portion of *ntanga* seeds which are first roasted and then pounded to a coarse flour in a mortar held between the legs of the girl's mother by the *mnyagu*. Pounding, like grinding, is symbolic of sex, and the women greeted the preparation of the ground *ntanga*[9] with raucous laughter. Cramming handfuls of ground seeds in their mouths, the women are led to the house where the *mwali* sleeps to act out forced entry to her chamber, singing demands for entry in response to the *mnyagu*'s lead all the time. When I participated in one such awakening, the women actually forced their way right into the girl's room. They crowded around the bed on which she lay wrapped from head to toe in cloth while the *mnyagu* violently shook her. Despite the songs about waking the novice she is not supposed actually to wake up, but to remain passive and silent, as if she were dead or sleeping. The novice was then carried on the back of an older woman to where a mat had been laid out in the middle of the yard, and was seated, as at the shaving between the legs of the woman who had carried her. This woman placed her hands over the ears and eyes of the *mwali*, who sat as she had sat before, passively with her head down. The *mwali* and the woman holding her were joined by another 'grandmother' of the girl, who sat across her feet. Her head and her shoulders were uncovered. Some of the children present were sent to fetch water. When they came back with small pots balanced on their heads, they were instructed by the *mnyagu* to begin dancing in a circle around the group on the mat, with the pots of water still on their heads. The old men came over and stood at the edge of the circle of women, who now joined the children, grabbing the pots of water from them and dancing around the mat. As they danced, with the pots of water on their heads, they deliberately spilled water onto the group seated on the mat. The children were sent back about five times to get more water. The women danced until the people on the mat were completely soaked. They threw water at each other and at the men who had come over to join them. They danced with each other, making lewd gestures, imitating lecherous men. Everybody got wet and slipped in the mud. When the *mnyagu* decided it was enough, the men moved back to where they had been sitting, and the women began to wash the *mwali*.

The *mnyagu* had placed some leaves called *lufumbeza* in a small shallow dish made from woven bamboo. The leaves are special and are used in various purification rituals. They smell sweet and, as they can stop people 'dreaming,'[10] they are used to wash the core bereaved at funerals. The leaves are left attached to the stem in bunches to make a loose bundle. Some water was poured over the leaves which were squeezed out into the dish. The *mnyagu* then poured some of this water over the girl's head and began, rubbing her head and body, to wash her. As she did this, she hit the girl's body with the bunch of wet leaves. This is '*kupunga*', meaning in this context to slap the body with medicine to cool it down and to prevent dreaming. Female relatives also of the *mwali* came forward to have their heads washed. A small child was made to sit between the legs of the *mwali* just as she sat between the legs of the old woman. She was made to wash this child, rubbing his body, just as the woman holding her rubbed hers. They sang a song about 'she is washing with the child'. The *mnyagu* said many times to the *mwali*, 'This is your child. Don't deprive him of anything!' The child was taken away and a *kanga* held over the group on the mat to form a sort of tent, under which the *mnyagu*, assisted by another of the *wamakolu*, could wash the girl's 'secret places'.

While the girl was being washed, an in-law of the girl's father prepared some finely ground salt, which she wrapped carefully in a maize leaf and tied into a package. This she gave to the father's sister of the girl, who tied it to a small stick and set off with it jauntily, going behind and around the house. Half dancing, half shuffling she vanished from sight. When she next came into view she was crouched and limping, resting on the stick as if she were an old man. Making for the group on the mat, she deliberately slipped, falling flat on her face in the mud right at the *mwali's* feet. Still on her knees, she greeted the group of women in quavering tones, handing the package of salt to the *mnyagu* who carefully untied it and handed it back. The father's sister then began to apply the salt in spots to the girl's body as if it were medicine, starting with the forehead and working down the body, chest, back and joints. While she did this she pulled a lecherous face. Then, crouching at the girl's feet, she began to lick all the salt off the girl's body. The women made loud comments of approval while this was being done, such as 'food without salt is not sweet' and 'food without salt doesn't taste'. The salt mime was explained to me in terms of fetching salt, which is a duty of husbands. This motif too recurs in similar rites throughout the area (Richards

1939: 56). In the Pogoro fetching of the salt, the woman sets out as a young husband and returns as a medicine giving elder, representing both the girl's future husband and her father. The salt is applied like medicine. Like medicine, it transforms the girl, making her 'good to eat'. The father's sister performs the salt mime because the girl's fertility comes via the *shirala* medicine from her father's side and, as one woman explained, it was the father's sister's brother who got the girl's mother pregnant. These mimes, and indeed the whole event, are also fun, an occasion for the women to act in a crude manner that would normally be considered outrageous.

The ceremony culminated once again in a public 'eating of cucumber seeds of the maiden', *kulia ntanga za mwali*, which had been cooked water into a coarse sticky paste. The paste was brought out in a dish, together with an enormous lump of *ubaga* made from millet the size of a football. The *mnyagu* broke off a large piece of this, dipped it in the *ntanga* and placed it between the hands of the *mwali*, who was still sitting still and silent on the mat. From this she then took a smaller piece of *ubaga*, coated it in the sauce and held it up, while the father's sister of the girl resumed her lecherous expression and followed the food with her eyes as it was waved before her. She began to dance, moving her head from side to side as she followed the food that the *mnyagu* held in front of her but out of reach. Eventually it was brought close enough for her to snatch with her mouth, licking her lips. The *mnyagu* rubbed the food on her face as she pushed it into her mouth. Another woman danced forward and the same thing happened, until everybody present, including the men and myself, had snatched with their mouths some of the food proffered by the *mnyagu*. The women said that, when they snatched the *ubaga* and the *ntanga*, they were pretending to be dogs. Indeed, the symbolism of predation is a recurrent motif across the region.[11] Although this is mainly for fun, it also makes explicit the fact that, now the *mwali* has been washed, there is no taboo on who may eat the *ntanga* nor on who can sleep with the *mwali*, who is, as in the salt ceremony, explicitly compared with food.

What was left in the dish was rubbed on the girl's body. She was again covered up and, 'carried' once more, was led back into the house where she was to stay until evening, when she could come out and wash. The ceremony was over and she could go to school in the morning. Everybody was fed a proper meal of maize *ubaga* and beans, together with what cucumber seed paste was left over. The group dispersed, some going over to the house of the girl's mother to dance. Although people refer to the day's events as 'taking the *mwali* out', they actually put the *mwali* back inside. This is not as contradictory as it seems. The *mwali* has been 'taken out', as having been washed, her period of seclusion is finished. Because the *mwali* ceremonies have become temporally disconnected with marriage, the actual formal 'coming out' now occurs later, at the handing over of the marriage payments when the bride enacts her 'coming out' of the house as she is presented to the groom's kin as a *mwali*, with her face covered and 'walking on her knees' out of the house. This ceremony is described in detail in Green (1993).

Containing female fertility

The *unyago* comprises several related themes which situate it within the anthropological category of *rites de passage* and, more fundamentally, within the total ritual repertoire not only of practice performed by persons defining themselves as Pogoro, but of south eastern and central African cultures more generally. As in other puberty and initiation rituals, the symbolic drama of events is structured around the transition of the novice from a state mirroring the passivity and asociality of death and birth to that of a person whose state and status enable her to participate fully in social activity (cf. Turner 1967, 1968; Comaroff 1985; Beidelman 1964; Godelier 1986, Bloch 1986, 1992). For the duration of her seclusion a novice is a *mwali kam numba*, a maiden of the inside of the house, kept inside, like a corpse prior to burial. The symbolism of the house equates what happens to the *mwali* with what happens to corpses, an identity reinforced by her behaviour and seclusion: silent, asocial and surrounded by women. Houses, or rather the insides of houses, are intimate places associated with sex, birth and death. The 'house' is a euphemism for marriage and the legal sexual relations that are assumed to take place inside it,[12] hence 'going outside' is a frequently used expression for adultery. Social activity happens outside the house in the public space of the yard (*luaga*), where men spend much of their free time sitting with friends.

But the *mwali* represents life, not death, and the power of female reproductive capacities through birth and female nurturance. The continuity of generations through women is vividly evoked by the image of the older woman washing the *mwali* sitting between her open legs, while the *mwali* simultaneously washes a smaller child between her own. The *mwali* is 'taught' the obligations of women, to have children, to feed people and especially to prepare food for her husband, at the same time as she is herself made ready for 'eating'. The capacity to feed and ensure the nurturance of others is regarded as the quintessentially female attribute (Beidelman 1997: 83), the appropriate expression of women's greater capacities for love and pity which ultimately derive from female experience, as it is culturally constituted around motherhood and birth. Consequently, fertility as reproductive capacity in the broadest sense is the objective of the rites, and this potentiality is both symbolised and conveyed by the cucumber seeds around which the entire sequence of the *unyago* is structured.

Cucumbers are a common feature of girls' puberty rites in the area (Swantz, 1970: 236; Turner 1968: 241). They reproduce quickly. More than their shape, it is the numerous seeds inside the fruit that make them particularly suited to an equation with fertility in general, and female fertility in particular. The *unyago* is structured around two occasions on which *ntanga* are prepared and eaten. In contrast to the eating of the *ntanga* at the start of the seclusion period, the eating of the second lot of *ntanga* is open to men and women of all ages, and is the culmination of the series of events which effect the 'bringing out' of the girl into the community. Although washing the *mwali* is an essential prerequisite to the public eating of the *ntanga*, and her cooling down is significant, the first eating of the *ntanga* by the *mwali* herself and the older non-sexually active women is what makes possible its general consumption weeks or even months later. Without their ingestion, the *mwali* would be unable to carry, bear and bring up children successfully. Unlike the *shirala* medicine, which conveys the capacity for fertility in a direct and immediate way, the cucumber seeds do not in themselves make the novice fertile. Without puberty and *shirala* they have no power. Rather, what they seem to do is to augment female fertility and then absorb the excess, which can then be contained in other people's bodies and made safe. Therefore the prohibitions which apply to the consumption of the first lot of *ntanga* paste are identical to those on fire, water and sexual contact that apply during the girl's first period. *Wamakolu* as older non-sexually active women have an obligation to eat the first lot of *ntanga*, containing within their bodies the fertility of the novice and preventing its dissipation.

The prohibitions relating to fire are the same as those relating to the eating of the *ntanga*, suggesting that the various prohibitions on the menstruating *mwali* here are not concerned with preventing the contamination of others, as Wilson suggests for the menstrual taboos of the Nyakyusa (1957: 131) nor with pro-tecting the woman herself from her own pollution (Buckley and Gottlieb 1988: 11). Because the *ntanga* can be eaten by anybody after the *mwali* has been washed on coming out of seclusion, it would appear that what the *wamakolu* are doing when they eat the first lot of *ntanga* is to contain the excess potency of the *mwali* until her state is sufficiently normal for there to be no risk to her if others eat it. The *wamakolu* are able physically to contain it because they are beyond reproduction themselves. They therefore do not channel away the *mwali*'s fertility, and, as women, they have already absorbed in their bodies this kind of excess potency, when their own periods started and when they themselves gave birth. The snatching of the *ntanga* by predatory dogs makes explicit the fact that there is no restriction on who may eat the *ntanga* nor, by extension, on the girl's participation in sexual activity. Turner describes a similar sequence for the Ndembu, in which people mimic hyenas, snatching the food as scavengers, which he interprets as stealing some of the girl's mother's fertility (1968: 226). This interpretation does not apply to the Pogoro rite, the whole point of which emphasises that the girl's fertility is no longer vulnerable to predation. This state is, however, short lived. Volatility returns with the powers generated by each birth, which are managed through identical restrictions on the exchange of food, fire and sex that apply to the house of a *mwali*.

8

Women's work

The embodied containment of contagious power by women in specific ritual categories is also a feature of funerary practices, together with the notion that containment cumulatively changes a person's substance. Bereavement, as a life experience, leaves a cumulative trace in people's bodies. This affects both men and women. The once bereaved acquire a degree of immunity from the ravages of death power, and can assume specific roles at the funerals of others. The funeral process is structured around the imagined transition of a dead person into a spirit, achieved through the manipulation of a series of parallel identifications between the dead person and the circle of key mourners, who are most closely identified with the body (cf. Goody 1962: 188; Wilson 1957: 49). It is the extent of this identification which makes possible the series of repeat funerals which constitute the extended funeral process without, as in the case of the secondary burials described by Hertz (1960) and others (Pina Cabral 1980; Bloch 1971, 1982; Huntingdon 1973), an actual body to rebury.

The identification between mourners and deceased is most pronounced for those women closely related to the dead, who wear around their necks strips of cloth (*lijemba*) representing both corpse and shroud until the funeral process is over. The identification between women and houses serves to identify female mourners with the corpse, and what happens to both the core bereaved and to the corpse closely parallels what happens to the *mwali*. While both men and women who have already been bereaved can contain the powers released by the deaths of others, women's obligations to contain death exceed those of men, even of those men most closely related to and thus identified with the corpse. These obligations commence at the very event which opens the funeral, after which mourning formally begins and are progressively lifted at two post-burial regroupings of mourners one, called *toa tatu*, shortly after the burial and the other, *sadaka ya mwisho*, up to a year later.

The bitterness of mourning

Unlike the Christian celebrations, from which people are increasingly excluded as invitation cards become, for the elite at least, the norm, nobody is excluded from the public events that comprise the funeral process. Participation in a burial, perhaps because it is the epitome of empathy, is regarded as the height of moral human sociality. Neighbours and kin are obliged to bury one another. Everything that happens at a funeral, *because* it happens at a funeral, amounts to 'working together' or 'co-operation'. The contribution of small sums of cash and items of food towards the funeral expenses is an integral part of this co-operation. People who do not attend the funerals of their relatives and neighbours without good reason are said to have 'no love for people' and may even be implicated in the death itself (cf. Goody 1962: 86). The obligation to participate in funeral activities falls heaviest on women. In the highlands communities older women who consider themselves to be devout Catholics compose an *ad hoc* corps of funeral specialists who direct the articulation of mourning through singing the Christian derived 'songs of suffering' (*nyimbo za mateso*) along with more traditional dirges. Older women also direct the preparation of funeral food and lead in the recitation of prayers by mourners at the funeral house. Such obligations entail significant demands on women's time. The death of a kinsperson necessitates remaining at the house of the dead for the fortnight period between the burial and *toa tatu*. Older women routinely attend the burials and *sadaka* for more distant kin and those unrelated to them but who lived in the vicinity. Many of these women are widows. They believe that, as one can be taken at any time God wants, one must be continually in a state of readiness for death. Attending other people's funerals is a necessary part of this preparation.

The activities associated with mourning do not begin at the moment of death. A funeral has to be formally opened, at an event called *lugutu* from the verb *-guta* to cry or mourn. It involves the killing of a chicken of the same sex as the deceased on the threshold of the house, while a male elder scatters some maize grains or pumpkin seeds from the dead person's store across the yard and implores the spirits of the dead to allow the events to proceed without discord. At the same time a female relative of the dead smashes a pot or a gourd signifying that wailing can begin. The essential act is the killing of the chicken, which is the 'work' of a woman, usually a 'sister' of the dead. The chicken is killed by smashing its head against the doorframe of the house so that it dies without shedding blood, in contrast to the usual way of killing chickens by cutting their throats with a knife, which anybody may do. The chicken is left where it lies for a time, before being taken away, plucked and cooked. Its meat is eaten by the old people who have already been 'died on' and who, because of their age, think of themselves as being close to death. If others were to eat the meat of this chicken they could bring death to their houses and families. I was told that old women are particularly suited to eating this meat. Not only are they likely to have already been 'died on', but having 'dried out', proximity with death will not harm their fertility. Also, as women, they should involve themselves fully in mourning, of which eating this chicken is part. As the *unyago*, when the novice is given a hen to tend as a child, chickens can stand for people in certain contexts and on certain occasions. The chicken at *lugutu* stands for the dead person, much as in Nuer sacrifice cattle are identified with the person on whose behalf the sacrifice is made (Evans Pritchard 1962: 263). However, the killing of the *lugutu* chicken is not a sacrifice or an offering to the dead. Rather, it is a replication of the death of the person who has already died in order that the powers it released may be safely contained. The spirits of the dead want blood because blood is the stuff of life. Spilled blood is death. The bloodless killing of the chicken is a way of containing death by having a death without blood, which is further contained physically by the already bereaved who consume its meat, just as the potent fertility of the *mwali* is contained by the *wamakolu* when they eat the first lot of cucumber seeds.

Houses and women's space

The word *shiwembo*, as well as denoting the funeral in its entirety, also refers to the stylised mourning dirges of the women. When the people already gathered at the house hear the pot smashing, a chorus of wails erupts from the women. Wailing and crying are the 'work' of women because women, having the capacity to 'pity' are 'able to suffer'. The bitterness (*lusungu*) felt by mourners is expressed in the old and ragged clothing worn at funeral events. Funeral food is similarly thought of as coarse, although it does not differ much, if at all, from the everyday food which people eat in their homes. Only coarse ground maize flour (*dona*) should be used in the preparation of the funeral meal. Onions must not be used and, partly because of the cost and partly because its consumption characterises celebrations, meat is rarely served on the day of the burial. Wailing continues periodically throughout the day. Women mourners arriving at the house of the dead pause and collect themselves at the edge of the compound, to prepare for their entrance at a slow pace and with arms raised in a striking gesture of loss. As they approach the yard and go right into the house, they wail in rhythm the name of the deceased or the kinship term by which they used to call them.

Men and women arrive separately. They will spend the whole day in separate groups in separate places, women inside the house or in the cooking area outside it. Women sit flat on the ground with their legs straight out in front of thcm. Men sit outside, leaning their backs against the walls of the house in the shade of the eaves, or squatting on makeshift stools. Men gather around the male representative of the bereaved to whom mourners give condolences and cash outside the house, which is packed full with women. The organisation of domestic space at funerals dramatises an intensification of the separation of male and female spheres of activity based on existing demarcations between male and female space. Most small houses are divided into two or four rooms, opening from a wide central corridor. The central corridor space is frequently used for cooking and is where the three hearthstones (*mafiga*) are set out. One hearth defines household, centred on the woman who feeds its members (cf. Harwood 1970: 23). On the death of a spouse, a payment called *vyamnumba* 'things of the inside of the house' is demanded by the female kin of the dead from the female kin of the survivor, in recognition of the intimate domestic services that they had received from the deceased. That this payment passes between women is significant. Women are more closely associated with these matters, and with the very house itself, than are men. It is where mothers and *mwali*s are secluded in order to safeguard their future fertility. Men and boys are on no occasion secluded inside, unless they are corpses or newborns. During funeral events, men sleep outside the house, not inside it. Women, if there is space, sleep inside. Both sexes sleep on the ground, on the dry banana leaves that have been spread throughout the house and yard for this purpose. They are a sure sign of a *msiba* and are used for sleeping at all funeral events. Sleeping on mats or beds is not permitted: it would contravene the ideal of suffering. Sex is absolutely antithetical to funeral events and is prohibited. Sweeping the homestead clear of banana leaves signifies the end of a stage of a funeral. It is most elaborate at the very end of the funeral process, when the yard is swept clean and the banana leaf shelter in which the funeral beer was placed is destroyed.[1]

Close relatives of the dead sit in the room with the corpse. Women prepare food outside huddled around large cooking fires. Funerals can attract a couple of hundred people, all of whom have to be fed. While women are busy with cooking and crying men and boys are sent to collect flour, food and firewood, and to purchase the necessities for the burial itself. Grain is pounded for the large meal served after the burial. The body is washed shortly after death by same sex people who have already been bereaved themselves and, dressed in good clothing, is laid out on a bed in one of the rooms for people to see. Men go inside the house to look at the body, but, unless they are the husband or the father of the dead, they do not remain long. A husband who has lost a wife is expected to stay with her body until the burial, as is a woman who has lost her husband. Spouses are not allowed to leave the house until the burial and are permitted neither food nor drink until after the burial. The relatives of the dead negotiate with affines over the various payments that should be made before the body is buried. These payments, of which *vyamnumba* is one, are *shirandira mashi*, 'for drinking water', because they should be made, or at the very least agreed, before the burial. If a woman dies before her husband has completed paying bridewealth, this should be paid, ideally in full, before the body can be buried.[2]

Burial

Just before the burial the body is undressed, washed again and wrapped in white cloth with the face left uncovered so that mourners may look for the last time and, as they bid farewell to the corpse, kneel and touch the cold forehead with their hands. Some thin, bandage-like strips are torn from the shroud[3] and set aside when the body is being dressed. These *ngoi* (strings) or *majemba* are worn tied around the heads of the female core bereaved. Apart from the widow and, perhaps, sisters of the dead, whoever else decides to wear these does so as a matter of choice rather than proscription. An older adult daughter may wear them but, in general, it is considered inappropriate for any but the old to do so, at least for an extended period of time. This is because a woman wearing *lijemba* is under the restrictions of mourning. She should not dress well nor use cosmetics on her body. Neither can she have sex. Old women said that, when they were young only very old women or widows wore *lijemba* because 'men are not able to suffer'. Loose threads are pulled from the frayed edge of the shroud and tied around the wrists of the dead person's small children to prevent them from 'dreaming' (cf. Goody 1962: 147). If a catechist or priest has come to do the service at the house this is read outside, when the body has been brought out and, either in a closed coffin or wrapped in a mat, placed in the centre of the yard. Small children, who are not permitted to see the body, are lifted over the coffin to 'jump the corpse' as a gesture of farewell. The body is taken out of the house, where it has been associated with women, by men (cf. Bloch and Parry 1982: 25) who now assume responsibility for its burial in the grave. The women inside the house, and the widower if a woman has died, follow the body out of it. A procession assembles, the core bereaved leading with the widow or widower in front of the body, then the men and, finally, the remaining women, and slowly wends its way to the burial site.

Burials themselves are brief affairs informed, as are the style of the graves, by Christian practice. They generally take place either in the churchyard or at the family's burial plot, usually at some distance from the house. Those who define themselves as Christian tend to define their families' burials as 'Christian burials', irrespective of whether a priest or catechist attends or of where the body is buried. Church cemeteries, the '*shamba la Mungu*' (the field of God) are reserved only for those meeting particular Christian standards. Once the burial is over people return to the homestead of the deceased in single file without looking back towards the grave. As they draw near, they pause to wash their hands, faces and feet. Those who have flour on their faces wash it off and women wearing shroud strips pull them down from their foreheads and wear the string around their necks, with the ends falling across the chest. A meal is served in the yard to all funeral participants under the direction of the male *mweni msiba* (literally 'person with the funeral', but in actuality a kind of funeral host) and other 'brothers' of the bereaved. Men and elders are served first. People are served and eat in small single sex groups gathered around one dish. The meal is an essential part of the burial. Eating together, as the idiom of sociability, is integral to the 'co-operation' that burying entails. Only after they have finished eating can people depart.

While the meal is served, or shortly after, the already died-on shave the heads of the core bereaved with a blade and water at the edge of the yard, which is thought of as an appropriate place for throwing rubbish. Only the head is shaved. The hair is left to lie where it falls. Because it is a funeral, the very purpose of which is suffering, soap is not used. The main bereaved are later taken, by same-sex people who have already been died on, to be washed with special leaves in a stream of running water. Only after this can they be given food. A wider group of kin and on occasion affines are shaved. Decisions regarding shaving are determined by individuals' feelings about the quality of the relationship with the deceased and their family. The core bereaved, those who define themselves as the immediate family of the dead, remain at the house of the dead for another one or two days until an event called *shasangira*. The composition of this category depends very much on personal choice rather than proscription and is an artefact of the performativity of kinship. It can include sisters-in-law or father's sisters of the dead, brothers-in-law and mother's brothers. Those defining themselves as core bereaved mark themselves out from the mass of mourners by smearing a mixture of flour and water across their foreheads. They remain at the house of the *msiba* after the burial, when neighbours and distant kin disperse. Women are more likely to define themselves as core bereaved than are men, and they are more likely to wear flour on their faces in a dramatic slash of white. These women spend much of the day of the burial in the same room as the corpse. It is these women, if they are older, who will mourn for an extended period of time. A widow should remain in a state of mourning, signified by the wearing of a strip of cloth, *lijemba*, representing the shroud, until the funeral process is finished.

The gradual removal of death

Death as an event encourages death, which the killing and restricted eating of the *lugutu* chicken is an attempt to contain. Death is also directly contagious. The corpse, as the dead thing itself, is the most contagious of all. The contagiousness of death permeates everything and everyone connected with the corpse. Only those who have already been 'died on' can involve themselves in the preparation and washing of the corpse, or take with them the vessels that were used in its preparation. Similar restrictions apply to the clothing of the dead, especially to that in which the dead person has been laid out. All those who have attended a funeral must wash as they depart, even if they have had no close contact with the body. Failure to do so would mean carrying death with them to their homes. The contagiousness of death affects particularly acutely those who are closely related to the dead and who are obliged to have close contact with them. Contagion is not solely a consequence of proximity, physical or otherwise, but of the identification between the core bereaved and the dead body around which the funeral process is structured (cf. Goody 1962: 188; Wilson 1957: 49). This identification is most apparent in the case of the main female mourners, who wear a piece of the shroud in which the body has been wrapped. Similarly, among LoDagaa the widow is 'dirty' and needs to be cleansed, not because of the physical intimacy which she had with the deceased while he was alive (Goody 1962: 193), but because of an identification with the corpse arising from their social relationship through which she is situated in the category of bereaved. Goody himself points to the parallel treatment by the LoDagaa of the core bereaved and the corpse. At one point, the widow is approached as if she were dead, when an offering is presented as if to an ancestor (1962: 188). This complex identification between corpse and mourners was explained in the following terms by one of Monica Wilson's Nyakyusa informants, 'What they do to the participants they do to the deceased...If they are not cleansed, he is still muddy' (1957: 49).

Main mourners are shut inside the house with the body and come outside with it, because they are being made physically to take on the death and carry it around with them as dirt. This is systematically removed in stages following the burial; at the various repeat funerals that make up the funeral process. The first of these stages is washing and shaving the core bereaved after the burial. Shaving the bereaved is commonplace in funeral rituals in Africa, practised by groups as diverse as Nyakyusa (Wilson 1957: 42), Lugbara[4] (Middleton 1982: 148) and Nuer (Evans Pritchard 1962: 152). It is not merely a ritual of separation, as Goody suggests for the funeral shaving of the LoDagaa (1962: 61) serving to separate the living from the dead, and, since they shave the corpse also, the dead from their previous life. It is a ritual of cleansing. In Pogoro practice shaving is a key component of purification rites that address imbalances between powers and return people to appropriate states, as we saw in the washing of the *mwali* and will become evident in the next chapter when we examine in detail practices for the suppression of witchcraft. At the same time, like the whitewashing of the faces, it serves to mark out the bereaved from other people. Dirt is relative to contexts associated with spirits and only becomes the target of reduction where relations need to be established between people and spirits. In everyday life this is on occasions where persons need access to the space of ancestral and territorial shrines. Physical processes associated with birth and death implicate the living person in more excessive dirt, locating them at the other extreme of the continuum away from the state of the *mahoka*. Because of the 'paradox of the ultimate unity of life and death' (Douglas 1966: 176) the same 'dirt' is a consequence of sex *and* death, birth *and* mourning, although on occasion, these two aspects of 'dirt' stand antithetically opposed. Taking on the dirt that these situations entail is a way of harnessing and containing the potency inherent in them, at the same time as seeking, through various rites of purification, to re-establish the ideal middle position appropriate for living people in a drama played out between two conceptually opposite places, the inside of the house and the cool shade of the forest, the place of the *mahoka*. The medium of cooling and cleansing, which gets people back into good 'states', is water. Its equivalent is the process of decay. This is what happens to the dead person's body and, by implication, to the hair and other stuff discarded at the place where domestic rubbish is thrown. This may be anywhere at the edge of the yard, away from the house. Places so designated are often clumps of banana trees, plants which are, as we have seen, associated with a prolific and natural fertility and which surround every yard.

The dirt of death is removed in stages from the circle of core bereaved that progressively shrinks at each of the repeat funerals following the burial of the body. Just as the dead person must be cleansed and cooled down in order to become a *lihoka*, so the women must be cleansed and cooled down in order for them to resume their normal positions, away from the 'dirt' of mourning. Strips of shroud are gradually discarded in a ritual that makes explicit reference to the burial of the body, both emphasising the identification between mourner and corpse and the end of the identification in successive stages that differentiate between the closeness to the deceased of various categories of female mourners. Close relatives of the dead remain at the funeral house for one or two days. On the morning of the second day after the burial, while it is still dark, the *shasangira* meal is prepared at the house. One of the older women, the *wamakolu*, takes some of the food in her hand and scatters it into the corners of the house. She does this silently. The food is left to lie where it falls. This is a *tambiko*, although an informal one, to the generalised and unnamed dead who are thought to be hovering around the homestead, indeed inside the very house itself, attracted by the death. Women here are set up as the arbiters of uncontrolled polluting death, while men negotiate formally with the ancestors.

After the *shasangira*, the women who have been wearing *majemba* go, before the sun has risen, to bury them by water. The shroud strips are buried in a shallow trench, made oblong like a grave, in the muddy soil at the edges of a permanent river. They are laid lengthwise on top of each other. Bereaved women close to the dead remove the strips which were torn from the shroud and replace them with a piece of cloth, which they wear around the neck as *lijemba*. Some spit water on to the strip as they lay it in the earth. To spit water, *kupeta mashi*, is a kind of *tambiko* to the spirits who trouble the living. It is a way of spitting out the trouble and the heat from the physical body of the group, while, at the same time, calming the *mahoka*. The women speak to the dead person as they bury the cloth saying, 'You have gone and left us. Don't come back.' They ask that '*nshimba zizizimiri*' – 'the bodies cool'. This is directed both at the person who has died and at those left behind. They cover the trench with earth, wash themselves in the stream looking only downstream as they do so, so as not to encourage the dead to return, and make their way to the house without looking back.

The female kin who are less close to the deceased do not replace their shroud cloth with fresh pieces of old cloth. Those closer to the dead do so, donning replacement strips, tied around their necks just like the original shroud. Depending on the woman's relation to the deceased, these are worn until around two weeks after the burial, at a collective meal called *toa tatu*, which in essence is a regrouping of mourners who were present at the burial. The core bereaved remain at the house until *toa tau* is finished. With the exception of the main female mourners, women wearing *lijemba* remove them and bury them by water prior to the funeral meal. Only the main female mourner continues to wear hers until the funeral is finally ended, as much as a year later at an event called *sadaka ya mwisho*. This event, formally marking the transition from person to spirit, is an occasion of sadness and celebration.[5] Wearing and discarding the shroud strips is explicitly associated with female ritual obligations as carriers of an embodied identification between dead and living that situates both within the liminality of mourning. A woman who has worn them many times explained that burying the strips by water calms the dead and they become still. This is possible because the shroud strips are the dead person and death in general, which the female mourners have been physically carrying around with them. Burying them 'like a corpse' makes them into the symbolic corpse of the second, third and fourth funerals, *shasangira, tatu* and *sadaka ya mwisho*, which replicate on a reduced scale the activities and organisation of space at the start of the funeral process, prior to the burial of the body.

Gender matters

The notion of cumulative changes in a person's makeup informs our understanding of the ritual obligations of women past their reproductive years, as mediators of both life and death. The fundamental identity between the powers of life and death implies that women's bodies can better contain them than male bodies can, because they have already been exposed to these powers, through engagement in reproductive processes and participation at funeral events that constitute essential elements of female growth as a process of becoming. In the case of the *wamakolu*, who are no longer involved in reproduction, the powers associated with life and death cease to be dangerously antithetical because they will neither transmit them to others through sexual activity nor affect their own fertility. While the embodiment of cosmological powers associated with the life process empowers women to assume specific ritual statuses in the management of reproduction and death, it also precludes their assumption of the status of shrine medium (*mbui*). This is only available to men who live their lives in a state as close as possible to that of the spirits. Before entering the sacred section of the forest, these mediums follow certain prohibitions that are designed to make them more like the *mahoka* than other living people. They abstain from sex, from smoking and from food. They observe permanently various other restrictions on dress and style of housing. Not only are their clothes held to be 'traditional', a piece of single coloured cloth wrapped around the body, they wear next to their skin a piece of white cloth, such as is used as a shroud or demanded by the *mahoka*. Just as it is taboo to dress a body in red, it is taboo for *wambui* to wear this colour. Red is associated with blood and with hot things. They avoid contact with death. They must not see corpses and, like pregnant women, they stand aside at the first stage of a funeral when the presence of the body makes death contagious.

The nature of female bodies, with their capacity to absorb power and be transformed by it, means that women cannot achieve the separation from life processes that being a shrine diviner entails. Even after the menopause, women continue to be involved in the life processes of others, as containers of both death pollution and female fertility. In contrast to the transmission of mediumship among the Shona, where female power gradually ebbs away from women's bodies leaving them appropriate vessels for possession by royal ancestor spirits (Lan 1985), Pogoro women never lose their association with life processes, and indeed, have specific ritual duties concerning the life processes of others.

'Women's work is weeping'

Women's ritual obligations and their duty of care extends into popular Christianity. The social experience of ageing and growth substantively transforms the constitution of the entire person, impacting on cognitive and emotional qualities that are enhanced with age. As women get older they are expected to become progressively more able to assume the emotional labour of suffering for themselves and others. The cultural emphasis on suffering as a value is doubtless influenced by Catholic iconography in which women's childbearing role is intimately related to the pain and fleshly suffering of Christ and to the emotional anguish of the mother who will eventually lose him (Walker Bynam 1987; Warner 1976). Weeping statues and representations of the Virgin reinforce this vision of compassionate Mary and of suffering mothers, promoting an almost visceral sense of identification between Mary's experience as a woman and women's experience more generally (Bloch 1993). Women's capacity to endure and feel empathy for the suffering of others stems from their culturally accorded role as mothers, who have a duty to care for other people. Motherhood in Ulanga, and in places like it, is premised on a particular experience of one's own body as a nurturer and carrier of the bodies of others; of children in the womb and on one's back and inevitably, as time passes, of the shroud representing the body of a loved one. It involves excruciating pain and suffering, incredible patience and often, almost unbearable loss. Love, loss and pain are the core emotional experience of being female, as it is culturally constituted, in which women as *mothers* care for others and manage their transition between life and death. This particular construction of femininity is experienced cumulatively through everyday living and participation in the gendered rituals that emphasise women's duties as carers and caretakers of life and death. Women's personal experience of caring and of loss creates empathy for the suffering of others, an empathy heightened by the overwhelming emotional resonance of the ritual occasions at which the vagaries of death and life are acknowledged. It is this lived experience (cf. Walker Bynam 1987: 281) of gender, rather than Catholic representations, which inform the religiosity of devout Pogoro Catholic women, centred on intense personal relationships with Mary and remembering the dead.

While men also attend church services, wear rosaries and pray at home, women's participation in Christian practices is more extensive, and certainly more intense. Women comprise the majority of participants in all night vigils held for Mary and those conducted at home as part of the funeral process, where members of the group singing hymns inside the house are mostly female, in contrast to the mixed sex group dancing what are locally defined as 'traditional' songs outside it. Weekday Masses attract women in larger numbers than men.

Women are more involved in the Legion of Mary and church sponsored lay organisations than their male counterparts, and regularly pray in their houses on behalf of family members, dead and living. Services held on Good Friday are dominated by women who sing the special sad 'songs of suffering', the very same songs which have come to constitute the legitimate expression of mourning at funeral events when they are sung for hours at a time. Because these songs are associated with funerals, singing them and hearing them evokes memories of the funerals of others and the pain of personal loss, creating an atmosphere of palpable sadness in the church. The Good Friday service is also understood, as the structure of the service intends, as the funeral of Christ himself (cf. Taussig 1980: 105; Rushton 1982: 156–7). The crucified Christ is taken down from his high position behind the altar and laid at its foot, for people to file up to and kiss, just as they bid farewell to a dead person immediately prior to burial by filing past the coffin and laying a hand on their forehead.

Although the events of Good Friday focus on the crucifixion of Christ, the re-enactment of his funeral in establishing the occasion of his death simultaneously effects the establishment of Mary as a bereaved mother. This understanding of Mary as a mother who has lost a son, and of Christ's death, rather than his life as significant,[6] is fundamental to women's core experience of Catholicism, founded on a relation of empathetic understanding between themselves and Mary. Valued as a mother, rather than as a virgin, Mary occupies heaven and earth simultaneously. An essentially ordinary woman, Mary's life is tragic, as a mother who both loved and lost a son. Mary thus understands the plight of women, and feels pity and compassion for them, just as women feel compassion for Mary and help her to remember Christ through mourning. Mary is not merely an intercessor with Christ and God, but a divine being in her own right to whom prayers and conversations can be directed. Unlike the figures of God and Christ, to whom one prays (-*sali*) or begs (-*omba*) Mary's humanity means that the conversational exchange is possible. People 'talk' to Mary (-*ongea*), and she listens because, understanding the suffering of others, she feels pity, just as women feel pity for Mary's own suffering.

The relation of compassion with Mary is founded on a perception of Mary as an ordinary woman, made extra ordinary only through her selection by God (cf. Bloch 1993). Tales of Mary's extraordinary nature stress her compassion and kindness, rather than her piety. The kinds of cultural elaborations of Mary as pure and without sin, associated with a particular moment of European Catholicism, are largely absent. Mary is not perceived as a unique kind of woman who has managed to transcend the ultimate contradiction between spirit and flesh which formal Catholic theology proposes. On the contrary, Pogoro women's representations of Mary emphasise her humanity as a bereaved mother, as a person who has had intimate contact with both birth and death, and who can therefore empathise with the suffering of others (cf. Walker Bynam 1987: 269). Contemporary Pogoro women's relationships with Mary cannot be explained by symbolic constructions of gender in which Mary is thought to appeal to women as a kind of role model of purity and transcendence of original sin (Rushton 1982; Warner 1976). Pogoro women do not regard Mary as a symbol of motherhood or virginity, but as a real woman who has lost a son and with whom a relationship of mutual compassion is possible. Similarly, women do not see themselves as being merely representatives of different gender attributes when they participate in gendered rituals. The whole point about such rituals is that the processes of transformation they effect do not occur as abstractions, divorced from the people who perform them (cf. Bloch 1992). Participation in rituals associated with fertility and death is imagined as physically and emotionally transforming those undergoing them and determines their capacities to assume gender specific ritual roles in the future.

Older women's involvement in funerary rituals and their obligations as mourners conveys an emotional resonance (cf. Kratz 1994: 130) which makes possible the cumulative experience of compassion on which their special relationship with Mary, the mother of a dead son, is founded. This cumulative gender differentiation which the embodiment of power entails means that women never become more 'like men' as they age and lose their reproductive capacity, which Herbert has suggested accounts for the special ritual roles of post menopausal women in other communities in Africa (1993: 231). On the contrary, through exposure to the powers released by the life process and an enhanced capacity to empathise, older women embody par excellence the female characteristics of nurturance, love and pity. Women's capacity for suffering and the expression of love, achieved through ageing and involvement in life processes is the culmination of their becoming, and of their identification with Mary as the basis of a personal piety founded on the imitation not of Christ, at his moment of death (Walker Bynam 1987: 257), but of his mother.

9

Witchcraft suppression practices and movements

This chapter examines the manifestation of public witchcraft suppression practices in Ulanga District, historically and in the present. Movements for the suppression of witchcraft have swept across south eastern and central Africa throughout the twentieth century. Perhaps the best documented is *kamcape*, observed at different places and points in its history by Audrey Richards, Max Marwick and Roy Willis. The practice of such movements tends to be similar. They are often associated with a single practitioner, either based at a cult centre or on whose authority itinerant specialists work. Their ritual practice is generally public, involving groups of people or even entire villages. It centres on the use of medicine that both suppresses the powers of witches and protects potential victims from witchcraft attack. Often, both witches and accusers participate and receive the same treatment, a key component of which entails the purification of clients. This is achieved by washing parts of the body in special medicines thought to have cleansing, as well as anti-witchcraft properties. The anti-witchcraft medicine of *kamcape* was explicitly associated with cleansing, the very name of the movement being derived from the verb 'to clean' or 'to scrub' (Richards 1935: 149; Willis 1968: 8; Marwick 1950: 100). In the Tanzanian movements, this purification sometimes involves shaving off the hair, hence witchcraft suppression practices are talked about in terms of 'shaving witchcraft' (Redmayne 1970: 114; Green 1994). These kinds of movements and their associated practices are not confined to the past, but seem to resurface periodically, often in the dramatic form of a touring witchfinder and his entourage conducting mass cleansings in the villages. This happened in parts of rural Zambia in 1989 when a Dr Moses performed anti-witchcraft rituals virtually identical in form to those associated with *kamcape* some twenty years previously (Auslander 1993: 172–4). Similarly, between 1988 and 1992, parts of southern Tanzania witnessed what appeared to be a revival of anti-witchcraft practices when the sheer number of people visiting one particular specialist attracted the attention of local government and the national media.[1] Anthropologists and historians have tended to regard such movements as essentially 'modern' phenomena because, if studied in isolation, they appear to have origins external to the societies affected by them, their emergence often coincides with periods of great upheaval and change, and their ritual sequence incorporates elements of Christian and bureaucratic practice.[2] Practitioners make use of official stamps, issue certificates of cleansing and are said to keep written records of all those who have received treatment. Some explicitly represent themselves, through their dress and demeanour, as a radical challenge to 'traditional' healers and diviners. The young men who brought *kamcape* medicines to villages made a point of wearing European style dress. They placed their anti-witchcraft medicine in glass bottles rather than gourds and horns, and used mirrors to identify and mystically record the identity of witches (Richards 1935; Willis 1968). Dr Moses adopted similar strategies, combining the practice of the office and the clinic with indigenous ideas about medicine, witchcraft and purification (Auslander 1993: 183). Despite condemnation by mainstream Christian churches, anti-witch specialists often claim to be working with, or for, Christian deities and saints (Richards 1935: 45; Auslander 1993: 172; Redmayne 1970: 106). And, in the face of government opposition, many claim to be working *for* the government, in the interests of 'development', by controlling the number of witches.

The evidence from Ulanga suggests that the public witchcraft suppression practices associated with anti-witchcraft movements cannot be understood simply as modern innovations. On the contrary, their anti-witchcraft practices only appear modern and innovative when the movements are considered solely in terms of themselves, divorced from the social contexts in which they operate. Despite those elements that seem to have foreign origins, the basic practice of these movements conforms to the sequence and structure of indigenous purification procedures routinely performed at life crisis rituals. It is only when the movements are examined in relation to the way that witchcraft is socially constructed that the central element of their practice, involving the *purification* of witches, makes sense. Purification is thought appropriate for dealing with witches because of the way that witchcraft is conceptualised in much of south eastern and central Africa, as a premeditated act, which, through the use of medicines, transforms the person into something dirty and anti-social. While the widespread acceptance of new movements beyond their areas of origin can be explained, in part, by their conformity to indigenous purification procedures, their periodic re-emergence, often at times of political and economic instability, owes much to the political pragmatism of village leaders and factions, and the dynamics of their relationship with local administrations (cf. Ross 1969: 62; Probst nd). These people may invite specialists in to cleanse villages or advocate that a large proportion of those involved in witchcraft disputes go to a particular specialist, creating the conditions under which a 'movement' for the suppression of witchcraft can apparently appear.

Modern movements for the suppression of witchcraft?

The resurgence in popularity of public anti-witchcraft practices during moments of apparent crisis has generally been explained by anthropologists in narrow terms of the classificatory potential of witchcraft ideologies, where attributes of witches are seen to be associated with what are negatively perceived to be attributes of 'modernity'. The manifestation of public anti-witchcraft practices at these moments has been viewed as a logical response to an increase in witchcraft accusations generated by the pressures of change (Richards 1935; Marwick 1950; Auslander 1993; Ranger (ms); Willis 1968; Iliffe 1979). According to this interpretation, practices directed against witches are not only concerned with witchcraft, but serve to express dissatisfaction with the present in a kind of cultural code. The manipulation of imported practices by anti-witchcraft specialists has encouraged observers to seek to understand these practices in terms of an assumed opposition between reified categories of 'tradition' and 'modernity', in which anti-witchcraft practices come to constitute a kind of symbolic commentary on social transformation. Anti-witch specialists utilise 'Western' artefacts and techniques as icons of 'modernity' in their struggle to eliminate witchcraft, thereby appropriating and controlling the modern symbolically, at the same time as, temporarily at least, restoring social cohesion and order.[3] On the face of it, this line of interpretation seems plausible. But it rests on unfounded assumptions, about the relation between witchcraft and social change on the one hand and, on the other, a perceived relation of opposition and exclusion between local categories of 'tradition' and 'modernity'. More fundamentally, in conflating the interpretation of witchcraft symbolism with the motivations of social actors it fails to take into account the actual social processes that bring anti-witchcraft specialists and villagers together. These processes rest on the articulation of local political institutions, including factions within villages, village leaders, district administrations and anti-witchcraft specialists themselves, as well as on the classificatory potential of both witchcraft symbolism and anti-witchcraft practices. In any case, there is no reliable evidence to support the view that witchcraft incidents and accusations actually increase at certain periods, despite the claims of village leaders. Apparent witchcraft panics legitimating the involvement of anti-witchcraft specialists must be understood in the context of actual relationships between different local political institutions.

Mass involvement in public anti-witchcraft practices is a consequence of the articulation of the relationship between villages as administrative units, villagers, state policy and anti-witchcraft specialists themselves. The politics of public witchcraft suppression practices are therefore quite distinct from the interpersonal dynamics of attack and accusation. Although the symbolic association of witchcraft with individualism, greed and exploitation underlies the classificatory appeal of witchcraft discourse in east central Africa, participation in anti-witchcraft activities is not concerned only with a politics of meaning via the ritual manipulation of ideas and representations. Participation in public anti-witchcraft practices is articulated with other forms of participation in institutions with political potential. The political potential of public anti-witchcraft practices rests on their manipulability as vehicles for the categorisation of certain individuals as sympathetic to the practice of witchcraft. This is possible even where anti-witchcraft practices do not differentiate between witches and non-witches because the logic underlying participation in such practices is that non-witches will obtain protection from potential witchcraft attack. As only actual witches stand to lose by participation, anybody unwilling to participate is likely to be suspected of witchcraft. For some individuals participation, or refusal to participate, can become a statement of allegiance to particular groups and interests, particularly where certain local institutions either strongly oppose or encourage participation.

National governments, district administrations and Christian churches in east and central Africa generally strongly oppose participation in anti-witchcraft activities, associating such activities with witchcraft and with atavistic unprogressive customs. Such practices may be dismissed as stupid, not modern and not conducive to development and anti-witchcraft specialists, who in the eyes of rural people provide a service to the community, condemned for exploiting a gullible rural population. In the view of governments, the educated elite and the majority Christian churches, any practice associated with witchcraft is to be dismissed as anti-development, even if it is directed against witches. The perception of anti-witchcraft specialists and their rural clients is quite different. They regard anti-witchcraft practices as *good* for development because they control the harmful activities of witches. They also reject the notion that such practices are not 'modern'. On the contrary, such practices address contemporary situations, making use of up-to-the-minute organisational techniques as well as acknowledging contemporary Christian identities. The fact that such practices are perceived as modern and pro-development by their proponents does not imply that they are not also regarded as 'traditional' in certain fundamental respects, and valued as such. As I have shown, practice defined as 'traditional' is not unchanging. As it refers to practices that address the quality of the relationship between living people and spirits, practice defined as traditional can, and does change, as long as the authority for this transformation can be shown to come from the spirits themselves. Anti-witchcraft practices are 'traditional' in so far as they conform to indigenous purification procedures. From the perspective of advocates of witchcraft suppression practices in Ulanga at any rate, participation in them is both pro-development and traditional. There is no necessary contradiction between the two categories of practices. Practices, which appear 'modern', can have 'traditional' ends, as for example in the case of the incorporation of Christian derived elements into local funeral practices (Green 1995). Categories of 'tradition' and 'modern' are associated with statuses and used for the temporal classification of practices and persons (Green 1999c). Similarly, people can be, and are, both traditional and modern at the same time. Though this possibility is denied by the progressive discourse of Church and state, it is made real by the implication of representatives of Church and state in anti-witchcraft activities. In the view of ordinary rural people, those who refuse to participate in anti-witchcraft activities are, despite their claims to the contrary, supporters of witchcraft and are therefore against development and against tradition. 'Progressive' opponents of anti-witchcraft activities lay themselves open to implication in the very activities that they condemn because they are seen to be supporting witchcraft.

The dynamics of classification are frequently self-consciously manipulated by advocates of anti-witchcraft practices to realise cleavages between different factions within communities (Parkin 1968) and between those communities and what are locally perceived as external institutions, especially district administrations and Christian churches. The repopularisation of self-proclaimed 'traditional' anti-witchcraft specialists in Malawi in the early 1960s was part of a strategic bid by chiefs who defined themselves as 'traditionalist' to embarrass and discredit progressive opponents of Banda's claim for power. Banda's opponents and Christians were tainted with witchcraft through their forced participation in anti-witchcraft activities (Ross 1969). The chiefs exploited the association of progressives with Christianity, with new forms of social organisation and new kinds of income opportunities. These were represented as individualistic and a direct challenge, not only to the power base of the chiefs, but to an image of community values privileging reciprocity at the heart of an authentically 'traditional' morality.

The social context of witchcraft

In Ulanga ideas about witchcraft are intimately connected to more general notions about morality, sociality and humanity.[4] The defining characteristic of witches is that they are people who are excessively greedy and anti-social, to the point where they quite literally embody the inversion of normal human attributes (cf. Beidelman 1963: 67). The core anti-social quality of witches is epitomised in what is said to be their inability to eat with people (cf. Middleton 1963: 263). This attribute of witches is fundamental because eating together, as the enactment of sociality, is regarded as the very essence of co-operation, to the extent that merely participating in the series of communal meals that comprise the funeral process constitutes 'co-operating' in the burial (Green 1996). Witchcraft attacks are spoken about in an idiom of corrupted consumption (cf. Rowlands and Warnier 1988: 122; Douglas 1982: 114). If victims of witchcraft are not eaten alive, they are poisoned by the harmful medicines placed by witches in their food. Envious, anti-social people transform themselves into witches through the use of medicines that empower them to harm others.[5] Other medicines can be used by anti-witch specialists to suppress the powers of witches, making it impossible for them to continue to practise their witchcraft, whatever their intention. As anti-witch specialists treat witches with medicines after shaving off the alleged witch's hair, the process for the suppression of witchcraft in Ulanga is called *kunyolewa*, meaning 'being shaved' (Green 1994), and described in terms of 'shaving witchcraft' (*kunyoa uchawi*).

Although individuals are often suspected of practising witchcraft, they are less frequently accused. The word 'witch' (*mchawi*[6]) was often used as a term of joking insult and abuse. A formal accusation of witchcraft is distinct from more subtly voiced suspicion. In the early 1990s it took the particular form of touching the accused person on the head with two one-shilling coins. This amounted to 'catching a witch' who could then be taken for 'shaving'. The expression 'going to be shaved' summarised what was, until recently, a rather protracted process involving anti-witch specialists, village authorities and disputants, which could take several weeks to complete.[7] The basic elements of anti-witchcraft practice took only a few hours, and centred on the use of medicine to suppress the powers of witches, and on shaving. Between around 1980 and her death in 1997 one particular specialist assumed responsibility for 'shaving witchcraft' throughout Ulanga district, a position since assumed by a successor. This specialist was an elderly Ndamba woman called Kalembwana, but known throughout the district as the *Bibi*, a term of respect meaning 'senior woman' or grandmother. Her practice was based at the edge of Ihowanja village, at the southwestern margins of the district.[8] The bulk of Kalembwana's clients came from Southern Tanzania, among them many Pogoro people from the Mahenge area. A substantial minority came from other parts of Tanzania, and from all social classes. Kalembwana claimed that her anti-witchcraft powers and ability to divine came from various spirits in the locality and had successfully transformed her ancestral shrine into a territorial cult. Like many other anti-witchcraft practitioners, she appealed to people of diverse cultural backgrounds, and to Muslims and Christians, by acknowledging the ultimate source of her power as God himself (cf. Redmayne 1970: 106).

Although people spoke of 'catching'[9] witches and taking them for 'shaving', the majority of Kalembwana's Pogoro clients chose to go voluntarily. This was because her anti-witchcraft practice was said not only to suppress the powers of witches but also to protect potential victims from witchcraft attack. It was also a precaution against a possible future accusation of witchcraft. Consenting to be shaved was not viewed as an admission of guilt but, on the contrary, amounted to an affirmation of innocence as only a witch would be reluctant to lose their witchcraft powers. For most people going to be 'shaved' was not particularly shameful or embarrassing, since consent implied they had nothing to fear. Occasionally coercion was applied to individuals who refused to participate. Such instances were often due to a person's association with the Church which forbade participation in anti-witchcraft activities. Others, particularly members of the small-educated elite, were reluctant to become involved in anti-witchcraft practices which they condemned as silly and demeaning. Once people arrived at Kalembwana's village for 'shaving' they were directed to a camp at the edge of the village that consisted of two long thatched shelters, arranged at right angles across a yard. One shelter was for women and children, the other was for men. Those coming for 'shaving' had to remain in the camp until they had been dealt with. Special restrictions applied to all those staying there. People could only leave and enter by the path that they used when they first arrived. They were not permitted to have sex, to wear shoes or to drink beer. Fire could not be given to, or taken from, people staying outside it. The atmosphere in the camp was calm and relaxed. Theft was said to be an impossibility. Distrust of alleged witches seemed minimal, largely because most people considered themselves wrongly accused and because of the conviction that 'shaving' would really deactivate witches.

In the dry season of 1990, up to forty people a day arrived at Ihowanja for 'shaving', and some 200 people were resident in the camp.[10] A further brief visit six years later suggested that being shaved at Ihowanja remained equally, if not more, popular, and for clients from even further afield. For economies of scale, 'shaving' was only carried out on certain days. This meant that some people had to stay in the camp longer than others. While they remained there they helped Kalembwana, by working in her fields and homestead, a practice that had led to the disapproval of the district administration.[11] I was told that the names of all those arriving for 'shaving' were formally recorded in a large book by Kalembwana's assistants. Those who had been 'shaved' were provided with a numbered certificate, confirming that they had undergone the anti-witchcraft procedure. Like the camp itself, which was not merely there for the convenience of visitors, the provision of documentation was viewed by clients and anti-witchcraft specialists alike as an integral part of the witchcraft suppression process.

Groups of people were 'shaved' together. Further restrictions were imposed on them from midnight the night before this was to occur. They had to abstain from sex and from smoking tobacco. They could not wash, nor use oil on their bodies and they could not change into clean clothes. Menstruating women could not be taken for 'shaving' until their period had finished. In the morning those going for 'shaving' were divided into two single-sex groups. Each person was made to carry a stick of firewood. In addition, some of the women carried a small quantity of maize flour and some salt for cooking. Others carried the chickens that they had brought with them from their homes in the knowledge that one bird per group of people coming together would be required for the ritual. The women wore old patterned pieces of cloth wrapped around their bodies, but, in striking contrast to everyday wear, with their breasts and heads uncovered. The men wore shorts without shirts or a cloth slung over the shoulder or tied around the waist. The wearing of other types of clothing was forbidden, as was wearing borrowed clothes and 'western' (*Kizungu*) artifacts such as wristwatches. The 'witches' were taken in their two groups to a place at some distance from the camp, away from the village, which was described to me as 'forest'.[12] Two shelters had been constructed there, one for each sex. The people were then made to sit on the floor of the shelters, which had been liberally sprinkled with anti-witchcraft medicine, awaiting their turn for 'shaving'.[13]

According to people who had been 'shaved', and to Kalembwana and her assistants, what happened next was as follows. The men were shaved first. Outside the shelters all the head and body hair, including the eyebrows, was shaved. The fingernails and toenails were pared. The cutting and shaving was done with what was described as a 'traditional' knife, in deliberate contrast to the ubiquitous razor blades of everyday use. The clothes which people had been wearing up to being shaved were thrown away, and clean clothes put on. These clothes were also described to me as 'traditional', in contrast to the western style garments that most people, especially men, wear normally. Back at the shelters, Kalembwana's assistants applied anti-witchcraft medicine, mixed with water to form a paste, to the peoples' heads. This was done in the line of a cross, with one smear of paste running from the forehead to the nape of the neck, and another over the crown from ear to ear. Meanwhile, more anti-witchcraft medicine had been mixed into the maizemeal and cooked, together with the chickens. Everybody ate this meal together. At various points in the proceedings oaths and curses directed against those returning to witchcraft were invoked. Finally people paid money for 'shaving'. In 1990 the fee was 152 shillings per person, the equivalent of about two days' casual labour. The two shillings component was handed over as coins. It was said to be the portion requested by Kalembwana's ancestral spirits, near to whose shrine the actual shaving occurred. This part of the payment appears to have remained constant, at least since Kalembwana began shaving witchcraft. The balance increases in line with inflation.[14] After the meal and the payment, the people then returned to the camp, and were free either to remain and rest or to begin the long return journey to their homes. *Kunyolewa* did not pick out and publicly identify witches. At no point was any distinction made between supposed witches and others going for shaving. Although people insisted that Kalembwana knew who the witches were and wrote down their names in a special book, everybody received exactly the same treatment.

Past practice

Kalembwana's witchcraft suppression practice is not a new phenomenon in Ulanga. But neither is it merely a repetition of past practice. It has much in common with a 'modern' witchcraft eradication movement, most obviously in the use of medicine and shaving, in its appropriation of bureaucratic practice and in its routinised approach to dealing with witches. Colonial records show that witches have been 'shaved' in Ulanga for at least the last eighty years.[15] Historians have pointed to a connection between the *maji maji* rebellion of 1905 and witchcraft eradication movements in Southern Tanzania, which also made use of special anti-witchcraft medicines and sequences of purification (Iliffe 1969: 508–9; Ranger 1966; ms; Gwassa 1973; Larson 1976: 103–5; ms). Current anti-witchcraft practice in Ulanga is very similar to that of the previous practitioners who had worked in the district, at least since the 1920s (Larson ms). Some of these were itinerant specialists, from other parts of Tanzania, who conducted mass rituals in villages.[16] They may have been influenced by, or been part of, movements such as *kamcape* that had reached parts of the south by the 1930s (Ranger 1966; ms; Larson ms; Willis 1968; Redmayne 1970). Others were more local, and, like Kalembwana, conducted their practice from a cult centre that was both a place of shaving and a shrine to territorial spirits.[17] Historical sources suggest that witchcraft suppression practices in Ulanga were not necessarily confined to large public events, nor were they always part of so-called eradication movements.[18] People involved in a witchcraft dispute would either go or be taken to a local doctor or diviner for shaving.[19] The prevalence of this practice was confirmed by a diviner of a territorial shrine (*mbui*), who said that his predecessors had routinely shaved witchcraft, but that now people preferred to visit those whom they regarded as having special anti-witchcraft expertise.[20] It seems likely that only the head hair or a section of it was shaved. Older informants state that the all-over shaving is an innovation of Kalembwana. While *kunyolewa* seemed quite different to a witchcraft ordeal, there were elements of ordeal in it (cf. Douglas 1963: 123–4). As in other witchcraft suppression movements, witches who returned to witchcraft were said to die should they remember their medicines at any point in the future, and a more immediate death was said to be a real possibility for the most intransigent of witches (cf. Ranger ms: 5; Auslander 1993: 173; Willis 1968: 4; Marwick 1950: 104; Redmayne 1970: 119).

The basic elements of current anti-witchcraft practice in Ulanga are the same as those associated with both public witchcraft suppression movements and more private anti-witchcraft practices. While these similarities might suggest an historical connection between them (Willis 1970: 131), there is little evidence to support the view that specific anti-witchcraft practices originate with organised movements and are simply appropriated by succeeding generations of specialists. The interpretation of current practice in Ulanga in terms of apparent historical continuities cannot explain why specific features in particular seem to characterise practices for the suppression of witchcraft, irrespective of who performs them. Nor can it elucidate the logic underlying witchcraft suppression procedure. In order to see why *shaving* witchcraft makes sense, we must look more closely at local conceptualisations of witchcraft and at the place of shaving in purification procedures.

Anti-witchcraft practice and purification procedures

Although witches derive their powers from the use of medicines there is more to the logic of 'shaving witchcraft' than the use of other medicines to suppress the powers of witches. Ideas about witchcraft are defined in the context of more general notions of personhood, which, as an attribute of the living is defined in relation to the attributes of the non-living, the spirits of the dead and those associated with territory. Just as the attributes of spirits are defined in relation to those of living people, the attributes of witches are defined in relation to those of living people and of spirits. The immorality of witches makes them not only anti-ancestor, but also anti-people. They behave in ways which proper people should not. Witches kill without a reason and they do not speak. Silence (*jiii*), characteristic of corpses, is *the* defining aspect of the unsocial associated with states of pollution and seclusion. The anti-social nature of witches is further manifested in their inability to eat with people. When they do eat, their chosen food is the flesh of the freshly buried dead. Their excessive greed results in an insatiable appetite for the vitality of others. Witches actively seek out the pollution of death and make use of the night, when other people sleep, to hover around graves and homesteads in their search for prey. They occupy the domain of living people, but at an inappropriate time. I have argued that Pogoro ritual deals with renegotiating the place of living people in relation to spirits, through shifting their position on the continuum between excessive physicality and its complete absence. Witchcraft has its place on the extreme physicality side of this continuum. The attributes of witches implicate them in a wholly negative construction of physicality, associated only with death, unlike human physicality which is also associated with life.[21] Consequently, witchcraft suppression practices centre on purification and replicate, in their form and structure, 'traditional' purification procedures performed in the context of life-crisis rituals.

Although Kalembwana makes a point of giving clients several doses of anti-witchcraft medicine, the core features of her practice centre on the cleansing of witches. This is cited by both clients and anti-witch specialists themselves as a precondition for the medicine's efficacy. Without cleansing the medicine will not take 'hold' or be incorporated into the bodies of witches. In order to cleanse witches Kalembwana makes use of a complex sequence of seclusion and purification which plays on the basic contrast between people and spirits, associating her practice with the spirits of territorial shrines and the legitimacy of 'tradition' in the dual sense of practice which refers to the past and which concerns the relation between people and spirits. The restrictions imposed at the camp place those waiting to be 'shaved' in a state of semi-seclusion, partially separated from the ordinary transactions of social life. Not wearing shoes, the restrictions on drink and the supposed impossibility of theft all hark back to an idealised 'traditional' morality, sanctioned by the spirits. The dress restrictions before going to be 'shaved' are those associated with territorial shrines, as are those concerning abstinence from sex and smoking, and the exclusion of menstruating women. These, along with the prohibitions on Western items such as watches, also associate people with a non-European past, the time of the ancestors, enacted in the present. Perhaps predictably, the shaving is done with what is described as a 'traditional' knife.

As well as situating anti-witchcraft procedures in the domain of 'tradition', Kalembwana's anti-witchcraft ritual resituates people associated with witchcraft in relation to spirits by establishing the utter dirtiness of witches. Those going to be shaved wear their own clothes, dirtied by their own sweat. They are forbidden to wash before going. Nor can they put oil on their skin. The women wear their breasts outside their garments. Not washing and exposing the breasts are practices that constitute mourning for the core bereaved during the first part of the funeral process, prior to burial. During this time, women are obliged to stay inside the house with the corpse, so taking on the pollution of death that is greatest before the disposal of the body. This dirtiness is made strikingly explicit in the case of the one-day funeral for a first child to die (*mjindu*).[22] As the mother shuffles out of the house on her buttocks, she is followed by female kin who cover her head with dirt and litter from the yard until they reach the rubbish heap where she is washed and shaved. This connection with funeral dress is made by those who have been 'shaved' at Ihowanja. It is most frequently commented on by women. The witches and those accompanying them are made to sit in their old clothes on a floor that has been sprinkled with medicine. They must be shaved before the medicine can be given to them properly, applied to their heads and eaten with food. The shaving is said by both clients and practitioners to be cleansing. Witches need shaving because, as I was told on numerous occasions, 'they are rubbish, dirt, shit'. Shaving is, for Pogoro people at least, intimately associated with cleansing and purification. It is always done together with washing. Peoples' heads are shaved on a number of occasions. These include being released from prison, on recovery from a severe illness, and, most commonly, after the burial of a close relative. A girl's head is shaved as part of the *unyago* puberty rites which are also structured around seclusion, silence, sequences of washing and shaving, and the giving of various medicines to augment and protect her latent fertility. Shaving the head, by changing the appearance, conveys, obviously, a change of state – from girl into *mwali*, from person into bereaved, and from witch into one who has been made unable to practise witchcraft. The shaving off of all a person's body hair at *kunyolewa* emphasises the intensity of their uncleanness. It also emphasises their humanity. Only living people can practise witchcraft, hence the hair and nails, parts of the body that grow and are visible and external signs of biological life, are removed and thrown away. Once they have been shaved and given medicine, the 'witches' can eat with other people, and doing so is the culmination of the event.

The emergence of anti-witchcraft movements

Kalembwana's witchcraft suppression practice conforms to the structure of Pogoro rituals in which purification is central. It also conforms closely to the structure of similarly oriented rituals performed by many other peoples throughout sub-Saharan Africa. These rituals deal with the shedding of pollution through sequences of seclusion, washing and shaving and, finally, the 'bringing out' of the person into the community. This ritual structure is evident in Lo Dagaa funerals (Goody 1962: 59–203), in Zulu healing rites (Ngubane 1977: 77–85, 113– 27) and in the Ndembu's *nkanga* ceremony for girls (Turner 1968: 201–57). There are numerous other examples.[23] This gives 'shaving' an instant validity in the eyes of clients who recognise it as an appropriate way of dealing with witches. That many of the witchcraft suppression cults in east central Africa have relied on similar sequences of purification, albeit augmented by elements of Christian or bureaucratic practice, perhaps explains their spread and acceptance beyond their areas of origin. But the underlying logic of witchcraft suppression procedures does not account for the periodic re-emergence of the kinds of public anti-witchcraft practices which constitute the so-called eradication movements. Their transient popularity cannot be explained simply by the existence of ideas about witchcraft, nor by an increase in witchcraft conflicts as a response to economic and social pressures as some writers have implied (Richards 1935: 458–9; Marwick 1950: 102; Willis 1968; 1970: 129; Auslander 1993: 189).[24] The marked increase in participation in public anti-witchcraft practices at specific points in history can only be understood by examining the complex processes through which such practices become public. Practices for the suppression of witchcraft have to be considered separately from the organised movements which occasionally assume responsibility for their performance. Anti-witchcraft movements are not autonomous religious institutions which periodically appeal to villagers. Their mass appeal is in fact *created* by their potential role in political processes, as is the very structure of their organisation.

Anti-witchcraft practices tend to be brought by specialists to villages. Alternatively, as was recently the case in Ulanga, the fact that witchcraft disputes were dealt with by village administrations meant that large numbers of villagers were sent to a particular anti-witch specialist.[25] These specialists, who are generally very few in number, could not by themselves ensure that their anti-witchcraft practices became part of a movement with what appears to be mass public appeal. In countries such as Tanzania and Zambia, villages are not mere aggregations of dwellings, but are units of local administration whose leaders have the official authority to impose decisions on villagers and to initiate collective action. In practice, the ability of village leaders to impose their will on villagers depends very much on personal factors and is not absolute. Factions within villages can attempt to persuade leaders to sanction decisions concerning the village, such as inviting in anti-witchcraft specialists. Once a specialist arrives to conduct a mass ritual, villagers have to participate or be suspected of witchcraft because the logic of such rituals is that they not only deactivate witches, but protect potential victims from witchcraft attack. In the case of *kamcape*, Dr Moses and the movement of witchfinders observed by Audrey Richards, headmen had invited specialists in to cleanse villages in response to pressure from specific factions within it. The co-operation of those who opposed their coming was coerced (Richards 1935; Auslander 1993; Willis 1968).[26] What appeared to observers to be a mass movement in the villages was *not*, in fact, a movement of villagers, but a consequence of specialists coming in to conduct mass cleansings. The young men who wished to implicate fellow villagers in anti-witchcraft rituals did not seek the assistance of anti-witchcraft specialists only because they were worried about witchcraft, but because they wished to challenge the authority of elders and village leaders, many of whom were publicly humiliated in the witch finding process. They did, however, make a point of vociferously articulating their concern with what they alleged were unprecedented levels of witchcraft activity. The fact that an increase in accusations is evident in historical records and in the contemporary discourse surrounding anti-witchcraft practices is not surprising. In many African countries attempts by the state to control any practices associated with witchcraft through legislation meant that village leaders had to obtain the approval of the district administration for participation in anti-witchcraft procedures. Any village chairman or headman requesting the administration's approval for an anti-witchcraft specialist was likely to claim that incidents and accusations of witchcraft had risen uncontrollably, whether or not there had been any real increase. Public anti-witchcraft practices are not simply a response to an increased incidence of witchcraft or anxieties about it but, on the contrary, create the context in which such allegations are likely to be made.

That requests from village authorities for anti-witch specialists often went to the local administration for approval has contributed to the popular perception of such specialists as actually being appointed by government to further 'development' by controlling the number of witches. This recognition is exploited by anti-witchcraft specialists themselves. The use of rubber stamps, certificates of shaving and 'official' letters summoning suspected witches for cleansing are recurrent features of their practice (Redmayne 1970: 110,124; Willis 1968: 6). There is no doubt that such practices enhance the authority of anti-witchcraft specialists, at the same time as undermining that of their opponents, including the majority Christian churches. As a woman who had been shaved five years previously said to me, 'If Kalembwana were really bad, as the Church says, then the government would not have her do this work.'

In reality, colonial and post-colonial governments in Africa have tended to be hostile to anti-witchcraft practices and to matters related to witchcraft. District administrations only sanction anti-witchcraft practices in the last instance in an effort to control them. Paradoxically, the constitution of villages as units of administration which have to comply formally with district policy means that district policy itself may play a critical role in making anti-witchcraft practices public. This factor accounts for the history of mass participation in anti-witchcraft practices in Ulanga district throughout the twentieth century where, in the early years of the British administration, public anti-witchcraft practices were discouraged in the belief that they could lead to a mass rising like the *maji maji* rebellion, which had relied on itinerant diviners taking medicine to rural homesteads. The popularity of a peripatetic anti-witchcraft specialist called Ngoja in the late 1920s caused the district administration and the loyalist headmen of the Pogoro council to unite in banning public shavings.[27] Special permission had to be sought for individual participation in anti-witchcraft activities. From around 1940, policy changed. It became common for itinerant anti-witchcraft specialists to tour villages, if invited by headmen, who had to seek the approval of the district administration. Requests were generally justified in terms of an increase in witchcraft activity and accusations, and the very real threat of social disruption implied. The authorities in particular took this seriously as the colonial administration struggled to implement its policy of closer settlement, relocating the rural population from scattered homesteads into compact villages which it was thought would facilitate the economic improvement of the district. The district administration permitted specialists to conduct mass shavings in the new settlements, for which they received a fee per head shaved.[28] In the 1950s population concentration ceased to be a priority for government. As settlements gradually disbanded, requests for mass shavings subsided. People returned to scattered homesteads, escaping the headman's control. The village was no longer a unit which could be subjected to or initiate collective action. Individuals involved in witchcraft disputes were once more allowed to visit specialists for 'shaving'.

After Independence, national policy with regard to witchcraft was carried over intact from the colonial period.[29] The district administrations' policy on anti-witchcraft specialists only changed as a result of the villagisation programme in the late 1970s, when the scattered population of Ulanga district was once more forced into concentrated settlements in order to bring about 'development'. In the years immediately following the move, some specialists were permitted to 'shave' villages, if a sufficient number of village officials requested it, or if it seemed to be the only way of preventing the break up of the new settlements. Village leaders again justified requests for shaving with a catalogue of witchcraft incidents and accusations.[30] As the new settlements were consolidated, the district administration put an end to the mass shavings and, by treating alleged incidents of witchcraft as civil disputes to be dealt with by village authorities, passively encouraged people to go to Ihowanja. Anti-witch specialists were discouraged from visiting villages, and found permission to travel the district withdrawn, on the grounds that their presence would disrupt agricultural production.[31] By the mid 1980s many people had returned to their pre-villagisation homesteads (Maghimbi 1990: 258). Villages ceased to be effective units of local control and the authority of village leaders diminished.

The ability of village leaders to impose decisions on a widely scattered population was limited. That requests for mass shavings have tailed off since the late 1970s is largely due to the disintegration of villagisation policies. While Kalembwana's legitimacy as a shaver of witchcraft in Ulanga was due to her elaborate ritual sequence, her virtual monopoly on anti-witchcraft practices is directly related to the articulation of district government policy with local political processes. This monopoly continued throughout the 1990s, based on reputation and on the strategic response of Kalembwana's kin to client demands and numbers.

The timing of anti-witchcraft movements

Mass movements for the suppression of witchcraft seem to undergo periods of revival at times of economic and political upheaval. This was the case for *kamcape* in all its various manifestations (Willis 1968; 1970: Richards 1935; Ranger ms). The more recent popularity of Dr Moses was also related to deepening economic crisis in Zambia and a widespread perception of rural decline (Auslander 1993). In order to explain the apparent periodicity of anti-witchcraft movements we have to consider why requests for anti-witchcraft specialists should coincide with periods of instability, implicating both a wider public and district authorities in anti-witchcraft practices. The answer lies in the specific role played by anti-witchcraft practices in political processes in which the public performance of such practices constitutes a powerful political institution. In east and central Africa political processes and participation are not confined to the state and party models of official political institutions. The exclusion of opposition and dissent from the sphere of formal political organisations, largely as a consequence of colonial policy and the subsequent establishment of post independence single party states, has ensured the perpetuation of other institutional forms through which the mobilisation of public opinion is possible. These institutions may not be formally recognised as political by governments that, until recently, worked to limit the existence of political organisations free of state or party control. Participation in formal political structures was further delimited by narrowly redefining the constitution of the legitimate sphere of political activity. Despite this, the political potential of various local institutions has always been tacitly acknowledged by the colonial and post-colonial governments which have struggled to control them (cf. Lonsdale 1986). In Tanzania, the abolition of chiefship, legislation restricting the activities of the traditional healing sector and attempts to curtail public involvement in anti-witchcraft practices were based on explicit recognition that such institutions posed a potential organisational challenge to the restricted sector of formal political control.

During the colonial period rural people had no official means of challenging government policy. Leaders were imposed, creating new structures of bureaucracy, justified with reference to the administration's view of 'traditional' society as hierarchical, rule bound and rigid (cf. Ranger 1983). After Independence, despite the imposition of a new structure of authority in rural areas, the basic structure of administrations remained intact. In many countries formerly independent local organisations and cooperatives were co-opted by the party machine. Policy implementation continued, as it had been during the colonial period, to be defined as a non-political matter of development. To this end, as Ferguson has shown for Botswana, policy decisions which effect rural areas were, and are, presented as technical solutions to problems of 'development' (1990). While the move towards ever increasing centralisation in single party states meant that villagers could not formally challenge policy decisions imposed from above, it did provoke the continuation of informal modes of political action, for example opposition to government agricultural schemes, refusal to co-operate with development initiatives and, in many places, withdrawal from cash crop production when the terms of trade mediated via parastatal marketing boards became unfavourable. In rural Tanzania, as in much of Africa, relations of coercion and opposition continue to be played out between a diverse range of institutions with political potential, among them the state, political parties and interest groups, the Christian churches and local social institutions through which political participation is possible (cf. Bayart 1986, 1993; Chabal 1986, 1994). In this context, the attitude of opposition of the state and the majority Christian churches to anti-witchcraft practices is a significant factor in explaining the timing of decisions to implicate all or some villagers in such practices.

Public anti-witchcraft practices as a political institution in Ulanga

In the history of anti-witchcraft practices in Ulanga District the political potential of participation has been strategically manipulated locally to target different people as representatives of different institutions at different points in history. These targets have included district administrations, village leaders as their representatives and, more recently, lay people who are closely associated with the Roman Catholic Church.[32] While these social categories are always potential targets for anti-witchcraft activities, the extent to which one category or another becomes the focus for anti-witchcraft practices at different times is directly related to the broader political and economic context in which certain persons as representatives of specific institutions come to be implicated in the kind of policies those institutions pursue locally. Consequently, while village officials are always vulnerable to enforced participation in anti-witchcraft activities, attempts to implicate local administrations and representatives of Christian churches in such activities are more likely to occur when local opposition to their activities is greatest. Village leaders themselves were, and are, frequently co-opted by the pressure to participate in public anti-witchcraft practices, or be suspected of witchcraft. Formal accusation has long been a means of getting rid of, or humiliating, unpopular leaders, imposed from above, who were loyal to district policy, rather than villagers' interests. In 1949, for example, a 'progressive' headman selected by the colonial authorities was taken by villagers for 'shaving', with the reluctant consent of the administration.[33] Just over forty years later, in 1991, attempts were made by some villagers to abduct their chairman and take him by force for 'shaving', partly because of conflict over his new wife, but also because of his close association with extractive and unjust party policies which villagers opposed. The chairman insisted that he was innocent of witchcraft but, aware that the accusation was explicitly political, refused to consent to being 'shaved'. For most of his opponents this merely confirmed that he was in fact guilty of witchcraft. His support in the village faded away and he was eventually replaced after an acrimonious public meeting.

Public participation in anti-witchcraft rituals was greatest during the two periods of forced resettlement, when village leaders responded to requests for mass shavings. While these were made practicable by the new administrative structure of village control, requests for anti-witchcraft practitioners peaked during these periods because they were an appropriate idiom for the articulation of opposition to state policies justified in terms of 'development'. The result was to implicate the pro-development state directly in dealing with witchcraft, and in dealing with it using mystical means, effectively undermining the administration's credibility as a progressive opponent of anti-witchcraft practices. Although the involvement of all the residents of a village in anti-witchcraft activities is, for the time being, a thing of the past in Ulanga, the group focus of Kalembwana's anti-witchcraft practices ensures that the political potential of participation remains significant. It is currently being played out between lay representatives of the Roman Catholic Church and their opponents.

Anti-witchcraft movements in general tend to attract the disapproval of mainstream Christian denominations (Auslander 1993; Green 1994; Richards 1935). While many such movements were explicitly hostile to Christian churches, to people closely associated with them and to mission Christianity, anti-witch specialists themselves have often claimed to have the support of Christian deities and saints. Anti-witchcraft movements, rather than being anti-Christian as such, are against the churches as exclusive and powerful institutions, with foreign origins, selectively benefitting those who are closely allied to them (cf. Ross 1969: 59). Such people are often seen to be wealthier than others and, by being 'good Christians' to be turning their backs on what are locally defined as

'traditional' obligations to assist kin and neighbours and to participate in collective activity (cf. Ranger ms: 28; Willis 1968: 11). Although the Church has
long been powerful and politically significant in Ulanga the current economic
climate and the failure of state service provision reduces alternatives and
increases the dependency of the rural poor upon it. The power of the Church is
now less constrained and freer of state intervention than at any time since the
start of the colonial period. It is therefore not surprising that since the late 1980s
people closely associated with the Catholic Church, including close relatives
of clergy and employees, have been accused of witchcraft in order to implicate
them in the anti-witchcraft activities which the Church condemns. Such people
may find themselves taken by force for 'shaving'. Alternatively, their reluctant participation results in a temporary public exclusion from the Church
defined Christian congregation in the form of a six-month ban on receiving
communion.

In the Pogoro communities of Ulanga people locally defined as 'good
Christians' continue to be implicated in anti-witchcraft activities. In July 1995
a rumour that the newly ordained Bishop had been attacked in his house by a
group of twenty witches spread rapidly, becoming the major topic of conversation at any social gathering. According to its retellers, the witches had broken
into the Bishop's bedroom and confronted him as he stood before them. The
witches had overlooked the fact that certain ritual specialists can see witches,
who are otherwise invisible to ordinary people. The new Bishop's power was
such that he saw the group and recognised them as witches. He grabbed the
telephone which was sitting on the table and called the other priests who occupied neighbouring rooms for assistance. Within seconds the witches were
surrounded and subject to a hail of sticks and fists from the angry Fathers.
Some of the witches were injured, at least two receiving broken arms. The fact
that some older men suspected had sustained arm injuries during this period
quite independently was taken by many as firm proof that the incident occurred,
although the clergy with whom I spoke maintained that nothing unusual had
happened. All those allegedly involved were closely associated with the Church,
either as employees or as leaders of lay organisations.

Although witchcraft suppression practices are always inherently political
at the interpersonal level, their public manipulation as a vehicle of rural opposition to state and Church seems to occur at specific points in history
where state and Church intervention or policy failure is greatest. Because the
state and Christian churches condemn practices associated with witchcraft as
anti-development, even if these are directed *against* witches, the perpetuation of
public anti-witchcraft practices can constitute a means of articulating opposition

to the development rhetoric and policy interventions of state and Church. Public anti-witchcraft practices in Ulanga entail a deliberate attempt by specialists to deal with witchcraft in what are locally defined as 'traditional' terms. This makes them an appropriate medium of opposition to the interventionist policies of Christianity and the State, which, in the local perception, have failed to bring about 'development'. Similar processes underlie the timing of public co-option in anti-witchcraft practices in other places and at other points in history where the political potential of public anti-witchcraft practices is seized by specific factions in a bid to articulate them with other political institutions. In Ufipa, Tanzania, the resurgence of *kamcape* was directly related to the political factionalism surrounding TANU's bid for power in the villages in the immediate pre-Independence period. *Kamcape*'s main advocates were pro-TANU youth seeking to discredit and challenge the control of traditionalist elders who stood to lose power in the new structure of administration (Willis 1968). This process of classification was played out in reverse in Malawi, where 'traditionalists' sought control of both public anti-witchcraft practices and their opponents. But, as the classificatory potential of anti-witchcraft practices is always ambiguous and virtually any social category can be associated with the negative qualities of witchcraft, such practices are not necessarily articulated with formal institutions and parties. In Zambia Dr Moses' followers targeted older women, whom they blamed for damaging young people's fertility, rather than targeting representatives of formal institutions, in a misplaced attempt to shift the responsibility for the AIDS pandemic away from the sexual exploits of male youth. Nevertheless, participation in public anti-witchcraft practices was articulated with disputes over the chiefship, conflicts over succession and between Christians and non-Christians (Auslander 1993: 175).

The timing of public anti-witchcraft practices does not derive from anything intrinsic to the practices themselves, but from the specific context in which they may be brought into a relationship with other local political institutions and made public. To interpret contemporary anti-witchcraft practices only in terms of symbolic politics is to ignore their role in concrete political processes. Anti-witchcraft practice is deliberately syncretistic, involving the use of imported artefacts and indigenous medicines and purification procedures. They can be claimed by traditionalists, as in Malawi, or by those seeking to challenge traditional holders of power, all in the name of a proper kind of 'traditional' morality, which, in the ideal, precludes the possibility of witchcraft. Anti-witchcraft practices are neither wholly 'modern', nor 'traditional', but for their proponents can represent the best values of both. This flexibility permits their political manipulation, making them into an appropriate trap for those who insist that progress is incompatible with tradition, and that the two categories of institutions, practices and people are mutually exclusive and antithetical. For others, however, such practices are merely a way of dealing with witchcraft. The political potential of anti-witchcraft practices depends on the institutional context of their performance.

10

Matters of substance

I have argued that the monopoly on witchcraft suppression practices associated with Kalembwana and her successors and for a time at least, with a
particular place was due to a combination of factors, including the policies of
local administrations and the cultural acceptability of 'shaving' as an effective anti-witchcraft strategy. This was not a new position. The south central
part of Tanzania had an established history of witchcraft suppressors who were
associated with virtual monopolies and booms in popularity, and the credibility that Ihowanja practitioners attained owed much to popular understandings
of this history. Similarly, the post-missionary Catholic Church of the 1980s
and 1990s owed much of its position and influence to the specific history of
the district, in particular to the vacuum of power created in the aftermath of
German colonial repression and the massive depopulation following the first
world war and tsetse concentration. The Church's retention of the institutional
structure established by the missionaries ensured that the expectations of hierarchy and patronage which characterised relations between mission and community were to persist long after the official end of the missionary era, at the
same time as these were subverted through increased demands by the Church
for local communities to provide material support. One consequence of this was
the popular articulation of the ambivalence with which the Church was regarded
through its enforced implication in the witchcraft suppression practices which it
opposed, and through the forced involvement of people closely associated with
it in anti-witchcraft activities. Another was the latent anti-clericalism which
has long been an attribute of Church–community relations (Larson 1976). This
ambivalence was not new. The missionary assault on what the Church represented as un-Christian custom and its persistence in the form of what is locally regarded as 'traditional' practice (*mila/jadi*) suggests that Christianity had
always been problematically perceived whether as, during the *maji maji* rising

for example, an index of subjection or more recently as a voluntary association of the elite.

The ambivalent perception of the institutional Church co-exists with a deep sense of being Christian as an embodied aspect of personal and emotional identity. We have seen in the previous chapters how this identity is constituted through practices such as baptism during which Christian substances are incorporated into the body, engendering a uniquely Christian kind of personhood as embodied being. This being is experienced processually through the life course, as it is ritually constituted, informed by emotion and experience through which the substance of the person is affected. In such contexts core experiences around birth and death which determine kinship become prime sites for the performance of ritual practice that derives its authority from predecessors. Such practice, which I have glossed, following Boyer (1990) as 'traditional', is not necessarily that which was performed in the past. Rather it is that which is legitimated by predecessors as those who were alive in the past. Such practice can and does change, as long as the authority for innovation can be represented as coming from ancestors or spirits. 'Tradition' in Ulanga's Pogoro communities is essentially a ritual status which can be, and is, performed by those defining themselves as Christian. Christianity and non-Christian practices can, and do, co-exist without necessitating a split between Christians and non-Christians. There is then no intrinsic 'rationality' of 'conversion' (Horton 1975). Anthropological understandings of Christianity as a miraculous system of intellectual power which will, to use the Comaroffs' memorable phrase, 'colonise the consciousness' (Comaroff and Comaroff 1991) of others are themselves the ideological products of a particular historical trajectory in the representation of Christianity in idealist terms as an inner matter of the spirit.

This book has shown how the mass adoption of Christian religious affiliation in a particular part of Southern Tanzania was strongly influenced by material factors, notably the brutal suppression of an anti-colonial rising which allowed the Catholic church to consolidate itself as a significant power broker in the southern region. It was ultimately mission control over schooling and the policies of colonial governments, rather than a desire for religious change, which promoted the increase in the numbers of Christians. The perpetuation of what I have characterised as missionary power relations long after the formal end of the missionary period helped maintain church power in the district, but it never managed to enforce its hegemonic interpretation over what it considered appropriate practice for Christians. Church definitions of Christianity and of who was Christian differed from those held by ordinary people. The failure of the Church to establish the authority on which orthodoxy depends means that the gap between formal Christianity and popular practice grows ever wider as people practise their own version of Christianity. Increasing disillusionment with clergy and with the Church as the 'religion of business' is fostering the emergence of a new form of post-mission Christianity in the diocese which is genuinely independent of mission as people define their own practice as Christian. This new Christianity prioritises the establishment of highly personal and unmediated relationships with Christian beings, in the process creating something very like the very kind of spiritualised individualistic understanding of Christianity that, formally at least, is espoused theologically by both the post-Vatican 2 Catholic Church and some Protestant churches. Significantly, while community disengagement from the institutional Church leads to increased emphasis on individualistic relations with the Christian divine beings, it perpetuates the institutional Church's sustainability crisis, reinforcing the dependence on business and the continued association between Church personnel and capital.

The contemporary position of the Catholic Church in Ulanga is not an inevitable consequence of missionary Christianity nor of political relations in that part of Africa but is, rather, influenced by the specific conjunction of events and relationships described in this book. These include the aftermath of *maji maji*, the emergence of ethnic identities, colonial regimes of local governance and the creation of a political vortex in which the influence and power of mission came to mediate between local communities and colonial states. That this power was largely imaginary outside the immediate context of the district is irrelevant. Swiss and German Catholic missions never caught the ear of British colonial governments or their secular administrators. What mattered for rural Catholics in impoverished districts was mission as *the* source of access to education and health services, emergency assistance and, for some, virtually the only stepping stone to non-agricultural employment or a life outside the area. Self government in 1963 and the *ujamaa* policies which aimed at autarky through the relocation of rural populations never seriously challenged the power of the missions and the increasing confidence of the new Christian establishment. Missionary influence remained strong in Tanzania and churches continued to be engaged in the provision of medical and social services. By the time the socialist policies were eventually abandoned, missionary control had formally acceded to local clergy, but dependence on mission funding and with it the perpetuation of missionary power relations remained. Clergy, like their missionary forebears, set themselves up as local elites controlling key resources for the poor while continuing to rely on the personal relations of patronage with European orders and with individual benefactors that ensured the resources on which the consolidation of influence depended. The Christian churches extended their role in service delivery and with it their influence as independent bodies, to some extent outside the narrow confines of what was officially recognised as the formal political arena. This position was, of course, highly political. Ex-mission churches were engaged both in the national politics of representing Tanzania's Christians to government and donors, at the same time as they were enmeshed in local relations of dependence and patronage within Christian parishes free of formal missionary control but dependent on missionary funding. The economic leverage gained by clergy as a result of missionary funds allowed individual clergy to consolidate patron–client networks within the diocese as well as invest in the education and futures careers of kin. The core staff of the diocese are well connected to important political figures in Tanzania and the Church is virtually guaranteed protection from public criticism as a result of this influence, which extends across other dioceses too.

The Christian churches in Africa cannot be viewed solely in the categories which they may claim for themselves, as religious or humanitarian institutions, divorced from the political world of social relations and vested interests, although they may perform humanitarian and religious services to communities. Such categorisations are themselves politically motivated. Christian clergy are social actors engaged in local and national political processes, as well as wider international agendas over which they have little control. Understanding the Church, in Africa or anywhere, means understanding these relationships. Understanding the contemporary hold of Christianities in much of the continent depends on recognition of this. Although it may appear that the missionary dream has been realised the reality is, as we have seen, more ambiguous. In parts of Tanzania at least personal relationships with Christian beings are superseding enforced orthodoxy as part of an essentially open system of social relationships with spirits. The theological assertions of Christianity matter less than the experience of Christian powers through the incorporation of Christian substances. Dealing ambivalently with Christianity is not a straightforward matter of either resistance or accommodation, colonisation or empowerment. Like witchcraft suppression practices and ideologies of witchcraft, Christianity is never solely reducible to any particular category. It can be at times repressive, at others empowering, on occasion a membership organisation, on others an aspect of personhood, but never solely a system of ideas divorced from the materiality of practices and the people who perform them. Whether at the level of the person who embodies Christian medicine in baptism or who wears a paper sacred heart of Jesus across their own for personal protection, or for the person who says 'I am Pogoro' meaning 'I am Catholic', thereby encapsulating the material history of colonial and post-colonial mission, Christianity in Southern Tanzania is always and inevitably a matter of substance.

Notes

1 Global Christianity and the structure of power

1 For accounts of mission involvement in service delivery in Kenya see Strayer (1978), for Rwanda, Linden (1977), and for Rhodesia, Murphree (1969).

2 For accounts of the histories of different missionary strategies in Africa see Hastings (1994) and Sundkler and Steed (2000).

3 Evans Pritchard remarks on the presence of a Catholic mission and states that though its influence was apparently minimal Christian Nuer had their own form of worship (1962: 48).

4 For accounts of this explicitly anti-syncretistic Christianity in Africa see Bond (1987) and Lan (1985).

2 Colonial conquest and the consolidation of marginality

1 Until 1974 Mahenge (Ulanga) District encompassed the present day districts of Ulanga and Kilombero. The boundaries of the old district are roughly coterminous with the boundaries of the present-day Roman Catholic Diocese of Mahenge.

2 Tanganyika also refers to the state prior to the union with Zanzibar and the formation of the United Republic of Tanzania in 1964.

3 This is a rough estimate based on figures supplied by the Ulanga District Council in 1990 and adjusted for population growth. Tanzania has not had a census since 1988 and does not include ethnic/cultural identity on census returns.

4 These figures are given in the 1998 Catholic Directory of Tanzania.

5 Gender and religiosity are discussed fully in chapters 6, 7 and 8.

6 See Gulliver's (1959) ethnographic map of Tanganyika published in the journal *Tanzania Notes and Records*.

7 This social constitution of kinship is the theme of chapter 6.

8 Lorne Larson, personal communication.

9 For a comprehensive account of the ecology and geography of the old Ulanga district see Jatzold and Baum (1968).

10 Apparently a mixture of millet flour and water.

11 The timing is derived from Bell (1950: 50).

12 In a brief piece reconsidering the origins of the *maji maji* war, the anthropologist Crosse-Upcott pointed out that, while the German authorities were unpopular, 'German personnel were too few in number and insufficiently mobile to mount a thoroughgoing reign of terror' (1960: 71). This is borne out by the evidence. In 1905 the total European population of the territory as a whole was 1873, 'of whom 316 were women and 205 children. In the districts directly concerned with the rising ... the total European population was 317, of whom 56 were women and 61 children ... The African population of the whole territory was estimated by the German governor at seven million' (Hassing 1970: 373–4).

13 There is some evidence to suggest that once the revolt was underway that water taken from other shrines in the region assumed the same status and power as '*maji*' (Crosse-Upcott 1960). This finding would seem to be supported by the existence of territorial shrines across what Lan, and others, have referred to as 'spirit provinces' in southern Tanzania (Lan 1985: 34).

14 At the time of the rising 'Liwale district was thickly populated and the triangular piece of country bounded by the Liwale and Mlowoka streams and the Kilwa-Songea road has been described as "nothing but houses just like Dar es Salaam" ' (Bell 1950: 44–5).

15 For a similar interpretation of the significance of ritual practice in the Mau Mau movement in Kenya see Green (1990).

16 For example, in Mahenge itself. Lorne Larson, an historian of Ulanga district, remarks that the Pogoro and N'gindo exhibited 'suicidal, ritualistic tendencies' during the rising, because of their faith in the properties of the water (1976: 112). This faith was apparently shortlived. According to Iliffe , 'At Mahenge the transition from confidence to doubt was illustrated by the three successive columns the first marching straight at the machine guns, the second using cover, and the third sending forward a single warrior' (1979: 180).

17 According to Bell's assessment of the evidence to support an alleged conspiracy theory for the origins and spread of the rising, the reasons for its expansion and popularity were straightforward. 'The secret of the rebellion ... can be summed up by the one word "OPPRESSION" ' (his emphasis) (1950: 55).

18 And others. Indeed, Monson refers to the incidence of 'armed uprisings and other anti-German initiatives in Mahenge, Njombe and Songea districts' (1998: 99).

19 Bismarck is reputed to have said 'To acquire territory is very simple in East Africa. For a few muskets one can obtain a paper with some native crosses' (quoted in Iliffe 1979: 90).

20 The boundaries were revised slightly in 1890 (Koponen 1994: 76).

21 In 1888 the DOAG had a mere 56 men to control an area twice the size of Germany (Koponen 1994: 78).

22 Personal communication Lorne Larson.

23 Some indication of the time scale and distances involved is given in Bell (1950: 49). A German force consisting of four Germans and eighty askari (locally recruited men) marched for twenty-nine days between Kilwa and Liwale, engaging in skirmishes on twenty-two days. During this time they 'failed to make communication with any other force'. Rebel forces routed other reinforcements from Kilwa and Songea heading for Liwale.

24 A full account of the history of Mahenge (Ulanga) district is given in Larson (1976).

25 As news of armed rebels reached Mahenge, missionaries and colonial staff went into hiding in the *boma*, and were well ensconced there by 23 August 1905. A mass attack on the 30 August resulted in the repulsion of Pogoro and Ngindo forces, but two days later an attack by the Mbunga who had crossed the Kilombero river precipitated a state of siege which was to last until the *boma* was formally retaken on 23 September (Iliffe 1979: 177–97).

26 In the entire outbreak only fifteen Europeans were killed by rebel fighters, compared to 73 askari and 316 ruga ruga soldiers. A further nine Europeans and three *askari* are reported to have died of disease (Koponen 1994: 597).

27 The famine policy was intentional. German military administrators believed that 'only hunger and want' could achieve 'a final submission' (Wangenheim, quoted in Iliffe 1979: 193).

28 For a fuller account of the reforms see Koponen (1994: 242); Iliffe (1969: 49–51) and Stoecker (1986: 148–61).

29 The Central Line Railway was originally to have been extended to run from Morogoro to Liwale. Following *maji maji*, the decision was taken in 1908 to extend it to Unyamwezi in the north west (Iliffe 1969: 72).

30 The policy was initially promoted in Tanganyika by Horace Byatt, Governor from 1922–5 (Graham 1976: 1).

31 Mahenge District Book, 1935, MF 17, TNA.

32 The Tanganyika African National Union became the *Chama Cha Mapinduzi* (Party of the Revolution) in 1977 after the union between TANU and the Zanzibar Afro-Shirazi Party.

33 The lack of ritual significance for Pogoro chiefs is also explained by the existence of a separation of powers between political leaders and the ritual specialists responsible for the fertility of the land.

34 The paradigmatic representation of the 'native' was always a male household head, rather like the representations of the 'modern farmer' in development discourses in Africa (Green 2000*a*).

35 Quoted in Graham (1976: 3).

36 Which had themselves reached endemic proportions due to disruption of the ecological balance caused by population shift in the aftermath of rinderpest and the importation of new diseases, parasites (such as jiggers) and disease strains with international trade (Kjekshus 1996).

37 Two other reserves in the area occupied by the present day Selous and Mikumi National Park were Motoro, just north of the Rufiji river and Mtetesi, situated due south of Liwale towards Nachingwea. Full details of changes in reserve boundaries are given in Matzke (1976).

38 J. P. Moffett, the officer in charge of resettlement, explained the policy in the following terms: 'It was found that tsetse was a lover of shade and that flies would not travel far across open country, almost certainly not across an area two miles wide. Herein lay the means of salvation. If man would live in open country instead of in thick bush he might hope for some measure of freedom from infection . . . If the naturally open space was unsuitable, then suitable areas would have to be made by clearing the bush. This would be no great hardship to him: he is, in fact, accustomed to it, 'shifting cultivation' being one of his practices. The great thing was to get as many

cultivators as possible to settle in the same area and to clear one continuous open space; in fact to make a 'concentration'. In practice, it was found that the smallest number of families who could live fly-free in a concentration was one thousand' (1939: 35–6).

39 The extent to which cattle were kept by Ulanga peoples in the nineteenth century is questionable. Historians refer to assets in the form of stock even among groups such as Pogoro, who today claim no affinity with cattle, the assumption being that the rinderpest epidemics of the 1890s wiped out the cattle population. However, if this were the case it is hard to understand why such groups completely failed to restock or the absence of referents to either cattle and small stock in their cultural practices such as bridewealth.

40 File T5/2 Tsetse Sleeping Sickness Concentrations General 1949–62, TNA.

41 File R20/5 *Mahenge Uandikishaji wa Vijiji*, File R20/7 Mahenge Operation *Vijiji* Tanzania (*Kihamo*), District Office Mahenge.

42 Villages were divided into ten house groups under the pre multi-party system, introduced in 1992, and thereafter into sections called *kitongoji*. Each *kitongoji* has a chairperson whose role is similar to that of the *balozi*, ten-house leader. In some villages both positions coexist, the *balozi* associated with CCM matters and the *kitongoji* representative with village government.

43 Although the export of slaves was a feature of the southern economy in the nineteenth century the numbers of slaves actually taken from southern communities was quite small and slavery, though significant, was not the determining feature of the economy (Kjekshus 1996: 21–4).

3 Evangelisation in Ulanga

1 See Murphree (1969) for Rhodesia, de Craemer (1977) for Zaire, Linden (1977) for Rwanda. For other parts of Tanzania see Thompson (1976: 36), Nolan (1977), Iliffe (1979), and Beidelman (1982).

2 The Protestant missions were also viewed with ambivalence, especially in the Muslim dominated coast where by 1893 eleven out of thirty-six missionaries had died, and £40,000 had been spent 'and the number of converts was twenty' (Smith 1963: 96).

3 All Roman Catholic missionary orders appear to have pursued similar tactics. Referring to Tanganyika in general, a commentator remarked in 1934 that, a great amount of baptising in *periculo mortis* goes on, so that the natives blame the mission for 'killing young and old by baptism' (Richter 1934: 47).

4 Some orders, for example the French 'Black Fathers', ran special catechetical classes to train laity for this purpose (Richter 1934: 40).

5 Baptism Book LBiii, Kwiro Parish.

6 This information comes from the Pastor of the Lutheran Church, Mahenge.

7 Ulanga Mahenge District Book, vol. 1. (no page numbers), microfilm 21, TNA.

8 See for example, file 461/10/29 Land Leases to Missions, 1927–42, TNA for conflict over land and trading. On witchcraft eradicators see below, chapter 9.

9 Balldeg Sisters from Switzerland.

10 Girls' puberty practices and the significance of seclusion are discussed in full in chapters 6 and 7.

11 See for example Culwick, G. M. (1939).

12 This practice occurred elsewhere and under missions of other denominations, for example, among the Zaramo the Lutherans secluded girls, with similar justifications (Swantz, L. 1966: 78).

13 DO's handing over report, 1934, in File No 61/141/G/Vol. 1,'Handing and Taking Over Mahenge District', TNA.

14 A typical agreement between a father and the mission is quoted here in full.'I, Liambandowe, have received from the Kwiro mission 50 shillings for returning, over the (bride)wealth for Afra, my child. I have received this money under the following conditions:1. Afra will stay secluded until she has a Christian marriage (*Afra akae utawani mpaka atafunga ndoa ya kikristu*). 2. When she has a Christian marriage, I shall return to the mission this wealth, 50 shillings. (*Atakapofunga ndoa ya kikristu, nitarudisha misieni Kwiro mali hiyo, shs.50*) Kwiro, 18.4.37. I agree, Daudi' (Mapatano File, Parish Office, Kwiro).

15 Mapatano File, Parish Office, Kwiro.

16 Letter from Bishop Maranta to DO, Kiberege, 12/10/1936, in File 46/10/29-1927–42-Land Leases To Missions, TNA.

17 The influence of the Church in what is now Kilombero is perhaps less so, due to a long history of Islamic influence and Lutheran engagement, and the economic strength of the district relative to Ulanga.

18 For transport, rather than ploughing.

19 In 1991, 56 lay people were permanently employed by Church organisations in Kwiro parish, the largest parish in terms of population as it includes the diocese headquarters. This figure does not include staff of the Friary and seminary. Smaller parishes are likely to employ catechists, now unsalaried, in addition to cooks and cleaners for parish houses, clerks, grinding mill operators, handymen and agricultural labourers for parish farms. Unlike government employees, Church employees are predominantly local. Many more people are employed on a daily or casual basis.

4 The persistence of mission

1 See Catholic Directory of Tanzania, 1988.

2 Based on the figures given for the Diocese of Mahenge in the 1998 Catholic Directory of Tanzania.

3 The Vicar General of the Diocese supplied this figure.

4 The majority of benefactors to Catholic clergy in Tanzania are German. See van Bergen (1981: 263).

5 Diocesan expenditure for the financial year 1991–2 was forecast at 35 million shillings. At the time, the official exchange rate was about 390 shillings to £1.

6 In German East Africa a law provided for the compulsory segregation of lepers. It was repealed in 1930, but voluntary segregation was encouraged by the British at treatment centres (Iliffe 1987: 218–20).

7 See Mahenge District Record Book, in Morogoro (Eastern Province) Provincial Book Vol. ii, Bagomoyo and Ulanga District Books, microfilm no: MF 17, TNA.

8 The parish clerk, Kwiro, supplied this estimate. Individual records are not kept.

9 Kodi ya maendeleo, 'development levy'.

10 For a very similar perception of the Church in Sri Lanka, see Stirrat (1992: 53).
11 Such houses are always said to be for a priest's relative, because priests have to live in parish houses which are the property of the church.
12 *Dona* is maize flour produced after dehusking and coarse grinding, whereas *unga* is the fine white flour. *Unga* costs twice as much to grind, as it has to go through the machine twice. *Dona* is associated with suffering and the absence of luxury, and is thus the appropriate food for funeral meals in contrast to *unga* based food which is associated with feasts.
13 For an account of the conception of 'projects' in Ulanga and in Tanzania more generally see Green (2000a).
14 It is used to refer generically to offerings or things done for the dead or the divines. In contrast, *tambiko*, refers only to offerings thought of as 'traditional'.
15 See chapter 9.
16 This attitude is evidenced in the recall to Rome in 1982 of Archbishop Milingo, best known for his healing ministry in Zambia (Gray 1990: 109).
17 See Lussy (1953) for a good example of the attitude of Capuchin Missionary priests to the Pogoro peoples and to traditional practice.
18 6/7/58, Tangazo File, Parish Office Kwiro (my translation).
19 This decline appears to be widespread. See for example the articles in the journal of the Pastoral Orientation Service, nos. 5 and 6, 1980 (Tabora).
20 Some people use the ma-prefix to denote the plural. In Ulanga they are also called *washinjashinja* – slaughterers.
21 This notion has widespread currency in Tanzania. 'Bloodsuckers' were originally thought of as Arabs, see Baker (1941), no doubt because of their association with the slave trade. Bloch (1971: 32) describes a very similar notion of 'heart thieves' for the Merina of Madagascar.
22 These types of allegations also occurred during the colonial missionary period. Interestingly, one of the priests accused of assaulting a young woman whose marriage he was arranging was Lussy, the author of several ethnographic papers. See the District Officer's 1934 report in file 61/141/G/ vol. 1, 'Handing and Taking Over Mahenge District', TNA.
23 See for example, Christian (1989: 152) for Spain, and Stirrat (1992: 52) for Sri Lanka.
24 For a description of their methods see Swantz, L. (1990).

5 *Popular Christianity*

 1 See chapter 9. The Nyakyusa also equated baptism with the giving of medicines. An informant told Wilson that Christians 'have a medicine. You are baptised with a medicine' (1957: 115).
 2 The constitution of female fertility and the significance of medicines in kinship are explored in the following chapter.
 3 The religiosity of older women in Catholic communities has been noted by Davis (1984) for the Mediterranean region, Pina Cabral (1986) for Portugal, Stirrat (1992) for Sri Lanka and Scheper-Hughes (1992) for Brazil.
 4 Battles over rain were common aspects of missionary strategy in Africa and of political conflict more generally where chiefs and royal lineages were associated

with control over the fertility of the land under their jurisdiction. See for example Comaroff and Comaroff (1991); Lan (1985) and Iliffe (1979).

5 Cf. Gray (1990: 103).

6 Mganga can mean medicine person, diviner, medium, doctor. The exact meaning depends on context. In this thesis it refers to specialists in 'traditional' medicine, who are not *wambui*. It can also mean, in Kipogoro, 'Witch'.

7 The understanding of Good Friday as funeral elsewhere is remarked upon by Taussig (1980) and Sallnow (1987) for Latin America; by Mosse for South India (1996), and Rushton (1982) for Greece.

6 Kinship and the creation of relationship

1 Kinship implies obligation and can be perceived as a cost. Moreover, the values attached to relationships are, as Guyer (1993) points out, differentiated along indices of value in which certain kinds of persons have very little value and could consequently be let go to form other social networks, or in the extreme examples about which Guyer is writing, sold into slavery.

2 The District Book hints to the instability of marriage as early as 1934, when many marriages collapsed before the completion of the bridewealth and the children remained affiliated to the family of their mother (Morogoro (Eastern Province) Provincial Book vol. 11: Bagomoyo and Ulanga District Books, Microfilm MF 17, TNA). What appears different about the contemporary situation is not so much the incidence of female-headed households but women's perception of this as a choice or strategy.

3 This was sufficient grounds for divorce in the native courts under the British (see District Book).

4 The Kiswahili *posa* and *mahari* are also commonly used.

5 From the Kiswahili for letter, chit, document. What it conveys in this context is a contract between the wifegivers and the wifetakers to the effect that the outstanding sum will be paid over later and that in the meantime the woman will not be 'taken' by anybody else.

6 The ceremony is described in detail in Green (1993).

7 From *-temeka*, to do brideservice, to clear grasses.

8 The District Book hints at the instability of marriage as early as 1934, when many marriages collapsed before the completion of the bridewealth and the children remained affiliated to the family of their mother (Morogoro (Eastern Province) Provincial Book vol. 11: Bagomoyo and Ulanga District Books, Microfilm MF 17, TNA).

9 And would be left at their mother's natal home in the event of her marriage.

10 The Luguru are a well-known matrilineal group in the region. See Beidelman (1967). For an interesting discussion on Luguru inheritance see Brain (1973: 128).

11 The General Rule set on 1 January 1935 states that the primary heir who is responsible for the distribution of a man's property and wives 'shall be a man's brother NOT his son or *mpwa*, and if no brother it shall be his son and not *mpwa*' (see Mahenge District Record Book, in Morogoro (Eastern Province) Provincial Book, vol. ii, Bagomoyo and Ulanga District Books, microfilm MF 17, TNA.

12 Swantz (1970: 88) and Beidelman (1967: xiv) describe similar debates among Zaramo, Kaguru, Luguru and other peoples occupying South Western and Eastern Tanzania.

13 As MacCormack points out, many of the terms used to talk about kinship and procreation are polysemous, conveying a range of associated concepts and ideas, from the physical to the cosmological (1982: 126).

14 See Mahenge District Record Book.

15 See Aijmer (1992: 10) for an account of Nyakyusa post-birth kinship practices. He states that, 'The Nyakyusa forge links between the new individual and the universe of kinship not in terms of sexual intercourse or conception, but only after the birth of the infant' through 'ikipiki medicine'.

16 The banana symbolism of the Nyakyusa is very similar, with plantains equated with the male and sweet bananas with the female (Wilson 1957: 37–8, 106).

17 Among the Vezo of Madagascar paternity is also conceptualised as a relationship which must be socially created, in contrast to 'natural' maternity (Astuti 1992).

7 Engendering power

1 It is believed that the unborn child would die if a pregnant woman were in close contact with death. Pregnant women can attend burials, but generally stay at the edge of the proceedings, well away from the corpse.

2 The girls' rites do not involve clitoridectomy or any other surgical alteration of the genitalia, which women consider detrimental to sexual pleasure. Both sexes consider male circumcision clean, but there does not seem to be any equation of male circumcision with manhood.

3 Cf. Swantz for the Zaramo (1970: 363).

4 Among the Ndembu the evidence of puberty is taken as the development of the breasts, not menstruation (Turner, 1968: 200).

5 Ubaga is also known as *ugali* in Kiswahili, a dish of cooked ground grain flour made with water, like polenta.

6 'Stepping on' is also an idiom for the expression of hierarchical (and extractive) relations.

7 Similar sequences are found in the Ndembu 'nkang'a' (Turner 1968: 198–259), the Ngulu 'guluwe' (Beidelman 1964), the Zaramo's girls rites (Swantz 1970: 363–93), and in the Bemba's 'chisungu' and related rituals (Richards 1982).

8 That is, are sexually promiscuous.

9 This association seems to be a recurrent feature of the region, see for example Beidelman (1964: 370) for the Ngulu and M. Swantz (1970: 376) for the Zaramo.

10 Dreaming here refers to seeing spirits in one's sleep.

11 Among the Cewa, girls were supposed to have first intercourse with someone other than their husband at the end of their first period. This man was called the 'fisi', 'jackal' (Richards 1982: 179).

12 Cf. Beidelman (1964: 379) for the Ngulu.

8 Women's work

1 This is described in detail in Green (1993).

2 This is called 'bridewealthing the corpse' (*kuheta mauti*).

3 The usual word for shroud is *sanda*.

4 Among the Lugbara, only women shave after funerals.

5 It is described at length in Green (1993).

6 Sallnow remarks on a similar emphasis in Latin American Catholicism, where Christ's crucifixion is emphasised to the extent that the cult of Christ is essentially a 'cult of death' (1987: 49).

9 Witchcraft suppression practices and movements

1 For a detailed account of the response of the District Administration to this see Green (1994).

2 The assumption that such movements are 'modern' is explicit in the titles of the papers by Richards (1935), Marwick (1950) and Auslander (1993). Other authors who address anti-witchcraft movements as innovative responses to 'modernity' include Ranger (ms), Willis (1968) and Iliffe (1979). Exceptions to this view are Parkin (1968), de Craemer et al. (1976) and Larson (ms), who all point to the continuity of such movements through history.

3 For example Richards (1935), Willis (1968, 1970), Marwick (1950) and, more recently, Auslander (1993).

4 See, for example, Eliade (1976: 91); Strathern (1982).

5 The use of substances classified as medicine is not confined to witchcraft and anti-witchcraft practices. As elsewhere in Africa, the category medicine denotes any kind of transformative substance. For an account of ideas about medicines and the transformative capacities of substances see Green (1996).

6 *Mchawi* is Kiswahili for witch. The Pogoro term is *mganga*, which is not widely used because of possible confusion with the Kiswahili meaning of the same term, which connotes doctor, healer or medical practitioner working in any tradition. Both Kipogoro and Kiswahili are spoken and used interchangeably by Pogoro people in Ulanga.

7 According to discussions with informants in 1995 the administrative complexities surrounding a visit to the *Bibi* have been substantially reduced, making the whole process less time consuming. Some people also said that less time was now required in the camp at Ihowanja, suggesting that increased payments could buy a quicker passage through the witchcraft suppression process. I do not know to what extent such claims are true.

8 I visited Ihowanja in September 1990 and again, briefly, in 1996. Kalembwana was still practising there in July 1996 and continued to be regarded as *the* anti-witchcraft specialist by Pogoro people living in the highlands.

9 'Catching' need not be physical. As in the French Bocage, described by Favret -Saada, by simply being accused a person is 'caught', trapped in the discourse of witchcraft (1980: 24).

10 Of those present, about half were under thirty and two thirds women, but, because it was common for accusers and accused to go together for shaving and for people to go to Ihowanja in groups, the age and sex composition of camp residents was not an indicator of those social categories most likely to be accused of witchcraft.

11 Correspondence in the Ulanga District Office (File N 10/10 Mahenge Witchcrafts (Cap 18)) from about 1983 expresses concern over both the alleged exploitation of rural people and the increasing popularity of Kalembwana.

12 As is common in Africa, 'bush' or 'forest' is defined in relation to areas occupied or cultivated by humans. Therefore, the 'forest' or 'bush' is any place not currently used for habitation or cultivation.

13 This gender divide was not unique to anti-witchcraft practices. Within the camp, and on the day of the ritual itself, the separation of men and women simply replicated the everyday separation of the sexes, which is especially marked at public events.

14 In 1985 'shaving' cost 42 shillings.

15 See T N A File 2/7 'District Office Mahenge-Ngoja, Cult of' 1932, and for correspondence relating to the case at SanguSangu see File 29/13 'District Office Mahenge-Misc/Witchcraft Case Kamsani Magungu and Five Others' 1949.

16 The two best known were Ngoja, who worked in the area in the late 1920s and early 1930s, and Songo who became popular in the late 1940s (Larson 1976). Accounts of these specialists are also given in the colonial files and district books in the Tanzania National Archive, Dar es Salaam.

17 Ngope, who later became an itinerant specialist conducting mass shavings during the British administration's implementation of their closer settlement policy in the 1940s (see below), was, according to Larson, also a Pogoro diviner of a territorial shrine, whose clients went to his shrine area for shaving (Larson ms).

18 The historical sources are limited. As Larson points out, during the British colonial administration many witchcraft matters were classified as 'secret'. The British destroyed secret files in 1960 prior to Independence (1976: 88).

19 See for example TNA File 29/13 District Office Mahenge-Misc/Witchcraft Case, Kamsani Magungu and Five Others, 1949. This file in the Tanzania National Archives, Dar es Salaam.

20 By the 'past' he was referring to the 1950s and 1960s.

21 See Huntingdon (1973: 72) for the very similar way in which witches are conceptualised among the Bara of Madagascar.

22 For a full account of the special funeral practices for the first child of particular parents to die see Green (1993).

23 For the Tshidi see Comaroff (1985), for the Nyakyusa see Wilson (1957), for the Gogo see Rigby (1968), and for the Ngulu see Beidelman (1964).

24 Auslander's interpretation is slightly different. Although he considers anti-witchcraft practices to be a symbolic bid to regain control over a disordered world, the world is disordered as a consequence of the economic and social conditions created by 'modernity' (1993: 189).

25 This was also the case for Chikanga's clients, many of whom travelled great distances to see him (Redmayne 1970).

26 For an account of explicit coercion in anti-witchcraft practices see Ross's account of forced participation in Malawi, in the context of Banda's struggle for power where participation was guaranteed by the presence of uniformed armed youth who constituted Banda's private army in the villages (1969: 70).

27 The Pogoro council banned Ngoja's agents in 1928 (Larson ms: 36). This was followed in 1932 by a province wide ban on itinerant anti-witch specialists. See Provincial Commissioner, Mahenge, to All District Officers, Mahenge Province, 22:2:1932 in T N A File 461/2/7. See also T N A File 2/7, District Office Mahenge,'Ngoja-Cult Of, 1932–'. These files are in the Tanzania National Archive, Dar es Salaam.

28 TNA file 10/13 – T5/2, Kiberege Station. 'Mahenge Sleeping Sickness Concentration-Correspondence relating to, 1941–'. This file is in the Tanzania National Archives, Dar es Salaam.

29 See Laws of Tanganyika, vol. 1, chapter 18.

30 For example, in 1976 the chairman of a particular village requested an anti-witchcraft specialist, citing a catalogue of witchcraft incidents in which some sixty people were implicated (File N 10/10–Mahenge Witchcrafts, Ulanga District Office, Mahenge).

31 File N 10/10 Mahenge Witchcrafts (Cap 18), District Office, Mahenge.

32 Although clergy may be suspected of witchcraft, they occupy an ambiguous relationship in relation to anti-witchcraft practices in that they may also be seen as ritual specialists who can potentially de-activate witches (Green 1994). This, together with the fact that the resources of the Church make the abduction of priests by advocates of anti-witchcraft practices impossible, means that clergy are not targeted directly.

33 See TNA File 29/13 District Office, Mahenge, Misc/Witchcraft Case-Kamsani Magungu and Five Others, 1949. This file is in the Tanzania National Archive, Dar es Salaam.

References

Abrahams, R. G. 1981. *The Nyamwezi Today. A Tanzanian People in the 1970s*, Cambridge, Cambridge University Press.

Aijmer, G. 1992. Introduction: Coming into Existence, in his (ed.) *Coming into Existence. Birth and Metaphors of Birth*, Gothenburg, Institute for Advanced Studies in Social Anthropology, 1–18.

Allen, T. 1991. Understanding Alice: Uganda's Holy Spirit Movement in Context, *Africa* 61(3), 370–99.

Asad, T. 1973. *Anthropology and the Colonial Encounter*, New York, Humanities Press.

 1993. *Genealogies of Religion. Discipline and Reasons of Power in Christianity and Islam*, Baltimore, Johns Hopkins University Press.

Astuti, R. 1992. *Learning to be Vezo. The Construction of the Person Among Fishing People of Western Madagascar*, PhD Thesis, University of London.

Auslander, M. 1993. 'Open the Wombs!': The Symbolic Politics of Modern Ngoni Witchfinding, in *Modernity and its Malcontents* (eds.) Comaroff J. and J. L., Chicago, University of Chicago Press.

Baker, E. C. 1941. Mumiani, *Tanganyika Notes & Records*, 11, 1–10.

Bayart, F. 1993. *The State in Africa. The Politics of the Belly*, London, Longman.

 1986. Civil Society in Africa, in Chabal, P. (ed.) *Political Domination in Africa*, Cambridge, Cambridge University Press, 109–125.

Beidelman, T. O. 1963. Witchcraft in Ukaguru, in Middleton, J. and Winter, E. H. (eds.) *Witchcraft and Sorcery in East Africa*, London, Routledge and Kegan Paul, 57–98.

 1964. Pig (Guluwe): An Essay on Ngulu Sexual Symbolism and Ceremony, in *Southwestern Journal of Anthropology*, vol. 20, 359–93.

 1967. *The Matrilineal Peoples of Eastern Tanzania*, London, International African Institute.

 1982. *Colonial Evangelism. A Socio Historical Study of an East African Mission at the Grass Roots*, Bloomington, Indiana University Press.

 1986. *Moral Imagination in Kaguru Modes of Thought*, Bloomington, Indiana University Press.

 1997. *The Cool Knife. Imagery of Gender, Sexuality and Moral Education in Kaguru Initiation Ritual*, Washington DC, Smithsonian Institution Press.

156

Bell, R. N. 1950. The Maji–Maji rebellion in the Liwale District, *Tanganyika Notes and Records* 28, 38–57.

Biermann, W. and Campbell, J. 1989. The Chronology of Crisis in Tanzania 1974–1986, in Omnibode, B. (ed.) *The IMF, The World Bank and the African Debt. The Economic Impact*, London, Zed, 69–88.

Bloch, M. 1971. *Placing the Dead. Tombs, Ancestral Villages and Kinship Organisation among the Merina of Madagascar*, London, Academic Press.

1974. Symbols Song and Dance and Features of Articulation, Is Religion an Extreme Form of Traditional Authority?, *Archives Européenes de Sociologie*, 15, 55–81.

1975. Property and the End of Affinity, in his (ed.), *Marxist Analyses and Social Anthropology*, London, Malaby, 203–28.

1978. Marriage Amongst Equals. An Analysis of the Marriage Ceremony of the Merina of Madagascar, *Man* (NS) 13, 21–41.

1982. Death Women and Power, in Bloch, M. and Parry, J. P. (eds.) *Death and the Regeneration of Life*, Cambridge, Cambridge University Press, 211–30.

1986. *From Blessing to Violence. History and Ideology in the Circumcision Ritual of the Merina of Madagascar*, Cambridge, Cambridge University Press.

1992. *Prey into Hunter. The Politics of Religious Experience*, Cambridge, Cambridge University Press.

1993. The Queen, the Slaves and Mary in the Slums of Antanarivo, in Humphrey, C. & Thomas, N. (eds.) *Shamanism, History and the State*, Ann Arbor, University of Michigan Press, 133–145.

Bloch, M. and Parry, J. 1982. Introduction: Death and the Regeneration of Life, in their (eds.) *Death and the Regeneration of Life*, Cambridge, Cambridge University Press, 1–44.

Boddy, J. 1989. *Wombs and Alien Spirits. Men, Women and the Zar Cult in North Sudan*, Madison, University of Wisconsin Press.

Bond, G. C. 1987. Ancestors and Protestants. Religious Co-Existence in the Social Field of a Zambian Community, *American Ethnologist* 14, 55–72.

Boyer, P. 1990. *Tradition as Truth and Communication. A Cognitive Description of Traditional Discourse*, Cambridge, Cambridge University Press.

Brain, J. L. 1973. Ancestors as Elders in Africa, Further Thoughts, *Africa* 43(2), 122–33.

1978. Symbolic Rebirth: The *Mwali* Rite Among the Luguru of Eastern Tanzania, *Africa* 48(2), 177–88.

Bravman, B. 1998. *Making Ethnic ways. Communities and their Transformations in Taita, Kenya, 1800–1950*, Oxford, James Currey.

Buckley, T. and Gottlieb, A. 1988. A Critical Appraisal of Theories of Menstrual Symbolism' in their (eds.) *Blood Magic. The Anthropology of Menstruation*, Berkeley, University of California Press.

Burridge, K. 1991. *In the Way. A Study of Christian Missionary Endeavour*, Vancouver, UBC Press.

Butler, J. 1993. *Bodies that Matter. On the Discursive Limits of 'Sex'*, New York, Routledge.

Callaghy, T. 1987. The State as Lame Leviathan. The Patrimonial Administrative State in Africa, in Ergas, Z. (ed.) *The African State in Transition*, London, Macmillan, 87–116.

Campbell-Jones, S. 1980. Ritual in Performance and Interpretation: The Mass in a Convent Setting, in Bourdillon, M. and Fortes, M. (eds.) *Sacrifice*, London, Academic Press, 89–106.

Camporesi, P. 1989. The Consecrated Host: A Wondrous Excess, in Feher, J. (ed.), *Fragments for a History of the Human Body, Part One*. New York, Zone, 221–37.

Cannell, F. 1999. *Power and Intimacy in the Christian Philippines*, Cambridge, Cambridge University Press.

Caplan, A. P. 1976. Boys' Circumcision and Girls' Puberty Rites among the Swahili of Mafia Island, Tanzania, *Africa* 46(1), 21–33.

Carmody, B. 1988. Conversion and School in Chikuni 1905–1939, *Africa* 58(2), 193–209.

Carsten, J. 1992. The Process of Childbirth and Becoming Related Among Malays in Pulau Langkawi, in *Aijmer* (ed.), 19–46.

1997. *The Heat of the Hearth. The Process of Kinship in a Malay Fishing Community*, Oxford, Clarendon Press.

Chabal, P. 1986. (ed.) *Political Domination in Africa. Reflections of the Limits of Power*, Cambridge, Cambridge University Press.

1994. *Power in Africa*, London, Macmillan.

1996. The African Crisis: Context and Interpretation, in Werbner, R. P. and Ranger, T. O. (eds.) *Postcolonial Identities in Africa*, London, Zed, 29–54.

Cheru, F. 1989. The Role of the World Bank and IMF in the Agrarian Crisis of Sudan and Tanzania. Sovereignty versus Control, in Omnimode, B. (ed.) *The IMF, the World Bank and African debt. The Social and Political Impact*, London, Zed, 76–94.

Christian, W. 1972. *Person and God in a Spanish Valley*, New York, Seminar Press.

Collier, P. et al. 1986. *Labour and Poverty in Rural Tanzania*, Oxford, Clarendon Press.

Comaroff, J. and Comaroff, J. L. 1991. *Of Revelation and Revolution. Christianity, Colonialism and Consciousness in South Africa*, Chicago, University of Chicago Press.

1992. *Ethnography and the Historical Imagination*, Boulder, Westview Press.

Comaroff, J. L. 1985. *Body of Power and Spirit of Resistance. The Culture and History of a South African People*, Chicago, University of Chicago Press.

Coulson, A. 1982. *Tanzania. A Political Economy*, Oxford, Clarendon.

Crosse Upcott, A. R. W. 1958. Ngindo Famine Subsistence, *Tanzania Notes and Records* 50, 1–20.

1960. The Origin of the Maji Maji Revolt, *Man* 97 and 98, 71–3.

Culwick, A. T. and G. M. 1935. *Ubena of the Rivers*, London, George Allen and Unwin.

1938. A Study of Population in Ulanga, Tanganyika Territory, *Sociological Review*, 30 and 31, 365–79 & 25–43.

1994. A Study of Factors Governing the Food Supply in Ulanga, Tanganyika Territory, in Berry, V. (ed.) *The Culwick Papers, 1934–44: Population, Food and Health in Colonial Tanganyika*, London, Academy Books, 65–75.

Culwick G. M. 1939. New Ways for Old in the Treatment of Adolescent African Girls, *Africa* 12, 425–32.

Davis, J. 1984. The Sexual Division of Religious Labour in the Mediterranean, in E. R. Wolf (ed.) *Religion, Power and Protest in Local Communities. The Northern Shore of the Mediterranean*, The Hague, Mouton, 17–50.

De Craemer, W. 1977. *The Jamaa and the Church. A Bantu Catholic Movement in Zaire*, Oxford, Clarendon Press.

De Craemer, W., Vasnina, J. and Fox, R. C. (1976.) Religious Movements in Central Africa. A Theoretical Study, *Comparative Studies in Society and History*, 18, 458–75.

Douglas, M. 1963. Techniques of Sorcery Control in Central Africa, in *Witchcraft and Sorcery in East Africa*, (eds.) Middleton, J. and Winter, E. H., London, Routledge and Kegan Paul, 123–42.

   1964. Matriliny and Pawnship in Central Africa, *Africa* 34(4), 301–13.

   1966. *Purity and Danger: An Analysis of Concepts of Pollution and Taboo*, London, Routledge and Kegan Paul.

   1982. *Natural Symbols. Explorations in Cosmology*, New York, Pantheon.

   (ed.) 1970. *Witchcraft Confessions and Accusations*, London, Tavistock.

Eliade, M. 1976. *Witchcraft, Occultism and Cultural Fashion*, Chicago, Chicago University Press.

Evans Pritchard, E. E. 1940. *The Nuer*, Oxford, Clarendon.

   1951. *Kinship and Marriage Among The Nuer*, Oxford, Clarendon.

   1962. *Nuer Religion*, Oxford, Clarendon.

Fabian, J. 1971. *Jamaa. A Charismatic Movement in Katanga*, Evanston, Northwestern University Press.

Favret-Saada, J. 1980. *Deadly Words. Witchcraft in the Bocage*, Cambridge, Cambridge University Press.

Feeley-Harnik, G. 1994. *The Lord's Table. The Meaning of Food in Early Judaism and Christianity*, Washington, Smithsonian Institution Press.

Ferguson, J. 1990. *The Anti-Politics Machine : 'Development', Depoliticization and Bureaucratic Power in Lesotho*, Cambridge, Cambridge University Press.

Fernandez, J. W. 1978. *African Religious Movements*, Annual Review of Anthropology 17, 195–234.

   1982. *Bwiti. An Ethnography of the Religious Imagination in Africa*, Princeton, Princeton University Press.

Fisher, H. 1973. Conversion Reconsidered. Some Historical Aspects of Religious Conversion in Black Africa, *Africa*, 43(1), 27–40.

Foucault, M. 1980. *The History of Sexuality. Volume One: An Introduction*, New York, Vintage Books.

Gifford, P. 1991. Christian Fundamentalism and Development, *Review of African Political Economy* 52, 9–20.

   1998. *African Christianity. Its Public Role*, London, C. Hurst and Co.

Gluckman, M. 1950. Kinship and Marriage among the Lozi, in Radcliffe-Brown, A. R. and Forde, D. (eds.), *African Systems of Kinship and Marriage*, London, International African Institute, 166–206.

Godelier, M. 1986. *The Making of Great Men: Male Domination and Power among the New Guinea Baruya*, Cambridge, Cambridge University Press.

Goody, J. 1962. *Death Property and the Ancestors. A Study of the Mortuary Customs of the LoDagaa of West Africa*, London, Tavistock.

Graham J. D. 1976. Indirect Rule: The Establishment of 'Chiefs' and 'Tribes' in Cameron's Tanganyika, *Tanzania Notes and Records* 77 and 78, 1–9.

Gray, R. 1990. *Black Christians and White Missionaries*, Newhaven, Yale University Press.

Green, M. 1990. A Reanalysis of Mau Mau Oathing Rituals. Political Ideology in Kenya, *Africa* 60 (1), 69–87.

1993. *The Construction of 'Religion' and the Perpetuation of 'Tradition' among Pogoro Catholics, Southern Tanzania*, PhD thesis, University of London.

1994. Shaving Witchcraft in Ulanga: Kunyolewa and the Catholic Church, in R. G. Abrahams (ed.) *Witchcraft in Contemporary Tanzania*, Cambridge, African Studies Centre, 23–45.

1995. Why Christianity is the Religion of Business: Perceptions of the Church among Pogoro Catholics, Southern Tanzania, *Journal of Religion in Africa*, 25(1), 26–47.

1996. Medicines and the Embodiment of Substances among Pogoro Catholics, Southern Tanzania, *Journal of the Royal Anthropological Institute* (NS) 2:1–14.

1997. Witchcraft Suppression Practices and Movements: Public Politics and the Logic of Purification, *Comparative Studies in Society and History* 39(2), 319–45.

1999a. Women's Work is Weeping: Constructions of Gender in a Catholic Community, in Moore, H. L., Sanders, T. and Kaare, B. (eds.) *Those Who Play with Fire. Gender, Fertility and Transformation in East and Southern Africa*, London, Athlone, 255–80.

1999b. Overcoming the Absent Father: Procreation Theories and Practical Kinship in Southern Tanzania, in Loizos, P. and Heady, P. (eds.) *Conceiving Persons. Ethnographies of Procreation, Fertility and Growth*, London, Athlone, 47–67.

1999c. Trading on Inequality. Gender and the Drinks Trade in Southern Tanzania, *Africa* 69(3), 403–25.

2000a. Participatory Development and the Appropriation of Agency in Southern Tanzania, *Critique of Anthropology* 20(1), 67–89.

2000b. Public Reform and the Privatisation of Poverty. Some Institutional Determinants of Health Seeking Behaviour in Southern Tanzania, *Culture, Medicine and Psychiatry* 24, 403–30.

Gulliver, P. 1955. A History of the Songea Ngoni, *Tanganyika Notes and Records*, 41, 18–30.

1959. A Tribal Map of Tanganyika, *Tanganyika Notes and Records*, 52, 61–74.

Guyer, J. 1993. Wealth in People and Self Realization in Equatorial Africa, *Man* (NS), 28, 243–65.

Gwassa, G. C. K. 1973. *The Outbreak and Development of the Maji Maji War*, PhD Thesis, University of Dar es Salaam.

Harding, S. 1987. Convicted by the Holy Spirit: The Rhetoric of Fundamental Baptist Conversion, *American Ethnologist* 14(1), 167–81.

Harris, O. 1981. Households as Natural Units, in Young, K. et al. (eds.) *Of Marriage and the Market*, London, CSE Books, 49–68.

Harwood, A. 1970. *Witchcraft, Sorcery and Social Categories among the Safwa*, Oxford, Oxford University Press.

Hassing, P. 1970. German Missionaries and the Maji Maji Rising, *African Historical Studies* 3(2), 373–89.

Hastings, A. 1978. *A History of African Christianity, 1950–1975*, Cambridge, Cambridge University Press.

1994. *The Church in Africa 1450–1950*, Oxford, Clarendon Press.

Hasu, P. 1999. *Desire and Death. History through Ritual Practice in Kilimanjaro*, Helsinki, Finnish Anthropological Society.

Haugerud, A. 1995. *The Culture of Politics in Modern Kenya*, Cambridge, Cambridge University Press.

Hefner, R. 1993. Introduction: World Building and the Rationality of Conversion, in his (ed.) *Conversion to Christianity. Historical and Anthropological Perspectives on a Great Transformation*, Berkeley, University of California Press, 3–44.

Herbert, E. 1993. *Iron, Gender and Power. Rituals of Transformation in African Societies*, Bloomington, Indiana University Press.

Hertz, R. 1960. A Contribution to the Study of the Collective Representation of Death, in *Death and the Right Hand*, translated by R. and C. Needham, London, Cohen and West.

Hoehler-Fatton, C. 1996. *Women of Fire and Spirit. History, Faith and Gender in Roho Religion in Western Kenya*, New York, Oxford University Press.

Horton, R. 1971. African Conversion, *Africa* 41(1 and 2), 50–71, 155–87.

1975. On the Rationality of Conversion, *Africa* 45(3), 219–35.

1993. *Patterns of Thought in Africa and the West*, Cambridge, Cambridge University Press.

Huntingdon, W. R. 1973. Death and the Social Order. Bara Funeral Customs (Madagascar), *African Studies* 32, 65–84.

Hvalkof, S. and Aaby, P. 1981. *Is God an American?: An Anthropological Perspective on the Missionary Work of the Summer Institute of Linguistics*, Copenhagen, IWGA.

Hyden, G. 1980. *Beyond Ujamaa in Tanzania. Underdevelopment and an Uncaptured Peasantry*, London, Heinemann.

Iliffe, J. 1967. The Organization of the Maji Maji Rebellion, *Journal of African History* 8(3), 495–512.

1969. *Tanganyika Under German Rule 1905–1912*, Cambridge, Cambridge University Press.

1979. *A Modern History of Tanganyika*, Cambridge, Cambridge University Press.

Jacobson Widding, A. 1987. *Notions of Heat and fever among the Manyika of Zimbabwe*, Working Papers in African Studies 34, Uppsala, African Studies Programme, University of Uppsala.

Jatzold, R. and Baum, E. 1968. *The Kilombero Valley (Tanzania). Characteristic Features of the Economic Geography of a Semihumid East African Floodplain and its Margins*, Munich, Weltforum Verlag.

Jilek-Aal, L. 1976. Kifafa. A Tribal Disease in an east African Bantu Population, in Westermayer, J. (ed.) *Anthropology and Mental Health*, The Hague, Mouton.

Jilek-Aal, L. et al. 1979. Clinical and Genetic Aspects of Seizure Disorders Prevalent in an Isolated African Population, *Epilepsia* 20, 613–22.

Kilumanga, R. A. 1990. *Historia ya Jimbo la Mahenge*, Peramiho, Peramiho Printing Press.

Kjekshus, H. 1996. *Ecology Control and Economic Development in East African History. The Case of Tanganyika 1850–1950*, London, James Currey.

Koponen, J. 1988. *People and Production in Late Precolonial Tanzania. History and Structures*, Helsinki, Finnish Society for Development Studies.

1994. *Development for Exploitation. German Colonial Policies in Mainland Tanzania 1884–1914*, Helsinki, Finnish Historical Society.

Kratz, C. 1994. *Affecting Performance. Meaning, Movement, and Experience in Okiek Women's Initiation*, Washington, Smithsonian Institution Press.

Lambek, M. 1981. *Human Spirits. A Cultural Account of Trance in Mayotte*, Chicago, University of Chicago Press.

Lan, D. 1985. *Guns and Rain. Guerrillas and Spirit Mediums in Zimbabwe*, London, James Currey.

Larson, L. E. 1976*a*. *A History of the Mahenge (Ulanga) District 1860–1957*, PhD thesis, University of Dar es Salaam.

1976*b*. Problems in the Study of Witchcraft Eradication Movements in Southern Tanzania, *Ufahamu*, (3) 88–100.

(n.d.) *Witchcraft Eradication Sequences among the Peoples of Mahenge District*, unpublished paper.

Leach, E. 1983. Melchisedech and the Emperor: Icons of Subversion and Orthodoxy, in Leach, E. & Aycock, D. (eds.) *Structuralist Interpretations of Biblical Myth*, Cambridge, Cambridge University Press, 67–88.

Leinhardt, G. 1961. *Divinity and Experience. The Religion of the Dinka*, Oxford, Clarendon Press.

1970. 'The Situation of Death. An Aspect of Anual Philosophy', in Douglas (ed.), 1970, 279–91.

1985. Self: Public and Private. Some African Representations, in Carrithers, M. et al. (eds.), *The Category of the Person. Anthropology. Philosophy, History*, Cambridge, Cambridge University Press.

Linden, I. 1977. *Church and Revolution in Rwanda*, Manchester, Manchester University Press.

Lockwood, M. 1998. *Fertility and Household Labour in Rural Tanzania Demography, Economy and Society in Rufiji District, c. 1870–1986*, Oxford, Clarendon.

Lofchie, M. 1993. Trading Places: Economic Policy in Kenya and Tanzania, in Callaghy, T. M. and Ravenhill, J. (eds.) *Hemmed in. Responses to Africa's Economic Decline*, New York, Columbia University Press, 398–462.

Lonsdale, J. 1986. Political Accountability in African History, in Chabal, P. (ed.) *Political Domination in Africa. Reflections on the limits of Power*, Cambridge, Cambridge University Press, 126–57.

Lugalla, J. 1995. *Adjustment and Poverty in Tanzania*, Bremen, Informationzentrum Afrika.

Lussy, K. 1953. Some Aspects of Work and Recreation among the Wapogoro of Southern Tanganyika, *Anthropological Quarterly*, NS 1, 26–27, 109–28.

Lutkehaus, N. 1995. Feminist Anthropology and Female Initiation in Melanesia, in Lutkehaus, N. and Roscoe, P. (eds.) *Gender Rituals. Female Initiation in Melanesia*, New York, Routledge, 3–29.

Mac Cormack, C. 1982. Health, Fertility and Birth in Moyamba District, Sierra Leone, in her (ed.) *Ethnography of Fertility and Birth*, London, Academic Press, 115–39.

Mackenzie, J. M. 1988. *The Empire of Nature. Hunting, Conservation and British Imperialism*, Manchester, Manchester University Press.

Maghimbi, S. and Forster, P. (eds.) 1992 *The Tanzanian Peasantry. Economy in Crisis*, Harlow, Avebury.

Maghimbi, S. 1990. *Rural Development Policy and Planning in Tanzania*, PhD thesis, University of London.

Mamdani, M. 1996. *Citizen and Subject. Contemporary Africa and the Legacy of Late Colonialism*, Princeton, Princeton University Press.

Mapolu, H. 1986. The State and the Peasantry in Shivji, I. (ed.) *The State and the Working People in Tanzania*, Dakar, CODESRIA.

Marwick, M. G. 1950. Another Modern Anti-Witchcraft Movement in East Central Africa, in *Africa*, vol. 20(2) 100–13.

Matzke, G. 1976. The Development of the Selous Game Reserve, *Tanzania Notes and Records* 79 and 80, 37–48.

Max, J. A. O. 1991. *The Development of Local Government in Tanzania*, Dar es Salaam, Educational Publishers.

Mbembe, A. 1992. Provisional Notes on the Postcolony, *Africa* 62(1), 3–37.

Mbosa, M. 1988. *Colonial Production and Underdevelopment in Ulanga District, 1894–1950*, MA thesis, University of Dar es Salaam.

McDannel, C. and Lang, H. 1988. *Heaven. A History*, New Haven, Yale University Press.

Middleton, J. 1963. Witchcraft and Sorcery in Lugbara, in *Witchcraft and Sorcery in East Africa*, (eds.) Middleton, J. and Winter, E. H., London, Routledge and Kegan Paul, 257–75.

1982. Lugbara Death, in Bloch, M. and Parry J. (eds.) *Death and the Regeneration of Life*, Cambridge, Cambridge University Press, 134–54.

Migdal, J. 1988. *Strong Societies and Weak States. State Society Relations and State Capabilities in the Third World*, Princeton, Princeton University Press.

Ministry of Health 1997. *Policy Implications of Adult Morbidity and Mortality. End of Phase One Report*, Dar es Salaam, United Republic of Tanzania.

Mitchell, J. 1997. A Moment with Christ. The Importance of Feelings in the Analysis of Belief, *Journal of the Royal Anthropological Institute* NS 3(1), 79–94.

Mlimuka, A. K. and Kabudi, P. J. 1986. The Party and the State, in Shivji, I. (ed.) *The State and the Working People in Tanzania*, Dakar, CODESRIA, 58–85.

Molyneaux, M. 1977. Androcentrism in Marxist Anthropology, *Critique of Anthropology* 3(9 & 10), 55–81.

Monson, J. 1995. Rice and Cotton, Ritual and Resistance: Cash Cropping in Southern Tanganyika in the 1930s, in Isaacman, A. and Roberts, R. (eds.) *Cotton, Colonialism and Social History in Sub-Saharan Africa*, London, James Currey, 268– 83.

1998. Relocating Maji Maji. The Politics of Alliance and Authority in the Southern Highlands of Tanzania 1870–1918, *Journal of African History* 39, 95–120.

Moore, S. Falk 1986. *Social Facts and Fabrications: "Customary" Law on Kilimanjaro, 1880–1980*, Cambridge, Cambridge University Press.

1988. Legitimation as a Process: The Expansion of Government and Party in Tanzania, in Cohen, R. & Toland, J. (eds.) *State Formation and Political Legitimacy. Political Anthropology Volume 1*, New Brunswick, Transaction Books, 155–72.

Mosse, D. 1996. South Indian Christians, Purity/Impurity and the Caste System: Death Ritual in a Tamil Roman Catholic Community, *Journal of the Royal Anthropological Institute* NS 2(3), 461–83.

Mtenga, R. 1971. The *Changing Patterns of Leadership among the Pogoro in Ulanga*, BSc dissertation, University of Dar es Salaam.

Munishi, G. 1995. Social Services Provision in Tanzania, The Relation Between Political development Strategies and NGO Participation, in Therkilsden, O. and Semboja,

J. (eds.) *Service Provision Under Stress. The State, NG's and People's Organisations in Kenya, Uganda and Tanzania*, London, James Currey, 141–51.

Murphree, M. W. 1969. *Christianity and the Shona*, London, Athlone.

Naali, S. 1986. State Control over Cooperative Societies and Agricultural Marketing Boards, in Shivji, I. (ed.) *The State and Working People in Tanzania*, Dakar, CODESRIA, 132–54.

Narayan, D. 1997. *Voices of the Poor. Poverty and Social Capital in Tanzania*, Washington, World Bank.

Ngubane, H. 1977. *Body and Mind in Zulu Medicine. Ethnography of Health and Disease in Nyuswa-Zulu Thought*, London, Academic Press.

Nolan, F. P. 1977. *Christianity in Unyamwezi*, PhD Thesis, University of Cambridge.

Nyerere, J. K. 1962. *Freedom and Unity. A Collection from Writings and Speeches 1952–62*, Oxford, Oxford University Press.

Parkin, D. J. 1968. Medicines and Men of Influence, *Man* (NS) 3(3), 425–39.

1980. Kind Bridewealth and Hard Cash: Eventing a Structure, in Comaroff, J. L. (ed.) *The Meaning of Marriage Payments*, London, Academic Press, 197–221.

Parkin, D. and Nyamwaya, D. 1987. Introduction: Transformations of African Marriage: Change and Choice, in their (eds.), *Transformations of African Marriage*, London, International African Institute, 1–16.

Peel, J. D. Y. 1968. *Aladura. A Religious Movement among the Yoruba*, Oxford, Oxford University Press.

Pels, P. 1999. *A Politics of Presence. Contacts between Missionaries and Waluguru in Late Colonial Tanzania*, Amsterdam, Harwood Academic Publishers.

Pina Cabral, J. de. 1980. Cults of Death in North-Western Portugal, *Journal of the Anthropology Society of Oxford* 9(1), 1–14.

1986. *Sons of Adam Daughters of Eve. The Peasant World View of the Alto Minho*, Oxford, Clarendon.

Poewe, K. O. 1978. Matriliny in the Throes of Change: Kinship, Descent and Marriage in Luapula, Zambia. *Africa* 48(3), 205–19, 48(4), 353–67.

Probst, P. (nd) *The Hybridity of Mchape*, paper presented to the Satterthwaite Colloquium on African Religion and Ritual, 1996.

Puja, G. et al. 1994. Girls in Education and Pregnancy at School, in Tumbo-Masabo, Z. et al. (eds.) *Chelewa, Chelewa. The Dilemma of Teenage Girls*, Uppsala, Scandinavian Institute of African Studies, 54–75.

Rafael, V. L. 1992. *Contracting Colonialism. Translation and Christian Conversion in Tagalog Society Under Early Spanish Rule*, Durnham, Duke University Press.

Ranger, T. O. (nd) *Mchape: A Study in Diffusion and Interpretation*, unpublished paper.

1966. *Witchcraft Eradication Movements in Central and Southern Tanzania and their Connection with the Maji Maji Rising*, University of Dar es Salaam Seminar Paper.

1983. The Invention of Tradition in Colonial Africa, in Hobsawm, E. and Ranger, T. O. (eds.) *The Invention of Tradition*, Cambridge, Cambridge University Press, 211–62.

Redmayne, A. 1970. Chikanga: An African Diviner with an International Reputation, in Douglas, M. (ed.) *Witchcraft, Confessions and Accusations*, London, Tavistock.

Richards, A. I. 1935. A Modern Movement of Witchfinders, in *Africa* 8(4), 448–61.

1939. *Land Labour and Diet in Northern Rhodesia. An Economic Study of the Bemba Tribe*, London, Oxford University Press.

1950. Some Types of Family Structure Amongst the Central Bantu, in Forde, D. and Radcliffe-Brown (eds.), *African Systems of Kinship and Marriage*, London, International African Institute, 207–51.

1982. *Chisungu. A Girl's Initiation Ceremony among the Bemba of Zambia*, London, Routledge.

Richter, J. 1934. *Tanganyika and its Future*, London, World Dominion Press.

Rigby, P. 1968. Some Gogo Rituals of 'Purification': An Essay on Social and Moral Categories, in Leach, E. R. (ed.), *Dialectic in Practical Religion*, Cambridge, Cambridge University Press, 153–78.

Ross, A. C. 1969. The Political Role of the Witchfinder in Southern Malawi During the Crisis of October 1964 to May 1965, in Willis, R. G. (ed.), *Witchcraft and Healing*, Edinburgh, Centre of African Studies, 55–70.

Rothschild, D. and Chazan, N. (eds.) 1988. *The Precarious Balance. State and Society in Africa*, Boulder, Westview press.

Rowlands, M. and Warnier, J. 1988. Sorcery, Power and the Modern State in Cameroon, *Man* (NS), 23(1), 118–32.

Rushton, L. 1982. *Religion and Identity in a Rural Greek Community*, PhD thesis, University of Sussex.

Sallnow, M. J. 1987. *Pilgrims of the Andes. Regional Cults in Cusco*, Washington, Smithsonian Institution Press.

Sangree, W. 1966. *Age, Prayer and Politics in Tiriki, Kenya*, London, Oxford University Press.

Scheper-Hughes, N. 1992. *Death Without Weeping. The Violence of Everyday Life in Brazil*, Berkeley, University of California Press.

Semboja, J. 1995. State Financing of Basic Social Services During the Structural Adjustment period in Tanzania, in Msambicha, L., Kilindo, A. and Mjema, G. (eds.) *Beyond Structural Adjustment programmes in Tanzania. Successes, failures and New Perspectives*, Dar es Salaam, Economic Research Bureau, 149–68.

Semboja, J. and Therkilsden, O. 1995. *Service Provision Under Stress in East Africa. The State, NGOs and People's Organisations in Kenya, Uganda and Tanzania*, London, James Currey.

Seppala, P. (ed.) 1998. *The Making of a Periphery. Economic Development and Cultural Encounters in Southern Tanzania*, Dar es Salaam, Mkuki na Nyota.

Simpson, A. 1996. *Religious Formation in a Postcolony: Ethnography of a Zambian Catholic Mission School*, PhD Thesis, University of Manchester.

Sivalon, J. C. 1995. The Catholic Church and the Tanzanian State in the Provision of Social Services, in Therkilsden, O. and Semboja, J. (eds.) *Service Provision Under Stress in east Africa. The State, NGOs and People's Organisations in Kenya, Uganda and Tanzania*, London, James Currey, 179–90.

Smith, A. 1963. The Missionary Contribution to Education (Tanganyika) to 1914, *Tanganyika Notes and Records*, 60, 91–109.

Spear, T. 1997. *Mountain Farmers. Moral Economics of Land and Development in Arusha and Meru*. Oxford, James Currey.

Speke, J. H. 1996. (1868). *Journal of the Discovery of the Source of the Nile*, London, Constable and Company.

Sperber, D. 1975. *Rethinking Symbolism*, Cambridge, Cambridge University Press.

Stirrat, R. L. 1992. *Power and Religiosity in a Post Colonial Setting. Sinhala Catholics in Contemporary Sri Lanka*, Cambridge, Cambridge University Press.

Stoecker, R. 1986. *German Imperialism in Africa: From the Beginnings until the Second World War*, London, Hurst.

Strathern, A. 1982. Witchcraft, Greed, Cannibalism and Death: Some Related Themes from the New Guinea Highlands, in Bloch, M. and Parry, J. (eds.) *Death and the Regeneration of Life*, Cambridge, Cambridge University Press, 111– 33.

Strathern, M. 1985. Kinship and Economy. Constitutive Orders of a Provisional Kind, *American Ethnologist* 12(2), 191–209.

Strayer, R. W. 1972. Missions and African Protest, in R. W. Strayer (ed.) *Protest Movements in Colonial East Africa. Aspects of Early Responses to European Rule*, Syracuse, Maxwell School of Citizenship and Public Affairs.

  1978. *The Making of Mission Communities in East Africa. Anglicans and Africans in Colonial Kenya*, London, Heinemann.

Sundkler, B. and Steed, C. 2000. *A History of the Church in Africa*, Cambridge, Cambridge University Press.

Sundkler, B. G. M. 1961. *Bantu Prophets in South Africa*, London, Oxford University Press.

Swantz, L. 1966. *Religious and Magical Rites of Bantu Women in Tanzania*, Dissertation, University of Dar es Salaam.

  1966. *The Zaramo of Tanzania*, MA thesis, Syracuse University.

  1970, 2nd edn 1986. *Ritual and Symbol in Transitional Zaramo Society*, Uppsala, Scandinavian Institute of African Studies.

  1990. *The Medicine Man among the Zaramo of Dar es Salaam*, Uppsala, Scandinavian Institute of African Studies.

Tambiah, S. J. 1968. The Magical Power of Words, *Man* (NS) 3, 175–207.

Tanner, R. 1967. *Transition in African Beliefs. Traditional Religion and Christian Change. A Study in Sukumaland, Tanzania, East Africa*, New York, Maryknoll.

Taussig, M. 1980. *The Devil and Commodity Fetishism in South America*, Chapel Hill, University of North Carolina Press.

Taylor, L. 1995. *Occasions of Faith. An Anthropology of Irish Catholics*, Dublin, Lilliput Press.

Thiele, G. P. C. 1984. *Development Plans and the Economics of Household and Village in Dodoma region, Tanzania*, PhD thesis, University of Cambridge.

Thomas, N. 1994. *Colonialism's Culture; Anthropology, Travel and Governance*, Cambridge, Polity.

Thompson, A. R. 1976. Historical Survey of the Churches in Education from Precolonial days to Post-Independence, in Gottneid, A. (ed.) *Church and Education in Tanzania*, Nairobi, East African Publishing House.

Tripp, A. M. 1997. *Changing the Rules. The Politics of Liberalisation and the Urban Informal Economy in Tanzania*, Berkeley, University of California Press.

Tsing, A. 1993. *In the Realm of the Diamond Queen. Marginality in an Out of the Way Place*, Princeton, Princeton University Press.

Turner, V. W. 1968. *The Drums of Affliction. A Study of Religious Processes among the Ndembu of Zambia*, Oxford, Clarendon Press.

  1967. *The Forest of Symbols*, Ithaca, Cornell.

Turshen, M. 1984. *The Political Economy of Health and Disease in Tanzania*, New Brunswick, Rutgers University Press.

Tvedt, T. 1998. *Angels of Mercy or Development Diplomats. NGOs and Foreign Aid*, London, James Currey.

Van Bergen, J. P. 1981. *Development and Religion in Tanzania. Sociological Soundings on Christian Participation in Rural Transformation*, Madras, Christian Literature Society.

Van der Geest, S. 1990. Anthropologists and Missionaries. Brothers Under the Skin, *Man* (NS), 25, 190–207.

Vaughan, M. 1991. *Curing their Ills: Colonial Power and African Illness*, Cambridge, Polity.

Walker Bynam, C. 1987. *Holy Feast and Holy Fast:The Religious Significance of Food for Medieval Women*, Berkeley, University of California Press.

Warner, M. 1976. *Alone of All Her Sex: The Myth and Cult of the Virgin Mary*. London, Weidenfeld and Nicholson.

Weber, M. 1985. *The Protestant Ethic and the Spirit of Capitalism*, London, Unwin.

Westerlund, D. 1980. *Ujamaa na Dini. A Study of Some Aspects of Society and Religion in Tanzania 1961–1977*, Stockholm, Almquist and Wiskell.

White, G. 1994. Civil Society, Democratisation and Development (1): Clearing the Analytical Ground, *Democratisation* 1(3) 375–90.

White, L. 1993. Vampire Priests in Central Africa: African Debates about Labor and Religion in Colonial Northern Zambia, *Comparative Studies in Society and History*, 35(2), 746–72.

Wijsen, F. J. S. 1993. *There is only One God. A Social Scientific and Theological Study of Popular Religion and Evangelization in Sukumaland, Northwest Tanzania*, Nijmegen, Kok.

Willis, R. G. 1968. Kamcape: An Anti-Sorcery Movement in South West Tanzania, in *Africa*, 38 (1), 1–15.

1970. Instant Millennium. The Sociology of African Witch Cleansing Cults, in Douglas, M. (ed.) *Witchcraft, Confessions and Accusations*, London, Tavistock.

Wilson, M. 1950. Nyakyusa Kinship, in Radcliffe-Brown, A. R. and Forde, D. (eds.), *African Systems of Kinship and Marriage*, London, International African Institute, 111–39.

1957. *Rituals of Kinship Among the Nyakyusa*, London, Oxford University Press.

Wilson, M. 1963. *Good Company. A Study of Nyakyusa Age Villages*, Boston, Beacon Press.

1971. *German Missions in Tanganyika 1891–1941. Lutherans and Moravians in the Southern Highlands*, Oxford, Clarendon.

1993. *Strategies of Slaves and Women. Life Stories from East Central Africa*, London, James Currey.

Zanolli, N. V. 1971. *Education toward development in Tanzania. A Study of the Educative Process in a Rural Area (Ulanga District)*, Basel, Basler Beitrage zur Ethnologie.

Index

Cambridge Studies in Social and Cultural Anthropology

*available in paperback